Academia in Crisis

Value Inquiry Book Series

Founding Editor

Robert Ginsberg

Executive Editor

Leonidas Donskis†

Managing Editor

J.D. Mininger

VOLUME 335

The titles published in this series are listed at *brill.com/vibs*

Academia in Crisis

The Rise and Risk of Neoliberal Education in Europe

Edited by

Leonidas Donskis†
Ida Sabelis
Frans Kamsteeg
Harry Wels

BRILL

RODOPI

LEIDEN | BOSTON

Cover illustration by Frans Kamsteeg. Used with permission.

Library of Congress Cataloging-in-Publication Data

Names: Donskis, Leonidas, editor.
Title: Academia in crisis : dystopic optimism and postalgic realism in
   university life / edited by Leonidas Donskis, Ida Sabelis, Frans
   Kamsteeg, Harry Wels.
Description: Leiden ; Boston : Brill-Rodopi, 2019. | Series: Value inquiry
   book series, 0929-8436 ; volume 335 | Includes bibliographical
   references and index.
Identifiers: LCCN 2019016584 (print) | LCCN 2019980141 (ebook) | ISBN
   9789004401587 (hardback : alk. paper) | ISBN 9789004402034 (ebook)
Subjects: LCSH: Education, Higher--Aims and objectives--Europe. |
   Universities and colleges--Europe--Planning. | Europe--Intellectual
   life--21st century.
Classification: LCC LA622 .A328 2019 (print) | LCC LA622 (ebook) | DDC
   378.4--dc23
LC record available at https://lccn.loc.gov/2019016584
LC ebook record available at https://lccn.loc.gov/2019980141

Typeface for the Latin, Greek, and Cyrillic scripts: "Brill". See and download: brill.com/brill-typeface.

ISSN 0929-8436
ISBN 978-90-04-40158-7 (hardback)
ISBN 978-90-04-40203-4 (e-book)

Copyright 2019 by Koninklijke Brill NV, Leiden, The Netherlands.
Koninklijke Brill NV incorporates the imprints Brill, Brill Hes & De Graaf, Brill Nijhoff, Brill Rodopi, Brill Sense, Hotei Publishing, mentis Verlag, Verlag Ferdinand Schöningh and Wilhelm Fink Verlag.
All rights reserved. No part of this publication may be reproduced, translated, stored in a retrieval system, or transmitted in any form or by any means, electronic, mechanical, photocopying, recording or otherwise, without prior written permission from the publisher.
Authorization to photocopy items for internal or personal use is granted by Koninklijke Brill NV provided that the appropriate fees are paid directly to The Copyright Clearance Center, 222 Rosewood Drive, Suite 910, Danvers, MA 01923, USA. Fees are subject to change.

This book is printed on acid-free paper and produced in a sustainable manner.

Printed by Printforce, the Netherlands

Contents

Notes on Contributors   VII

Introductory Thoughts   1
    Tamara Shefer

1   Toward an Educational Dystopia? Liquid Evil, TINA, and Post-academic University   11
    Leonidas Donskis

2   Academic Homecoming. Stories from the Field   36
    Frans Kamsteeg

3   Universities as Laboratories. Internationalisation and the Liquidity of National Learning   53
    Stefano Bianchini

4   Liberal Arts to the Rescue of the Bachelor's Degree in Europe   82
    Samuel Abrahám

5   Academia in the Fast Lane vs. Organisational Ethnography and the Logic of Slow Food   111
    Harry Wels

6   Timescapes in Academic Life. Cubicles of Time Control   129
    Ida Sabelis

7   A Nomad of Academia. A Thematic Autobiography of Privilege   150
    Joost van Loon

8   The Truth is Out There: 'Educated fo' Bollocks. Uni's Just Institutional Daylight Robbery'. Universities in Crisis? What's New?   169
    Simon J. Charlesworth

Epilogue   195
    Ida Sabelis

Index   199

Notes on Contributors

Samuel Abraham
is President of Bratislava International School of Liberal Arts/Managing Director of ECOLAS. He studied International relations at the University of Toronto and at Carleton University in Ottawa where he obtained his PhD in Comparative Politics and Political Philosophy in 2001. He is co-founder and managing director of ECOLAS – Europe – a Consortium of Liberal Arts and Sciences building a network of over twenty liberal arts schools and programs in Europe (www.ecolas.eu). In 2006, he founded Bratislava International School of Liberal Education (BISLA) where he serves as a Professor and rector (www.bisla.sk). He is author of numerous articles dealing with politics, political philosophy and education.

Stefano Bianchini
is Professor of East European Politics and History at the University of Bologna and Rector's delegate for relations with Eastern Europe. Former director of the two-year Interdisciplinary MA in East European Studies (MIREES: a joint diploma of the Universities of Bologna, St. Petersburg, Vytautas Magnus at Kaunas, and Corvinus of Budapest), he is visiting professor of the State University of St. Petersburg and Executive Editor of *Southeastern Europe*, Brill, Leiden, a blind peer review international journal indexed by Scopus and Web of Science ESCI, among others.

Simon Charlesworth
is unemployed and lives in Wath Upon Dearne, Rotherham. He is the author of, among other work, *A Phenomenology of Working Class Experience* (Cambridge University Press, 2000). His research interests include Phenomenology, Sociology of Praxis, mental health and the role of institutions in the reproduction of social exclusion.

Leonidas Donskis†
1962–2016, was born in Klaipėda, Lithuanian SSR, Soviet Union. He was a Lithuanian philosopher, political theorist, historian of ideas, social analyst, and political commentator, professor of politics and important academic leader, dean and professor Vytautas Magnus University, Lithuania, Honorary Consul of Finland in Kaunas and deputy chairman of the Lithuanian Jewish Community. He was also the Member of the European Parliament (MEP) from 2009 to 2014. As a public figure in Lithuania, he acted as a defender of human rights

and civil liberties. A centre-liberal politician, he has always been opposed to all extreme or exclusionary attitudes and forms of violent politics. Instead, he stressed the importance to coexist with democratic programs of other non-exclusive ideologies, and moderation (adapted from https://en.wikipedia.org/wiki/Leonidas_Donskis). He published widely – for all audiences and with a decisive intellectual curiosity, broad knowledge and wit.

Frans Kamsteeg

is Associate Professor of Organisation Studies at Vrije Universiteit Amsterdam. He holds a BA in History, and a PhD in Social Sciences. He teaches qualitative research methods and organisational culture theory. His most recent research focuses on culture and identity aspects of institutional merging in South African Higher Education. He extensively wrote on religious change and Pentecostalism in Latin America, and identity work in Dutch civil society organisations. In 2009 he co-edited *Organizational Ethnography. Studying the complexities of everyday life* (Sage).

Joost van Loon

is Chair of General Sociology and Sociological Theory at the Catholic University of Eichstätt-Ingolstadt in Germany. He is the author of several monographs, among which *Media Technology: Critical Perspectives* (McGraw-Hill, 2008) and *Risk and Technological Culture* (Routledge, 2002). He is also editor-in-chief of the journal *Space and Culture*.

Ida Sabelis

is Associate Professor at the Faculty of Social Sciences, department of Organisation Sciences, Vrije Universiteit Amsterdam and former director of the MSc Programme Culture, Organisation and Management; co-founder of Kantharos, the first consultancy for Diversity in Organisations in the Netherlands; former Joint Editor in Chief for the Journal *Gender, Work and Organization*. Her publications deal with gender diversity, ecofeminism, the positioning of sex workers, cycling cultures and time studies – all centring around human rights' issues coupled with calling attention to global environmental and social hazards. She currently works with Harry Wels on a biography of Nola and Nick Steele, nature conservationists in Kwazulu-Natal, South Africa.

Tamara Shefer

is professor in the Women's and Gender Studies Department, Faculty of Arts, University of the Western Cape, South Africa, and former deputy dean of teaching and learning in her faculty. Besides her scholarship on intersectional sexualities and gender, she has had a long interest in the politics of higher education and scholarship, particularly within patriarchal and (post)apartheid contexts with focus on socially just and feminist pedagogies. Her most recent work is *Socially Just Pedagogies in Higher Education: Critical Posthumanist and New Feminist Materialist Perspectives* (2018, Bloomsbury Press) co-edited with V. Bozalek, R. Braidotti and M. Zembylas.

Harry Wels
is Associate Professor at Vrije Universiteit Amsterdam and African Studies Centre Leiden. Harry has been in academia all his professional life. He loves his work and the academic environment in almost all aspects. He hopes to continue working in academia. In his repertoire of publications over the years, this chapter stands out as unique.

Introductory Thoughts

Tamara Shefer

Located far from the geopolitical context of the authors in this volume, in the post-apartheid South African context of decades of 'transforming' higher education, re-energised by the last few years of young people's calls to decolonise the university, it was with some surprise that I found myself identifying, at multiple moments, with the sentiments and arguments expressed in this volume. Indeed, I doubt there are many scholars located in any university across the globe at this moment in time who will not recognise and find resonance with the powerful narratives articulated here, notwithstanding their predominant location in a European and a global northern context.

This book joins a growing and increasingly urgent conversation about contemporary hegemonic practices in the university in globalised contexts shaped by neoliberal capitalist imperatives. While our different historical and geopolitical contexts clearly present nuanced experiences for us in our different nation-state materialities, we also have much in common given the seamless, 'liquid' flow of globalised institutional frameworks and of higher education in current times. For example, at the same time as we in South Africa have been over the last few years facing probably one of the most intense challenges to 'business as usual' in the academy, the neoliberal, consumer capitalist grip on our universities was similarly intensifying. As Achille Mbembe (2015a, n.p.), well known critical humanities scholar, puts it:

> While this mini cultural revolution was unfolding, the post-apartheid governing classes further ensconced themselves in a bureaucratic rationality that considered market metrics the ultimate indicator of who and what mattered.

This is, in my view, one of the major contributions of this book: to provide a theoretically informed and 'evidence-based' account of the shape of this 'bureaucratic rationality'. In this respect the book adds to and strengthens the larger critique of the local and globalised neoliberalisation of the university. Many of the chapters position themselves within the foundational framework of Bauman's 'liquid modernity' (Bauman, 2000) and Bauman & Donskis' further iterations of 'moral blindness' and 'liquid evil' (Bauman & Donskis, 2013; 2016) to advance the critique of the university under these conditions and to craft a powerful and detailed picture of how neoliberal discourse and practices currently shape universities globally. Given the centrality of Bauman and Donskis' thinking and the way in which an engagement with the late Leonidas Donskis in person, and through his intellectual brilliance has so clearly been a key part of the conceptual and inspirational development of the book, it is particularly significant and poignant that Leonidas is an author of a chapter in the book and acknowledged as editor on the book. Having had the privilege to spend time with Leonidas when he visited South Africa to present a generous series of lectures related to his then newly launched book with Bauman (Bauman & Donskis, 2016) and having been present with some of the authors at a panel related to this book at a memorial conference for Leonidas in Kaunas in 2017, I am intensely aware of how important he was to the scholars here, as he was to so many across the globe. This chapter, indeed a special gift to the book and its readers, may well have been one of the last pieces of scholarship he worked on, and his legacy is threaded through the pages of this book as a continuing inspiration from this wonderful thinker and friend.

The chapters together and separately advance the account of this insidious creep of neoliberalism in contemporary universities, showing how it is entangled with global hegemonies of capitalism and the reproduction of the continued relations of power on the basis of classed, gendered, raced, aged, sexualised, citizenship, embodiment, and other social divides – what Donskis refers to as 'the unholy alliance of local and international ideologues of neoliberalism, libertarian preachers of free-market fundamentalism, and political technocrats', which is argued and shown to place immense pressures on both academics and students. Aptly described by Van Loon, such an entangled force 'intervenes, seduces, manipulates and then withdraws again in the shadows, like an intangible, shallow Prometheus. What this label "neoliberal" perhaps more accurately stands for is the recapturing and securing of a reproduction of a social order most commonly described as "capitalist" (Boltanski & Chiapello, 2017), but manifesting itself in a more limited fashion as the naturalisation of white, male bourgeois privilege'.

A range of profoundly negative and destructive effects of the 'unholy alliance' are described and unpacked in the different chapters. Donskis for example speaks about 'the post-academic university', which for him, as for others in this book and in other scholarly works, results in a 'shallow scholarship', articulated so well as:

> An awkward amalgam of medieval academic ritual, specialisation, a blatant and blunt denial of the role of the humanities in modern society, managerialism and shallowness allows a perfect scene for such a

post-academic university, the playground for enormous pressures, the latter coming from technocratic forces disguised as the genuine voices of liberty and democracy – first and foremost, the market-oriented forms of determinism and fatalism with no room left for the principle of alternative, including critical thought and self-questioning.

A key project of many of the chapters is the helpful and well-argued critique of the marketisation (described elsewhere as 'uberisation', 'Macdonaldism') and corporatisation (with digitalisation as a key component) of the university, shaped by larger global capitalist imperatives. Such a framework, aptly described as a 'cookie factory' that, as Sabelis puts it, 'sells students as products and treats staff as machines' is shown to be underpinned by utilitarianisation and individualised competition (between scholars and institutions). Kamsteeg notes:

> Universities have turned from homes of 'gay science' into orphanages of knowledge, transforming all their inhabitants into market competitors in a rat race for producing knowledge (citations), and pushing knowledge consumers (students) through the pipeline of the knowledge economy jungle.

Being determined by economic forces and deploying a market model of organisation is flagged by authors as being far removed from other historical traditions and intentions of the academy, in particular its role in contributing to social justice. And certainly, notions of university autonomy and academic freedom are argued to be 'dangerously approaching the point of no return when they will be on the way to becoming zombie concepts' (Donskis). Part of this corporatised and market-driven hegemony is a calcification of disciplinary divides and exacerbated privileging of those parts of the university viewed as 'useful' to market forces with a marginalising and devaluation of those not, in particular the humanities, arts, and social sciences. Abraham for example provides a detailed elaboration of European undergraduate programmes to expose the reinforcement of rigid disciplinary boundaries and resistance to interdisciplinary and transdisciplinary contexts of scholarship. The marginalising of the arts and humanities in particular is also well elaborated by Bianchini and Donskis.

The impact of this market model on academics and their scholarship is taken up in various ways in many of the chapters. The pressure on scholars to maximise efficiency and output and conform to bureaucratic surveillance in this respect is well articulated in Van Loon's autobiographical narrative:

All of a sudden, I had to organise my life and studies to maximise efficiency rather than the pursuit of knowledge or research-related interests, face considerable future debt and worry about how to transform my university degree into an asset on the labour market.

Similarly, Sabelis, echoing a number of other authors, argues how 'the neoliberal turn was able to transform institutions of higher education into self-referential, self-valorising quality-machines, whose "impact" was exclusively measured by its ability to meet the needs of business and government'. The drive for competitive individualised or institutionalised performance is implemented through audit and accountability cultures, 'tick boxes', layers of bureaucratisation, accountability methodologies and 'technologies of quantification. This has of course nothing to do with good research or good teaching, but with the ability to optimise quantification' (Van Loon). As Charlesworth suggests, 'the appearance of a process is materialised via administrative acts' that police scholars to conform to what is considered normative and appropriately reflective of the institution. Through such normative processes, a culture of violence is legitimised: this author shares a personal narrative of how he tends to avoid eye-contact due to personal reasons – incidentally a practice also normative in many African cultures when communicating with authority – and gets punished for this in an interview by a senior authority, abusively told that 'he will not get a job if he doesn't make eye contact'. What seems an isolated and unusual incident tells a huge story of the coercive nature of higher educational institutions and constraining expectations of performance based on a particular, arguably male and Eurocentric mode of establishing academic authority. Notably, the continued hegemony of white middle-class men and whiteness, middle-classness, and masculinity in the global power structures of the academy and the stigma of working class in the university is highlighted in a number of chapters (notably, Van Loon and Charlesworth). I cannot resist recounting a personal story here in which a colleague was reviewing a new staff member who has a more gentle, responsive way of engaging, yet is extremely productive and produces excellent teaching and pedagogical work. The colleague under review was criticised for not being more assertive and dominant in her ways of teaching and academic engagement, indeed, a critique that arguably buys into a masculinist, Eurocentric mode of scholarly engagement, made all the more curious coming from a highly critical post-colonial feminist scholar. Importantly, chapters also raise the way in which current hegemonic practices in the university make unimaginable and impossible an ethics of care and appreciation of relationality and multiple forms of scholarship (for example, Sabelis).

Some of the chapters speak powerfully to a further area of concern, that is, the side effect of current hegemonic practice in the academy, related to temporality and time. Wels talks about 'fast lane' scholarship, which results in more superficial, output-orientated scholarship. 'Fast food for the mind' and 'clock time rationality', Sabelis argues, cuts out quality, moreover 'cuts out time for the really interesting work'. And Kamsteeg elaborates on the numbing effect of the bureaucratic surveillance culture with its multiple tick boxes and forms, overwhelming academics with administration, severely undermining time and energy for intellectual pursuit. Linked to this as well as the accelerated output culture, Wels decries the lack of reading, or the ability to keep up with new literature in our areas of research:

> Part of intellectual slow food is slow reading for which there is no longer sufficient time in academia.

Sabelis also highlights the lack of divide between work and the rest of a scholar's life, using rich vignettes to illustrate how the work day for an academic never ends, whether we are in the office or not.

> Office times meander right through the times we spend at home, or on vacation, or wherever else in the world.

One of the most destructive effects of the multi-layered operations of contemporary orthodoxies in higher education, as elaborated by the authors, is the fragmentation, isolation, insecurity, and fear, endemic to the competitive, individualised imperatives as well as to the particular pressured temporalities outlined, which characterise contemporary scholarly life. We are made to feel alone in our time pressures and individually responsible and individually judged, often for systemic inadequacies, and as Van Loon puts it 'the institutional processes of higher education function to value and devalue, not simply by means of imposing a grading system, but also by means of *personalising* this (de)valuation'.

To add insult to injury in this overwhelmingly troubling picture is the repression of any resistance: the 'Stoners' will be banned (see Kamsteeg). And authors such as Van Loon and Sabelis point to the lack of organised resistance in universities, also shaped by the lack of time or space on the treadmill to organise and resist so that we are 'seduced into compliance' (Sabelis, epilogue).

Another significant negative effect offered for consideration by authors is the damage and devaluation of current teaching and learning practices, and the way in which the privileging of research in the neoliberal system of auditing reduces the student to 'just a number to justify the research status and existence of a professoriate' and the construction of 'teaching as a necessary burden', as Abraham puts it. Massification and loss of quality in teaching through the emphasis on the rapid and quantity-oriented production of graduates (Kamsteeg and Abraham) is arguably particularly felt by undergraduate students 'who come less and less in contact with their research-driven professors who often ignore and disdain their teaching responsibilities' (Abraham). In this kind of institutional framing, 'students in academia are treated like particles in a process of industrial rationalisation and commodification' (Wels). This produces compliant students with little curiosity, on the one hand, but also students who take on the identity of 'client' and 'calculating consumer', on the other, thus undermining the project of critical thinking and curiosity so central to scholarly practices (Kamsteeg and Wels).

The culture of insidious violence shaping academics' experiences, as argued earlier, has negative spin-offs on students too, as flagged by a number of chapters. As Charlesworth argues '(A)cademics can simultaneously materialise the appearance of their professionalism whilst acting in ways that are, fundamentally, abusive …'. Authors also illuminate how the reproduction of power inequalities and the reiteration of existing social privilege through higher education has been strengthened in the current context so that those with power already – across class, citizenship, gender and other lines of privilege – continue to benefit most, so that a university degree is 'merely an affirmation of their (the privileged) entitlement to superiority … both the beneficiaries and executives of the "neoliberal turn"' (Van Loon). While for those already poor, authors like Charlesworth share narrative testimony to the inability of a university degree to make a difference, in his informants' views:

> University connects to nothing. It connects us only with instability. It's just an unofficial dole office.

Authors go on to highlight one of the subtle ways in which the university continues to contribute to bolstering existing power relations, that is, through a process of erasure, the ignoring of difference of power and privilege, which, as Charlesworth argues, 'usually reduces to ignoring those who are discrepant so that good conscience can be realised via a field of co-presence that is ethnically cleansed via the anonymity arising from the way, surreptitious, interpersonal forms are used to ensure the devalued have no reason-for-being-anywhere'.

A further negative spin-off for students within the fast scholarship paradigm is how the university gears itself towards short term results, summed up by Sabelis as 'timescapes of employability', underpinned by 'a reductionist discourse of employability'. On the other hand, Van Loon reflects on the growing pool of unemployed doctoral students and graduates endemic to current practices in universities focused on increasing postgraduate output. Such a 'reserve army' is ultra-exploitable, and he argues the 'liquidation of the academy required such a standing reserve exactly because it enabled those privileged enough to work within it, to continue the institutionalised pretence of value accumulation'.

Achille Mbembe (2015b, p. 18) argues that:

> Today, the decolonising project is back on the agenda worldwide. It has two sides. The first is a critique of the dominant Eurocentric academic model ... The second is an attempt at imagining what the alternative to this model could look like.

In line with Mbembe's summing up, a further contribution of this volume that I value is that it not only offers a critique but also some direction for change and the beginnings of alternative imaginaries for higher education. The chapters speak, in diverse and overlapping ways, to resistances and calls to different ways of thinking about the university and scholarship. While some may be informed by a nostalgic link to more traditional notions of the academy, others speak to specific resistances linked to the growing discomforts outlined in the critique. Authors such as Wels and Sabelis strongly call for a 'slowing down', both as practice and resistance to current orthodoxies. Implicit in many of the chapters is a call for greater attention to an ethics of care in the university, at multiple layers, including self-care. In this respect, some authors also argue for the importance of destabilising the tired binarism of body and mind and the erasure of affect and emotion in the dominant canon. Attention to pedagogical and scholarly practices and rethinking these within a framework of facilitating student agency in becoming globally conscious citizens, as Kamsteeg puts it, to 'take societal responsibility on the basis of a thorough, emotionally grounded morality that is inclusive and diverse' as well as an emphasis on generating knowledge that draws on the past to provide and think about the future within the project of facing multiple global challenges. In calling for the university to re-awaken to its political role, the authors suggest the deployment of transnational opportunities, shown to be not only a disadvantage but also a resource for social justice mobilisation (for example, Van Loon and Bianchini). Authors like Abraham and Donski also make an impassioned demand for the re-centring of liberal arts and humanities, with a particular emphasis on critical education in scholarship and politics. Importantly, we are reminded of the agency and indeed responsibility of scholars, especially those more secure in their position, to resist. Van Loon for example suggests 'the Robin Hood approach, in which we form our own small (Gideon's) bands of Stoners and "fight" the system wherever it manifests itself by surprise and with playful acts of defiance'. Resistance and solidarity are both implied here as well as a challenge to the alienating normative conditions of the academy. Bianchini sums up succinctly in his call on the university to 'show the courage of innovation, to break obsolescent and centralised rules, expand flexibility in the forms and quality of teaching, produce new synergies for the society, cope with the reorganisation of the human life and its relations, according to the quick changes imposed by the space-time compression'.

While I have emphasised the contributions of this book at an international level, of course the book has much to offer at a more regional level as well. Since it is predominantly European based, notwithstanding global resonances and some reference to North America and Southern Africa too, different chapters offer a rich unpacking of particularities and nuances of current and historically located European contexts. This is especially so in Donskis' chapter in terms of tracing large political and social shifts across the centuries from medieval to enlightenment to modern, and how this shapes academy. Furthermore, the chapters authored by Abraham and Bianchini present a comprehensive picture of current policies within the European Union (EU) in relation to higher education, a keen historical overview of the academy in Europe aimed at understanding the 'dismal stage of the undergraduate studies in Europe today' (Bianchini), as well as a rich historical overview of European liberal arts and its transnational roots and shifts and changes over the centuries. Bianchini for example flags the post-Cold War as a period of reimagining the university and unpacks policies of internationalisation and transnationalism resulting in student and faculty mobility, and how these impact on the globalising effect of particular traditions of scholarship, serving to disrupt rigid nation-state insularity. In this respect, the book insists on the specificities of our contexts and their histories, and illustrates how contextual archival and current work provides valuable insight for understanding the current context, particularly helpful for scholars wishing to understood higher education and areas of contestation in contemporary European contexts. We also get a good sense of current nuances and differences in the way in which neoliberal practices are infiltrating and shaping universities in different national contexts across North America and Europe through the biographical account of Van Loon and his own experiences in different universities across these contexts.

On the other hand, as my subjective responses to this work attests, the book is not simply of value in European contexts. On the contrary, since we live in a globalised world and an increasingly globalised academy, which remains dominated in many parts by the north and west (indeed the very European context so well unpacked here), this book of course has large resonance and value for global southern critiques and transnational thinking around the future of the university, particularly in terms of critical, social justice and decolonial projects, or whatever term is drawn on at a particular moment.

As one emerges from reading these essays – their different tones and emphases notwithstanding – what stands out is a bold and dedicated passion for social justice, for imagining a different academy that can make a difference. Also evident in all the authorial voices, even though they are diversely located in terms of careers, disciplines, geopolitical contexts and individual lives, is their long embeddedness in the matters they address, and a courage to share personal experiences and challenges as well as an honesty in recognising their own complicity. In many ways I find that these chapters model an alternative scholarly practice that speaks to the critiques they make, even while following what appears to be a normative scholarly product such as an edited volume. The valuing of affect and subjective experience models resistance to the binarisms of body/mind, emotion/rationality, femininity/masculinity that underpins the historical traditions of colonialist, empiricist scholarship that have been instrumental, or at best complicit, in the practices of racist genocide, class exploitation, and environmental destruction that are implicated in our current global and planetary challenges. In this respect, I especially admire how the authors resisted the normative tradition of 'writing themselves out' of the academic story they told; rather, most chapters are threaded through with a subjective voice, sharing at times uncomfortable personal stories. Such personalised narratives, as a strong thread through many of the chapters, counteract traditions of objectivity and 'othering' of the subject of study. They not only provide anecdotal evidence and richness to the text but also model a project of destabilising dominant academic discourse and institutional practice in which embodiment, emotions, and experience are erased. Also, very special about this collection of essays is how the authors dialogue with each other – every author has read and enthusiastically engaged in everyone else's piece and the conversations and resonances are a golden thread through the text. Again, this serves as a positive intervention in our individualised and competitive hegemonies where scholars tend to cite others in a kneejerk attempt to prove our own authority rather than to engage meaningfully with their arguments, or when we read only to undermine and devastate others in our self-aggrandisement project, as prescribed by current orthodoxies. Here something else is happening: authors are reading each other constructively, to dialogue with each other's arguments, to add emphasis to what is being said by others, and/or to complement their own understandings for a strengthened analysis.

To sum up, this rich volume of essays reminds us, as Alexis Shotwell (2015, p. 7) puts it, that: 'We're complicit, implicated, tied in to things we abjure'. But the incisive analyses in this book also fine-tune our critique and reflexivity with respect to our positionality in our complicity and implicated-ness. This book inspires the reader with a critical hope to open up spaces for resistance and change, even if only in small pockets and through slow movements, and to allow a different 'imaginary' of what the university can be and do.

References

Bauman, Z. (2000). *Liquid Modernity.* Cambridge, Polity Press.
Bauman, Z., & Donskis, L. (2013). *Moral Blindness: The Loss of Sensitivity in Liquid Modernity.* Cambridge, Polity Press. (especially Chapter 4).
Bauman, Z., & Donskis, L. (2016). *Liquid Evil: Living with TINA.* Cambridge, Polity Press.
Mbembe, A. (2015a). The politics of 0%. *City Press*, 1 November 2015. Retrieved from https://citypress.news24.com/Voices/The-politics-behind-the-0-20151030.
Mbembe, A. (2015b). Decolonising knowledge and the question of the archive in public lectures at Wits Institute for Social and Economic Research (WISER), 30 Apr 2015. Johannesburg, South Africa. Retrieved from http://www.staugustine.ac.za/sites/default/files/ctools/13.%20Mbembe%20-%20Decolonizing%20Knowledge...%20%282015%29.pdf.
Shotwell, A. (2015). *Against Purity: Living Ethically in Compromised Times.* Princeton, NY, Princeton University Press.

CHAPTER 1

Toward an Educational Dystopia? Liquid Evil, TINA, and Post-academic University

Leonidas Donskis

Abstract

This chapter was written in the spring of 2016 and discussed during one of our last meetings as a group with a drive to produce our book 'on academia'. Leonidas Donskis received comments to this chapter, but did not manage to digest these. We left the chapter as it was, with some minor editorial changes. Actually, thinking about educational dystopia is our common project, exactly to help raise discussion about what can be termed the post-academic university. *Towards an Educational Dystopia?* is thus a root piece for this book.[1]

Keywords

academic cultures – identity – history – TINA – neoliberalism – power

1   Bound to Choose between Two Educational Philosophies?

Within European academic tradition, universities have always been associated not only with the increase of scientific knowledge and scholarly enterprise in general but also with cultivation of the soul and virtue. University culture embraced all forms of life and tendencies of thought characteristic of a given historical epoch. For instance, universities sustained and supported aristocratic culture. Earning the degree of doctor of philosophy was nearly the same as becoming part of the nobility. At the same time, universities were instrumental in the process of gradual democratisation of social life – for nobody was able to be a scholar by birth. It was a matter of achievement, rather than ascription.

---

1 We, the other editors, decided to insert this abstract as explanation and acknowledgement – we cannot compose an abstract for Leonidas Donskis, only attempt to bring his legacy further.

Suffice it to recall that the rector, in medieval universities, was elected a scholar whom his[2] or her peers regarded as the most deserving and learned.

Therefore, one part of an academic's identity has always been linked to accommodation of tradition, whereas another part represented the idea of achieving and accomplishing something that comes from your conscious endeavour. The latter tendency obviously anticipates the modern world where the logic of identity lies in self-cultivation and self-discovery, instead of the once-and-for-all established identity. This is to say that European universities attempted to preserve what we would describe now as the canon, yet they were bound to question and change European legacy from time to time. The interplay of tradition and modernity, or the canon and its reinterpretation, has always been at the core of university life.

However, some pivotal modern ideas did not emerge at the universities. Instead, they came from alternative sources and movements. At this point, it suffices to recall the Renaissance with its idea of *studia humanitatis*. The medieval model of scholarship and university education, with its focus on in-depth knowledge, specialisation, and separation of the faculties of the soul and competences, would never have allowed anything like *studia humanitatis*. The idea that we can reconcile natural sciences to arts, allowing the latter to become the core of education, is an inescapable part of humanist education, which was the outcome of *studia humanitatis*. The idea that an enlightened individual can cross the boundaries of disciplines encompassing poetry, philosophy, fine arts, and natural sciences, was the first step in what we now call cross- and inter-disciplinary scholarship. In its initial and original form, the idea of *studia humanitatis* dates back to Cicero who, as Alan Jacobs reminds us, 'in his *Pro Archia*, refers to the *studia humanitatis ac litteratum*: humane and literary studies' (Jacobs, 2015, p. 66).

The idea of liberal/humanist education emerged in Renaissance Europe opposing the scholastic/conventional university model of education. Yet it was accepted later. Most importantly, Renaissance scholars, from Coluccio Salutati to other great Florentine humanists and Neo-Platonists, stressed the critical importance of humanist education and its relation to civic virtue and patriotism. The paradox is that one of the most important traits of modern education – civic virtue and leadership – emerged in a setting, which was more of an anti-university model of learning. On the other side, we could mention the Enlightenment with its salon culture and ideas of the republic of letters, toleration, and civil loyalty, which has little, if anything at all, to do with university

---

[2] We acknowledge the 'he' here as potentially sexist language. However, in those medieval universities, women were not openly present as scholars, as far as we know.

culture of that time. Yet these things became crucial for European modernity, although they did not originate in the academic world.

What was crucial for the Renaissance was the idea that the human world was a perfect testimony of nearly divine powers of human creativity and, therefore, was able to establish a symbolic partnership between God Himself and the human being (this idea belongs to Comte Giovanni Pico della Mirandola). This paved the way not only for the humanities as the realm of human self-fulfilment but also for Giambattista Vico's assumption that human sciences were more important than natural sciences, since only the almighty God was able to know the world that He created. Once philology in the sense of Vico was the human world par excellence, it required the further step towards recognition of the autonomy of the human world.

Renaissance scholarship would have been unthinkable without the union of literature and philosophy, form and content, beautiful language and wisdom, strict logic and graceful metaphor, theorising and joking, *philosophia perennis* and comedy. The concept of the carnival of the language can be applied to Thomas More's *Utopia*, Erasmus's *Encomium Moriae* (Praise of Folly), and to the whole linguistic and poetic universe of Renaissance scholars.

Putting aside the stylistic and literary devices characteristic of Renaissance *studia humanitatis* and philosophical writings, we have to remember that non-affiliated or independent scholarship was also the phenomenon of the Renaissance. The type of an independent and traveling philosopher who is not affiliated to any university yet remains quite influential – the type that embraces René Descartes, Benedict Spinoza, Gottfried Wilhelm von Leibniz, John Locke, and Voltaire, to mention just a few – is too obvious to need emphasis. The same applies to the circle and the society – new organisations that became quite prominent outside the academic world.

Although the educational and political ideas of the Renaissance became part of European academic tradition, the aforementioned medieval model was still there. The tensions between medieval/specialised and Renaissance/Liberal Arts education are still quite strong, so we would deceive ourselves by asserting that they are just a trace of the past. It is difficult to say which of these models prevails now – maybe we could more or less safely state that a sort of fragile equilibrium has been reached. Yet the propensity to think that a scholar has no real existence beyond their college or university is most telling and betrays the conviction that we have no real existence beyond our institutions, which is a hundred per cent medieval idea.

To sum it up, civil society and civic virtue are difficult to sustain and cultivate without liberal arts education. Historically speaking, civil-mindedness and the spirit of liberality greatly benefited from the tensions between universities and their rivals, such as humanist circles, societies, philosophical salons, and coffeehouses. Therefore, the strength and the flexibility of universities lay in their ability to internalise what they had long denied and what once was in strong opposition to them.

The Renaissance was the epoch of utopias. Yet utopia, in the way that humanity knew it for centuries, is dead now. This signifies the arrival of what Zygmunt Bauman calls liquid modernity as opposed to solid modernity. Utopia got privatised, becoming merely a dream of the middle classes. Privatisation of utopia means the new condition under which no society is deemed to be good and just: only individual life stories can be success stories. As such, they tend to become our new utopian dreams in a utopia-free, or dystopia-ridden, world.

We live in a world without alternatives. TINA, the acronym for There Is No Alternative (first forged by Margaret Thatcher, and then wittily redefined and reinterpreted by Zygmunt Bauman), allows a point of departure when dealing with this uniquely new and unprecedented phenomenon – namely one's ultimate belief in social determinism and market-based fatalism, the major difference before earlier decades and our time being the fact that, whereas Sigmund Freud's dictum informed us that biology is destiny, our dictum could be that economy is destiny.

Hence, the transformation of evil from solid, equipped with black-and-white social optic and Manichean divides, into liquid evil with its Don Juan-like powers of seduction, lies, manipulations, and abandonment. Most importantly, liquid modernity and liquid evil would be unthinkable without the world without alternatives.

2 Liquid Evil and Living with TINA

As mentioned, we live in a world without alternatives. It's a world that propounds a single reality and a world that labels as lunatics – or eccentrics in the best case – all those who believe that everything has an alternative, including even the very best models of governance and the most profound ideas (not to mention business and engineering projects). The world has probably never been so inundated with fatalistic and deterministic beliefs as it is today; alongside serious analyses, as if from a horn of plenty, flow prophesies and projections of looming crises, dangers, downward spirals, and the end of the world. In this widespread atmosphere of fear and fatalism, the conviction arises that there are no alternatives to contemporary political logic and to the tyranny of economy or to attitudes toward science and technology and the relationship between nature and humanity. Not by any stretch is optimism the foolish exultation that we are here in this place and that our surroundings are warm, fuzzy, and comfortable; rather, it is the belief that evil is transitory and does not vanquish humaneness (or only briefly when it does). Furthermore, optimism means a belief that hope and alternatives do indeed always exist. The conviction that a pessimist is an all-round loftier and nobler being than an optimist is not simply a relic of the modern, Romantic sensibility and worldview – it is something greater.

This profound juncture goes all the way back to the monumental conflict between Christianity and Manichaeism – after Augustine (who, by the way, defeated his inner Manichaean and became one of the Fathers of the Catholic Church). Christians held evil to be a state of errant or insufficient goodness that could be overcome, while Manichaeans held good and evil to be parallel but irreconcilable realities. Optimism is, above all, a Christian construction – it's based on the faith that good can overcome evil and that unexplored possibilities and alternatives can always be found. But we live in an age of pessimism. The twentieth century was excellent proof evil was alive and well, and this has reinforced the positions of modern Manichaeans. They saw a world that could be temporarily abandoned by God but not by Satan.

One question, though, remains unanswered: How meaningful is Manichaeism today? Disbelief that God is all-powerful, and that He is Love, is something that might have been greatly reinforced in the wake of the many atrocities of the twentieth century. Mikhail Bulgakov's enduring work, *The Master and Margarita*, is imbued with a Manichaean spirit – the novel makes numerous mentions of the concepts of 'Light' and 'Dark' developed by the Persian prophet and eponymous architect of this belief system. The interpretation of evil in this great twentieth-century East European novel is one that asserts the self-sufficiency of evil. This interpretation of Christianity is close to that of Ernest Renan in his *Life of Jesus*, a study with which Bulgakov was quite familiar.

Even Czeslaw Milosz considered himself something of a closet Manichean. After his encounters with the incomprehensible evils of the twentieth century – which arose in a world no less rational and humanist than our own that had created world-leading cultures (such as in Russia and Germany) – Milosz came to see evil as an independent and self-sufficient reality or, at least, as a dimension that is not in any tangible sense affected by progress or modern forms of sensibility. He noted that French philosopher Simone Weil was also a closet Manichaean; she conferred a millenarian meaning on the phrase 'Thy Kingdom Come' in The Lord's Prayer. There's a good reason why Milosz taught a course on Manichaeism at the University of California, Berkeley. By his own admission, in his book *Milosz's ABC's*, he situated the opening act twentieth century evil in the story of Bulgaria's Bogomils and the martyrdom of the Cathars in Verona and other Italian cities. All of the great East Europeans were Manichaeans to some degree – from Russia's Bulgakov through to George Orwell (who was an East European by choice).

Meanwhile, we live in an era of fear, negativity, and bad news. There's no market for good news because no one is interested in it. (Although a fun and adventure-filled apocalyptic story is something quite different.) It is this that gives rise to the wholesale sewing of panic and the industry of fear – 'breaking news' that relies on commentaries with large discrepancies and wherein the commentators often contradict themselves. Although some of these are occasionally insightful and well-reasoned, most are hysterical and defeatist.

What does the concept of liquid evil signify? How can it be best understood in our times of mutually exclusive qualities and characteristics that a number of phenomena bear? I would argue that liquid evil, contrary to what we could term solid evil – the latter being based on white-and-black social optic and the resilience of evil easily identifiable in our social and political reality – assumes the appearance of good and love. More than that, it parades as a seemingly neutral and impartial acceleration of life – the unprecedented speed of life and social change implying the loss of memory and moral amnesia; in addition, liquid evil walks in disguise as the absence and the impossibility of alternatives. A citizen becomes a consumer, and the dominant value of neutrality hides the fact of disengagement.

Individual helplessness and forsakenness coupled with the state's denial and refusal of its responsibility for education and culture, goes along with the heavenly marriage of neoliberalism and state bureaucracy both of them insisting on the individual's responsibility not only for their life and choices in a free-choice-free world, but for the state of global affairs as well.

George Orwell clearly saw that the new forms of evil tend to walk in the guise of good and love. Thou shalt love Big Brother. To the contrary of the predecessors of Oceania's Party, Jacobins, Bolsheviks, and Nazis alike, no martyrdom is allowed. Your life will go unnoticed, and nobody will know anything about your existence. Or you will be swiftly and silently reformed to force you to assume and adopt the vocabulary that you had long denied passionately and consistently. Evil is not obvious and self-evident anymore. Low intensity political oppression and human rights violations as well as low intensity military conflicts obfuscate and obliterate the dividing line between war and peace. War is peace, and peace is war. Neither good news nor bad news remain unambivalent and clear nowadays: even if there is no war or any other calamity going on, it becomes impossible to discuss it without scaremongering and the fear industry. Good news is no news. Bad news is the news by definition.

Therefore, by liquidity of evil, I assume that we live in a deterministic, pessimistic, fatalistic, fear-and-panic-ridden society, which still tends to cherish its time-honoured, albeit out of date and misleading, liberal-democratic credentials. The absence of dreams, alternatives and utopias is exactly what I would take as a significant aspect of the liquidity of evil. Two ideas of Ernst Bloch and Karl Mannheim proved prophetic: whereas Bloch regretted that modernity lost the warm and humane spirit of a utopian dream, Mannheim strongly felt that utopias were effectively translated into political ideologies, thus stripping them of alternative visions and thus confining them to the principle of reality, instead of imagination. The liquidity of evil signifies the divorce of the principle of imagination and the principle of reality, the final say being conferred for the latter.

The seductive powers of evil are coupled here with disengagement. For centuries, as we know, the very symbol and embodiment of evil was the Devil, whether making his appearance as Mephistopheles in the legend of Faust ranging from medieval tales to Christopher Marlowe's *The Tragical History of the Life and Death of Doctor Faustus* and Johann Wolfgang von Goethe's *Faust*, or as Woland in Mikhail Bulgakov's *The Master and Margarita*. This was the old news, though. The old 'good' Devil represented solid evil with its symbolic logic of the quest for human souls and active engagement in human and earthly matters. He simply pursued his goal trying to reverse and delegitimize the established social and moral order.

This is to say that solid evil was a sort of amorally committed and actively engaged evil with a solemn promise of social justice and equality at the end of the time of the world. Liquid evil, on the contrary, comes up with the rationale of seduction and disengagement. Whereas Prometheus and Satan, according to Vytautas Kavolis, an American sociologist of culture and civilisation analyst of Lithuanian background, as we will see soon, were the two protagonists of subversion, uprising, and revolution, the heroes of liquid evil attempt to strip humanity of its dreams, alternative projects and powers of dissent. In doing so, they act as protagonists of counterrevolution, obedience, and submission. The logic of solid evil was to win the soul and to conquer the world by imposing the new rules of the game; yet the logic of liquid evil is to seduce and retreat, changing its appearances all the time. 'Seduce and disengage' – this is the very motto of the Proteus-like hero both of liquid modernity and of liquid evil. I know what is to be done, yet I refuse to engage leaving my object or seduced victim to her or his own devices – that's the name of the game. From now on, one's sinking in the ocean will be called freedom.

In his analysis of the emergence of the symbols of the rebellion/subversion of the established order, Vytautas Kavolis traced the symbolic designs of evil, understood as interpretive frameworks within which we seek the answers to the questions raised by our time, interpreting ourselves and the world around us. In his analysis of the emergence of the symbols of the rebellion/subversion of the established order, Kavolis traced the symbolic designs of evil understood as interpretive frameworks within which we seek the answers to the questions raised by our time, interpreting ourselves and the world around us.

Prometheus and Satan are taken here as core mythological figures and symbolic designs to reveal the concepts of evil that dominated the moral imaginations of pre-Christian and Christian thinkers and writers. Whereas Prometheus manifests himself as a trickster hero whose challenge to Zeus rests not only on his natural enmity to the Olympic gods but also on his compassion for humanity as well, Satan appears in the Bible as the one who subverts the universal order established by God and, therefore, bears full responsibility for all manifestations of evil that result from this subversion.

Kavolis' work in cultural psychology provides a subtle and penetrating analysis of the models of evil as paradigms of secular morality and of the models of rebellion as contrasting modes of cultural logic. In doing so, he offers his insights into the emergence of the myth of Prometheus and that of Satan. Prometheus emerges in Kavolis's theory of the rise of modernity as a metaphor of technological progress/technologically efficient civilisation combined with a kind of sympathetic understanding of, and compassion for, the urges and sufferings of humankind. Satan is interpreted as a metaphor of the destruction of legitimate power and of the subversion of the predominant social and moral order.

In this manner, Kavolis developed some of his most provocative and perceptive hints as to how to analyse the symbolic logic of Marxism and all major social or political revolutions – aspects of which are at some points Promethean and at others Satanic. Each modernity – for Kavolis spoke of numerous and multiple 'modernities', each of them as ancient as civilisation itself – or civilisation-shaping movement, if pushed to the limit, can betray its Promethean and/or Satanic beginnings (Kavolis, 1977, pp. 331–344; Kavolis, 1984, pp. 17–35; Kavolis, 1985, pp. 189–211; Kavolis, 1993).

A valuable implication for literary theory and critique, this standpoint underlined Kavolis's insights into Herman Melville's *Moby-Dick* and Mary Shelley's *Frankenstein*. With sound reason Kavolis noted that even the title of Shelley's novel, *Frankenstein, or the Modern Prometheus*, was deeply misleading – the obviously Satanic character, Frankenstein, who challenged the Creator of the Universe and of the human being, was misrepresented there as a sort of modern Prometheus.

Our freedom today becomes localised in the sphere of sheer consumption and self-renewal. Control, surveillance, dispositional asymmetry of power parading as freedom of choice, fear industry, and privacy exposure games make up a complex combination of the sociocultural condition that we metaphorically call here TINA and liquid evil. Promise to allow and foster freedom, equality, justice, reason, pursuit of happiness, human rights, powers of individuality and association, social mobility, and living without borders to all humanity, and then disappear suddenly, leaving individuals in their countless identity games, mistaken for freedom, while also reminding them that it is up to them to solve the world's problems without relying much on institutions, fellowship, and engagement – this is the liquid evil's tried and true strategy.

This is why I assume that the real symbol of liquid evil is a kind of Big Mr Anonymous (whom we will discuss more explicitly soon), or a collective Don Juan. Don Juan, in Zygmunt Bauman's eyes, is modernity's real hero. Don Juan is the face of modernity whose power lies in constant and incessant change. At the same time, his is the power of self-concealment and retreat for the sake of an asymmetry of power. Solid modernity was about the conquest of territories and their utilisation for the sake of the state of any other power structure. Liquid modernity is about a hide-and-seek power game, be it a military strike followed by retreat or any other destabilising action. Therefore, liquid evil, in terms of military campaigns, tends to disrupt economy and life in certain territories or societies by bringing there as much chaos, fear, uncertainty, unsafety, and insecurity as possible, instead of assuming responsibility and burden for remaking or transforming them. At this point, terrorism appears as a pure expression of liquid evil. Imperialism is about solid power games, yet terrorism is always about the liquidity of evil – even its sinister logic of speaking up in favour of society coupled with disdain for a concrete society that is sacrificed for individualised power games should not deceive us.

The seducer, who retreats by leaving the void, disenchantment, or death, is a hero of liquid evil. The existential Don Juan comes to establish the asymmetry of power whose very essence lies in being able to observe the other without being seen himself. 'Chi son'io tu non saprai' (Who I am you do not know) – these words from Wolfgang Amadeus Mozart's opera *Don Giovanni*, written by the librettist Lorenzo Da Ponte (who had Don Juan getting intimate with two thousand women) reveal the crux of the modern manipulator's asymmetry. You do not see me because I will withdraw and leave you when it will no longer be safe for me to stay with you and reveal too much of myself and my hidden suffering or weakness. Who I am you will never know, although I will find out everything about you. Yet there is an illusion left to the objects of obscure desire that they would get as much attention and self-revelation as they could possibly need. An anonymous internet comment delivering toxic lies, mortally wounding, hurting, and brutally insulting us, that is, individuals with our first and last names, is nearly a perfect expression of the liquidity of evil that operates on the ground and is deeply entrenched in our mundane practices. Who I am you do not know.

3 Rational Impersonalism and the Culture of Determinism

A curious philosophical book, disguised as an innocent fable and published at the beginning of the eighteenth century, may throw new light on the mixed logic of modernity. The book is Bernard Mandeville's *Fable of Bees: Private Vices, Publick Benefits* (two successive editions in 1714 and 1723). Originating in 1705 as a sixpenny satire in verse, titled *The Grumbling Hive; or, Knaves Turn'd Honest,* later it developed into a book by the addition of 'Remarks' and other pieces. A witty and subtle attack against three vices, Fraud, Luxury, and Pride, the poem offered a strong argument, presenting a hive as a mirror of human society. Like society, the hive lives in corruption and prosperity. Yet it feels nostalgia for virtue and keeps praying to recover it. When the prayer is granted, everything changes overnight beyond recognition: There is no more vice, but activity and prosperity disappear. What replaces activity and prosperity are sloth, poverty, and boredom. Last but not least, all this happens in a considerably reduced population.

The essence of what I would define as Mandeville's paradox is that individual vice in universalistic morality can turn into a public benefit, whereas individual virtue does not necessarily increase the well-being of society. Once society can benefit from our pursuit of our own interest, we cannot lightly dismiss private vices. Mandeville achieves something similar to Machiavelli's effect: No one single truth exists in social reality, and every coin has two sides as far as human interaction and social life is concerned. Nothing personal lurks behind the predominant social and moral order, and nobody can be blamed in person for the shortcomings and imperfections of our life. Our jealousy and greed just happen to coincide with other individual's wishes and desires.

Public benefits result from private vices just as common good comes from our realism, sober-mindedness, and imperfection. Like Machiavelli, Mandeville deprives us of One Single Truth in social and political life. Nothing is certain and obvious here. A greedy but laborious fool can be more useful for society than an idle sage – here we can clearly hear the early voice of modernity with its ambivalence, scepticism, and relativism.

What can be found behind the fictional paraphernalia of Mandeville's *Fable of Bees* is Pierre Bayle's *Dictionnaire historique et critique*. Mandeville's scepticism, antirationalism, relativism, along with a strong emphasis on psychology and sensualism, relates him to French theoretical and intellectual influences, Bayle and Pierre Gassendi. Incidentally, Adam Smith knew this fable through Francis Hutcheson. The following winged expression of Smith's has really much in common with the intrinsic logic of Mandeville's paradox: 'It is not from the benevolence of the butcher, the brewer, or the baker that we expect our dinner, but from their regard to their own interest' (for more on this, see Donskis, 2009).

Here we can hear the birth-cry of 'rational impersonalism', as Ken Jowitt would have it (see Jowitt, 1993). Impersonalism, ambiguity, and ambivalence, coupled with what Max Weber once described as 'the iron cage', are those intrinsic forces that make modernity and capitalism in particular so deplorable and hateful in the eyes of those who want to restore what has been irreversibly lost by our modern world – namely the predictability, clarity, visibility, stability, and certainty of social reality; safety and security; political passions and social upheavals; emotional intimacy; human fellowship; a sense of community.

Yet this is all but one side of the coin. The celebration of rational impersonalism and our private vices turned into public benefits reflected an uncritical and unreflective attitude of a post-Communist society. The fable of bees by Mandeville seems to have been nearly a perfect narrative for a transitory period in a society where economic and moral individualism was long suppressed and then released with no ability to counterbalance the portrayal both of self and the world around oneself in black and white. A gradual destruction of the public domain, without which democratic politics become impossible, was not on the minds and lips of those who celebrated the free market and the invisible hand as just another term for democracy.

These are all the incarnations of fatalistic beliefs in the infallibility of the inevitable decline. In fact, here we hear the voice of the culture of determinism, as Vytautas Kavolis once had christened this phenomenon. He suggested that this phenomenon is deeply rooted in a modern system of moralisation, which he termed the culture of determinism. Kavolis puts it thus (Kavolis, 1993, p. 48):

> A modern amoral culture, in the sense that it tends to eliminate the notion of individual moral responsibility without taking collective responsibility seriously, is the *culture of determinism*. In this culture it is assumed that individuals are shaped and moved by biological or social forces in all essentials beyond the control, or even the possibility of major choices, of individuals affected by them. The four major intellectual foci of this culture are the theory that 'biology (or racial inheritance) is destiny', the belief that the human being is and should be nothing but a utility-calculating, pleasure-maximising machine; the conviction that

the individual is, in currently existing societies, only a victim of the 'oppressive', 'impoverished', 'devitalising', or 'traditionally constricted' social conditions of his or her existence (without the ability to become an agent of his fate and assume responsibility for her actions); and the notion that he can be helped out of such conditions solely by the 'guidance of experts' who have a 'rational social policy' at their disposal, in the determination of which those who are to be helped participate merely as instruments of the experts.

Kavolis's concept of a modern amoral culture sheds new light on why victimised groups or societies relate to the ruling elites as patients to diagnosing and curing specialists. At the same time, it allows us an essential comprehensive point of entry: we can understand why and how victimised culture manifests itself as the culture of destiny and determinism – in contrast to the culture of freedom and choice. This concept reveals the links between all kinds of deterministic theories, especially in the social sciences. Kavolis starts by quoting Sigmund Freud's dictum, 'Biology is destiny', and then goes on to show other modes of discourse that speak out in favour of inexorable laws of racial inheritance, history, milieu, societal life, social organisation, and so forth. A modern amoral culture denying individual responsibility and moral choice, or the culture of determinism in Kavolis's parlance, is a system of moralisation disseminated in the modern moral imagination.

Hence, we can identify what might be called natural innocence and victimisation. According to this attitude, people cannot in principle control biological or social forces. On the contrary, particular individuals and even entire societies are shaped and moved by those forces. Since the world is controlled and dominated by powerful groups, clandestine international organisations, or secret agencies and their elusive experts, individuals cannot assume moral responsibility for their actions. Nor can they influence or change the state of affairs. Such an attitude is characteristic of marginalised and victimised groups, but it is equally characteristic of the kind of consciousness shaped by anti-liberal and anti-democratic regimes.

In fact, several foci intersect and meet here: the culture of determinism is clearly on the tip of iceberg when dealing with what might be termed the clash of the culture of choice and the culture of destiny, both deeply embedded in the mind-sets, the political and moral rhetoric and practices of Eastern and Central European elites. It is hardly accidental that the intellectual and moral heroes of Eastern Europe in the late 1980s and the early 1990s were Karl R. Popper and his talented, though deeply unconventional, disciple George Soros: both were preaching the open society – the one with no monopoly of truth, and also devoid of any determinism-and-fatalism-ridden perception of reality. I would also add to this congregation of Eastern and Central European heroes of transformation the iconoclastic and sceptical gift of Ernest Gellner, and the profoundly democratic lessons of Ralf Dahrendorf drawn from the transformation and also from the new disenchantment of the world in the Weberian sense, which Dahrendorf articulated in his epistolic dialogue with an imagined Polish gentleman, *Reflections on the Revolution in Europe*, modelled as a concept after Edmund Burke's classical – and profoundly conservative – reactions to the French Revolution.

Popper's polemical oeuvre *The Open Society and its Enemies* became a must-read in the 1980s, and quite understandably so. It was against everything we were taught to believe in: the idea that there must be the centre of gravity and the predictable logic in every segment of life; the idea of inexorable laws of history and social development; the conviction that great thinkers are all-natural born democrats and confessed liberals nearly by definition. Popper destroyed this set of clichés and naïve assumptions as a house of cards. Moreover, another study on the unquestionable value of the unpredictability and spontaneity of human life and societal existence, *The Poverty of Historicism*, appeared as a direct confrontation with Karl Marx (and what else we needed in the 1980s, one would think). Yet in addition to Marx, the gallery of thinkers dethroned by Popper included Oswald Spengler, Arnold J. Toynbee, and other heroes of the cyclic interpretation of history and culture. In those days, we firmly believed that there *was* an alternative, there *should* and there *must* be one, no matter what is happening to us.

How ironic, then, that at the beginning of the twenty-first century, we find ourselves in the world of TINA disguised as a world of rational choice, profit-enhancing, and pleasure-maximising forces of the free market. Eastern and Central Europe – with a special role conferred to the Baltics – became the long and winding road from the TINA of Marxism-Leninism to the TINA of Neoliberalism.

4   Death of Privacy and the Cult of Self-Exposure

In this age of our painful quest for attention and of our obsessive self-discovery and compulsive self-exposure, we constantly need a new promise and a repeatedly reinforced illusion that you, a Plain Jane or a Simple Simon, can gain world attention too. Not just stars and world leaders but you, an ordinary mortal, can be important to someone because of the way you look or act or live or because of what you have or do or desire or because of what you find funny or worth showing or talking about – in short, things all too human and easy to understand. We have begun acting like emigrants even when we no longer set foot outside our own house or home town: thirsting for companionship and authentic human ties we think this, when it happens, is a short-lived miracle that will end soon; therefore, we must intensify this experience, for we don't know when it will come our way again.

Simply put, our freedom today becomes localised in the sphere of consumption and self-renewal but it has lost any connection with the most important thing: believing that you can change something in the world. This belief was shared by all the great prophets, theoreticians, ideologues, and writers of modernity. Today all the great utopias are dead. We are living in a period of dreary novels of warning and dystopias, though even the latter quickly turn into objects of easy, uncomplicated consumption. The sense of determinism and fatalism, strengthened not only by our failure to understand why and how economic systems fail and why we are beset by social crises but also by our total dependence on far-away markets and currency fluctuations in distant lands, fosters the illusion that we as individuals are able to change things only by spontaneous reactions, acts of benevolence and compassion, kind words, and intense communication. All that is left seems to build down to technical instruments and more intense human relations. During outbreaks of the plague in Europe, the logic of carnivals, mass feasting, and even orgies was predominant as well.

Technology and social networks have become new forms of control and separation. You see everyone; they all expose themselves, register, and take part, fine: you only need to figure out how to keep everyone in a scheme in which there are no possibilities of hiding something from the controlling structures of the state. Privacy is dying in front of our very eyes. It simply no longer exists – not only because there no longer are any messages unread and uncontrolled by outsiders nor things that, as classical literature testifies, a human being had the right and even duty to take with himself to the grave. What has disappeared is simply what used to be rightly called a secret – it has become either a good traded over the counter, an object of exchange, a password to momentary and short-lived success, or else a weakness showing you have something to hide, thus enabling blackmail and the exertion of pressure to rob you of your last vestiges of dignity and independence. People no longer have secrets in the old, honourable sense and don't even understand what that could possibly mean.

People gladly publicise their intimate life in exchange for momentarily having the spotlight turned on themselves: such feasts of exhibitionism are possible only in an age of unsteady, twittering connections and of unprecedented alienation. Some of those who expose themselves on Facebook are like those whose blogs resemble burps and belches in which they, full of narcissism, heave up their crises and frustrations; others are merely temporarily overcoming their feelings of isolation and insecurity. In this sense Facebook was indeed a brilliant and timely invention, after all. Just when social separation and isolation became unendurable, when it was no longer bearable to watch bad television and to read the sadomasochistic press, Facebook came into the world.

But with it also came possibilities of mortal danger and fatal evil. For Facebook embodies, as you might say, the essence of the DIY phenomenon: do it yourself. Take off your clothes, show us your secrets – do it yourself, of your own free will, and be happy while doing it. DIY. Strip for me, babe.

What has happened to our privacy? This question is being addressed nowadays with ever-increasing frequency. Of American society and its privacy crisis, Sarah E. Igo writes (Igo, 2015, p. 18):

> Certainly, if recent popular titles are to be trusted – *The End of Privacy, The Unwanted Gaze, The Naked Crowd, No Place to Hide* (two different books!), *Privacy in Peril, The Road to Big Brother, One Nation under Surveillance*, and perhaps the creepiest entrant, *I Know Who You Are and I Saw What You Did* – we Americans are in the midst of an unparalleled privacy crisis. On one side are the Snowden revelations, Google Glass, drones, smart refrigerators, and commercial algorithms that seem to know us better than we know ourselves. On the other is the individual quest for self-exposure in an ever-expanding universe of social media: Here, it is not the state or corporations that seem to imperil privacy but, rather, willing exhibitionists, eager to dispense with the concept altogether as they share intimate details of their personal lives with strangers.

There was a time when secret services and the political police worked hard to extract secrets and to get people to open up the details of their private and even intimately personal lives. Today these intelligence services should feel simultaneously exhilarated and unneeded: what should they do in a situation where everyone is telling everything about their own business themselves? But even if people don't disclose what they're doing, whom they dislike, and how they got rich, they still willingly reveal who they communicate with and who they know. And it's impossible not to participate in that structure. If you leave it, you lose your sense of past and present, you sever contact with your classmates and your colleagues, you don't pay your dues, and you get separated from your community. In virtual reality and in Facebook what vanishes is a fundamental aspect of real freedom: self-determination and a free choice of association rather than being sucked into a friendship simply because technology does not allow you to lead a civilised life otherwise.

But what does this say about our society? We are led to disturbing conclusions about human freedom no less than to an unwanted but warranted recognition that all of humanity is indeed becoming a nation that, though displaced and humiliated, is liked and hallowed: a Facebook nation. In the contemporary world, manipulation by political advertisement is not only capable of creating people's needs and their criteria of happiness, but also capable of fabricating the heroes of our time and controlling the imagination of the masses through successful biographies. These abilities make one pause for thought about a 'velvet' totalitarianism – a controlled form of manipulating consciousness and imagination that is cloaked as liberal democracy, which allows the enslavement and control of even the critics.

What remains deeply underneath is increasing social control and mass surveillance, which reveals what happened to politics outpaced by technology. Whether we like it or not, technology does not ask us if we desire it. Once you can use it, you must do so. The refusal relegates you to the margins of society left without being able to pay your dues as a tenant or to participate in a public debate. The state, which does not use mass surveillance, becomes unable to justify its excessive use of secret services and spying techniques. Curiously, this tendency goes hand in hand with the spread and explosive proliferation of the forms of self-display and confessional culture in general, whether in popular or even in highbrow culture.

With sound reason, then, Sarah E. Igo concludes (Igo, 2015, p. 28):

> What if confessional culture is simply an avenue for turning the surveillance society inside out? One commentator writes that 'our physical bodies are being shadowed by an increasingly comprehensive "data body", a body of data, moreover, that 'does not just follow but precedes the individual being measured and classified' ... If this is the case, continuous visibility on one's own terms (whether through ACT UP, reality television, or Facebook) begins to look like a strategy – if not an unproblematic one – of autonomy, a public way of maintaining control over one's private identity. A culture of self-display may, in this way, be an obscure legacy of the 1970s, the outgrowth of identity politics and new media formats, but also a half-century's reckoning with data banks and bureaucratic surveillance.

Therefore, technology will not allow you to remain on the side-lines. *I can* transmutes into *I must*. I can, therefore I must. No dilemmas permitted. We live in a reality of possibilities, not one of dilemmas. This is something akin to the ethics of WikiLeaks, where there is no morality left. It is obligatory to spy and to leak, though it's unclear for what reason and to what end. It works in both ways: for and against the state, yet it never assumes responsibility for a truly anguished individual. It's something that has to be done just because it's technologically feasible. There's a moral vacuum here created by a technology that has overtaken politics. The problem for such a consciousness is not the form or legitimacy of power but its quantity. For evil (by the way, secretly adored) is where there is more financial and political power. If this is so, we deal a blow to ethics, since technology comes to fill the gaps left by politics and public morality: once you are connected, you are absolved and relieved. The media is the message, and living online becomes an answer to the dilemmas of our modern existence.

A total abolition of privacy leading to manipulation with human secrets and abuses of their intimacy, which appears as a nightmarish vision of the future in such dystopias as Yevgeny Zamyatin's *We* and George Orwell's *1984*, was foreseen, anticipated, and wittily depicted in early modern European literature. As mentioned in our *Moral Blindness* (2013), suffice it to recall Luis Vélez de Guevara's *El Diablo cojuelo* (*The Devil on the Crutches*, or *The Limping Devil*), a seventeenth-century text where the devil has the power to reveal the insides of the houses, or a variation of this theme in Alain-René Le Sage's novel under that same title in French, *Le diable boiteux*. The astonishing fact remains, though, that what early modern writers took as a devilish force aimed to deprive human beings of their privacy and secrets has now become inseparable from the reality shows and other actions of wilful and joyful self-exposure in our self-revealing age.

Two of the manifestations of the new evil: insensitivity to human suffering, and the desire to colonise privacy by taking away a person's secret, the something that should never be talked about and made public. The global use of others' biographies, intimacies, lives and experiences is a symptom of insensitivity and meaninglessness.

5   Big Mr Anonymous

As mentioned, the net society is the fear-ridden society. It becomes a perfect place for the entire fear industry and organised scaremongering. It highlights and exposes the rise of technocracy disguised as democracy. At the same time, the net society and its public domain nourish and nurture such indispensable constituent parts of technocracy as value neutrality and instrumentalism in all their manifestations. In this culture of constant fear, scaremongering, reform, and incessant change, shallowness becomes an asset rather than a liability. In fact, the culture of fear and is the culture of shallowness, and vice versa. Yet shallowness is 'miscalled' here as adaptability and flexibility (just like 'simple truth miscall'd simplicity' in William Shakespeare's 66th sonnet). This results in shallow institutional practices, countless and meaningless strategy games, and empty rhetoric. Vocabularies become separated from concepts, and end up as senseless language games and sets of hollow terms behind hollow concepts.

I had once asked the Russian writer Andrei Bitov to comment on the phenomenon of the superfluous human being in Russian literature. In a literary seminar that was taking place in Sweden's Visby he was speaking about Alexander Pushkin, who not only used this concept but elucidated the phenomenon itself as well in his novel-in-verse, *Eugene Onegin*. Be that as it may, prior to this work and Mikhail Lermontov's *A Hero of Our Time*, the first to call attention to the superfluous human being in Russia was Alexander Herzen, who immediately after the crushing of the Decembrist Revolt realised that there were people in Russia who would never find a place in politics or even society. They were in the wrong historical period and the wrong part of the world. Something or somebody made a mistake here: maybe it was God or history perhaps, or was it fate? Perhaps they had to be sacrificed in the name of a brighter future, as in a Greek tragedy. Bitov told me, without any agitation, that everything might be simpler still: there are, to tell the truth, situations, epochs, and societies, in which human beings are just redundant.

It strikes me that our epoch, too, can do perfectly well without human beings. We just don't need each other for any social plenitude, for human fulfilment. *Pars pro toto* is enough. We need parts instead of the whole. During elections, we need some votes; in a situation requiring the lowering of production costs, we need cheap labour; in order to create a safe, trustworthy, and business-friendly environment we need what's called solidarity (in other words, renouncing protest and not defending one's rights, instead choosing emigration or degradation). In some cases, an anonymous mass is precisely what fills the bill: it is intensely desired and eagerly sought after by vote-hunting politicians who before every election day remember emigrants as an indispensable part of their electorate while electronic voting (that we are about to, but haven't yet adopted) is going on. In other cases, this mass is what politicians try to run away from because they understand perfectly well that the problems causing people to leave everything behind in their homeland and move abroad are not capable of being solved in economically weak countries no longer separated by borders from economically stronger ones.

Ratings are impossible without an anonymous mass of spectators and voters; that's why we love the aforementioned Big Mr Anonymous for as long as he legitimises us with his faceless, soulless loyalty. We cannot do without this mass if we are politicians, television producers, stars, or anyone else claiming the right to be publicly known with a recognisable face and name. But as soon as this mass stops legitimising us and turns to us, not in gestures of recognition and thus of repeatedly recreating us, but in demanding from us that we take notice of their individual names and faces as they step out of this anonymous mass and thereby take on personal features of human pain, drama, and tragedy, then we begin to wish and wash this mass away. Why? It's because we almost instinctively realise that its problems – the problems of the individual souls making up this mass – are insoluble in a world in which everything they seek has been promised to them but without their having been told when and at what cost all this will be available to them. In their own country? At home? Why no, no way.

Where are the great promises of modernity to be found? Mobility, freedom of movement, and the freedom of choice – weren't these promised to them? And wasn't one of the promises a world without borders as well? But such a world wouldn't be conducive for small, economically and politically infirm countries to gain strength. In such a world, powerful states would get stronger and weak ones would get weaker still. Wasn't it promised to us that we'd be able freely to cross any European border?

I'll put the situation in the words of a character in Marius Ivaškevičius's play *Expulsion* as staged by Oskaras Koršunovas. Eglė, the (anti)protagonist, says that crossing the border will be easy but there's one thing you'll have to leave behind, one thing you won't be able to take with you: your self-worth. When did this change happen: before the expulsion or after it? And what kind of expulsion are we talking about here? Is it a self-expulsion in the sense of *let's get out of here*? Or is it an expelling in the sense of *let's get rid of it* – a deliberate jettisoning of something that painfully testifies to your own or the system's faults? Moreover, will you be allowed to be yourself? Or will you have to transform yourself into a monkey, a pitiful socio-political parakeet parroting the accent, vocabulary, manners, tone, timbre, and body movements of upper-class people?

The collective actor in the drama of expulsion is Big Mr Anonymous. By the latter name I have in mind the whole anonymity-enabling system that consists of operators and those operated upon; of repressive organs and their victims trying to survive. The direct actors, who first of all possess nicknames and only then have first and last names, constitute our Lithuanian *precariat*. This is globalisation's new lower class in place of Karl Marx's proletariat: they are the precariously, unsafely situated people living in a zone of ever-present danger and risk. Nothing is guaranteed to them, they can't be certain about anything; their sense of security has been taken away from them forever. At the same time, Big Mr Anonymous, as was suggested earlier, may well be understood as a system of seduction equipped with the power to withdraw from our sense of responsibility for our neighbours, ourselves, and the world around us, and from our sensitivity as well. Nothing personal, just business…

Yes, they can attain some prosperity, but only through a kind of social suicide by becoming part of the great Nothing in a foreign country. This *precariat* embodies and serves the global network of anonymous persons and organisations, a network that starts with statistics and ends with a really existing variety that is held to be sufficient proof of the fact that society allows the impregnable existence of shocking social contrasts and inequalities. These will be liberally explained away by cultural differences and their right to exist in dignity, to be as they are and to be left alone, without imposing sensitivities and interpretations that are foreign to them, or even giving them any political or economic power. Thus, you become part of the work force, with the right to imitate the right local accents and the consumption patterns of the jet-set classes, but without the right to your own authentic historical-political narrative and your own cultural ways of interpreting yourself.

6   Postscript: Zombie Concepts and Shallow Universities

In our book of dialogues, *Moral Blindness* (2013), Zygmunt Bauman and I have discussed a disturbing phenomenon, which I would describe as a post-academic university. An awkward amalgam of medieval academic ritual, specialisation, a blatant and blunt denial of the role of the humanities in modern society, managerialism and shallowness allows a perfect scene for such a post-academic university, the playground for enormous pressures, the latter coming from technocratic forces disguised as the genuine voices of liberty and democracy – first and foremost, the market-oriented forms of determinism and fatalism with no room left for the principle of alternative, including critical thought and self-questioning.

The sole mission and raison d'être of the post-academic university seems to lie in its overt shallowness, flexibility, submissiveness to the managerial elites, and also in adaptability to the calls and assignments coming from the markets and the political elites. Hollow words, empty rhetoric, and countless strategy games appear as the quintessence of this sort of tyranny of shallowness best embodied in the post-academic university. It is a strategy without a strategy, as the latter becomes merely a language game. The Wittgensteinian idea of language games was applied by Gianni Vattimo to describe technocracy walking in disguise as democracy, or present politics without politics, both reduced to a series of language games. As Zygmunt Bauman would have it, present strategies without strategies, or politics without politics, are tantamount to ethics without morality.

'Outside the Church there is no salvation' (*extra ecclesiam nulla salus*) – this expression is ascribed to Saint Cyprian of Carthage, a bishop of the third century. We have a modern equivalent of this sort of civilizational logic, though, since ours is a corporate and quasi-medieval world where individuals do not have their existence outside of an institution which frames and moulds them. The Academia is the New Church nowadays. This is why the role of dissent, secular heterodoxy, and alternative in this world is far more problematic and complex than it may seem at the first sight.

The post-academic university becomes a place to practice shallowness disguised as flexibility and adaptability. Lecturing becomes merchandise, and so does academic performance as such. The unholy alliance of state bureaucracy and neoliberal practices – deregulation, dissemination, and privatisation coupled with bureaucratic control – results in the academic community becoming a tiny and insignificant minority in what we call nowadays the academia. Enormous economic and political pressure coming from the university management and the state establishment makes academic and intellectual freedom vulnerable and fragile. In some cases, there is an obvious backlash – especially in Eastern and Central Europe where nobody spoke about students as workforce for more than twenty years. Strangely enough, the propensity to assess universities as suppliers of workforce is getting increasingly stronger now. In the 1990s, Kavolis warned his Lithuanian fellow academics and state officials about the grave dangers and devastating consequences of the cult of pure specialists, which he noticed in Lithuania at that time.

This propensity goes hand in hand with marginalisation of academics, scholars and students in terms of their autonomy and their involvement in the debates about the future of their respective universities. Whereas in nineteenth-century Russia Alexander Herzen and Alexander Pushkin wrote about the superfluous human being, we may well call faculty in present universities if not superfluous, then at least not decisive and central when it comes to the visions and articulations of academic life and the future of universities. The 'publish or perish' imperative having been replaced with the 'publish and perish' one, it is evident that permanent uncertainty, unsafety, and insecurity becomes one of the *conditions sine qua non* of academia. Therefore, endless and never-ending reforms of the academic system and universities allows the state bureaucracy and university management to keep scholars in suspense without their being able to participate in the symbolic construction of reality otherwise than through their subordination and subjugation to that system.

Ulrich Beck and Zygmunt Bauman wrote about zombie concepts – concepts that capture and describe non-existent things, or phenomena that do not exist nowadays anymore (see Bauman & Donskis, 2013). Hollow words, empty phrases, and shallow rhetoric – all these signify the arrival of the state of affairs when words and their frames of meaning bid farewell to one another. They simply part leaving no trace. The concepts of university autonomy and academic freedom are dangerously approaching the point of no return when they will be on the way to becoming zombie concepts – the enormous pressure put on the academia by the unholy alliance of local and international ideologues of neoliberalism, libertarian preachers of free-market fundamentalism, and political technocrats will sooner or later nullify the remnants of the time-honoured autonomy and independence of universities.

High schools, colleges, and universities are increasingly being confined to a playground for culture wars; yet things are even worse with various sorts of pilot projects of management and business administration being tested and tried out in universities with the sole reason of exclusion of corporate relations-free and independent academics from the public domain where they serve as naysayers and social critics. Therefore, such terms as responsibility and academic ethics become obsolete and superfluous, since they can barely shed any light on zombie concepts and reality they are bound to represent – for how can you represent the domain from which you are excluded by anonymous and irresponsible agencies of power structure that aim to manage, control, and reform you without your consent and even without consulting academic community? What is any sort of never-ending academic reform if not exercise of power using the news about it as a mere fait accompli? Policy makers do their utmost to reform universities without bothering themselves with the reform of the political system itself or politics at large; therefore, the longer you keep reforming the academia, the more insecure and unsafe academics become, which means that the imposed from above and vertical reform diminishes their powers of social criticism.

In addition to the explosive proliferation of zombie concepts, present-day universities have fallen prey to privatisation of utopia as a blueprint for a viable moral order and as a dream of a good and just society. For a long time, we knew utopia as a framework for a symbolic design within which we could explain ourselves and the world around us, allowing room for value and dream. Yet since utopia bowed out to the dream of a good and just society becoming a personal success story re-enacted by every single celebrity and their accounts of success and Cinderella-like miracle of social metamorphosis, this has dealt a painful blow to all visionaries of university life.

For how can we return to the university as a place of reconciliation of fact/truth and value, expertise and intimacy, verification and trust, free individual and critical community in a world which increasingly declares and takes pride in its value neutrality/ethical detachment euphemistically termed efficiency, adaptability, and flexibility? Here, again, we are in the realm of shallowness miscalled the ability to change, adapt, and be flexible. Bad news for the academia that still nurtures the dream of bridging the past, the present, and the future, thus confronting value neutrality, instrumentalism, and ethical detachment whose social effects have already proved disastrous for the modern world.

To have a plausible political-historical narrative nowadays means to have viable politics, rather than policies masquerading as politics. Politics becomes impossible without a good story in the form of a convincing plot or an inspiring vision. The same applies to good literature. When we fail a method in our scholarship, or when a method fails us, we switch to a story – this sounds much in tune with Umberto Eco. Where scholarly language fails, fiction comes as a way out of the predicament with an interpretation of the world around us.

The funny thing is that politics does not work without our stories. This is to say that modern politics needs the humanities much more than politicians suspect. Without travel accounts, humour, laughter, warning, and moralising, political concepts tend to become empty. With sound reason, therefore, Karl Marx once wittily noted that he learned much more about the nineteenth century's political and economic life from Honoré de Balzac's novels than from all economists of that time put together.

This is the reason why Shakespeare was far and away the most profound political thinker of Renaissance Europe. Niccolò Machiavelli's works *Florentine Stories* and *Discourses on Livy* tell us much about his literary vocation and also about the talent of a storyteller – no less than exuberant comedies penned by Machiavelli, such as *The Mandragola*.

Do we tell each other European stories nowadays to enhance our powers of interpretation and association, and to reveal one another's experiences, traumas, dreams, visions, and fears? We don't, alas. Instead, we have confined the entire European project merely to its economic and technical aspects. Stories lay the foundation for Giovanni Boccaccio's masterpiece *Decameron*; nothing other than stories about human suffering, whatever their blood and creed, made Voltaire's philosophical tales, such as *Candide, ou l'Optimisme* (Candide, or Optimism), truly European stories.

This reference as well as the human reality behind it crossed my mind almost immediately when I started teaching the course on politics and literature at the University of Bologna. The reason was quite simple: I had the entire fabric of Europe in my class, as the course was given within the East European studies program with the participation of students from Western, Central, and Eastern Europe, including non-EU countries such as Albania, Croatia, Kosovo, Macedonia, Russia, Serbia, and Ukraine.

We easily surpassed and crossed the boundaries of an academic performance and discussion, for it was human exchanges on the newly discovered and shocking moral blindness of classmates or neighbours, human dramas of high treason, moral treachery, disappointment, cowardice, cruelty, and loss of sensitivity. How can we miss the point talking past and present to each other or listening to someone else's drama that it was Dante who coined the phrase 'the cult of cruelty', and the English writer Rex Warner who forged the phrase 'the cult of power' – political idioms that we use constantly without being aware of the fact that they are not straight out of the vocabulary of today?

Suffice it to recall that the real founding fathers of Europe, Renaissance humanists Thomas More and Erasmus of Rotterdam made friends in Paris conjointly translating Lucian from Greek into Latin, and also connecting their friend, German painter Hans Holbein the Younger, to the royal court of the king of England, Henry VIII. Whereas the great Flemish painter Quentin Matsys saved for history the face of their friend in Antwerp, Peter Giles, Hans Holbein the Younger immortalised the faces of his benefactor Thomas More and Erasmus of Rotterdam.

Yet the bad news is that politics has colonised culture nowadays, and this has gone unnoticed, albeit under our noses. This is not to say that culture is politically exploited and vulgarised for long- or short-term political ends and objectives. In a democratic political setting, culture is separated from politics. An instrumentalist approach to culture immediately betrays either technocratic disdain for the world of arts and letters or poorly concealed hostility to human worth and liberty. However, in our brave new world, the problem lies elsewhere.

We don't need the humanities anymore as a primary driving force behind our political and moral sensibilities. Instead, politicians try to keep the academia as unsafe, uncertain, and insecure as possible – by reshaping, or 'reforming' it, into a branch of the corporate world. By and large, this idea of the necessity to politically rationalise, change, reshape, refurbish, and renovate the academia is a simulacrum, in Jean Baudrillard's terms. It conceals the fact that the political class and our bad policies are exactly what desperately need that change and reform. Yet power speaks: if I don't change you, you will come to change me.

We stopped telling moving stories to each other. Instead, we nourish ourselves and the world around us with conspiracy theories (which are always about the big and powerful, instead of the small and humane), sensationalist stuff, and crime or horror stories. In doing so, we are at peril of stepping away from our innermost European sensibilities, one of which has always been and continues to be the legitimacy of opposing narratives, attitudes, and memories. Human beings are incomplete without one another.

References

Bauman, Z., & Donskis, L. (2013). *Moral Blindness: The Loss of Sensitivity in Liquid Modernity*. Cambridge, Polity Press.

Donskis, L. (2009). *Troubled Identity and the Modern World*. London, Palgrave Macmillan.

Igo, S.E. (2015). The beginnings of the end of privacy, *The Hedgehog Review, 17* (1), 18–29.

Jacobs, A. (2015). The witness of literature: a genealogical sketch, *The Hedgehog Review, 17* (2), 65–77.

Jowitt, K. (1993). *New World Disorder: The Leninist Extinction*. Berkeley, Berkeley: The University of California Press.

Kavolis, V. (1977). Moral cultures and moral logics. *Sociological Analysis, 38*, 331–344.

Kavolis, V. (1984). Civilisational models of evil, In Coleman Nelson, M., & Eigen, M. (eds.), *Evil: Self and Culture*, Alphen aan de Rijn, Human Sciences Press.

Kavolis, V. (1985). Logics of evil as secular moralities. *Soundings, 68*, 189–211.

Kavolis, V. (1993). *Moralising Cultures*. Lanham, Maryland, University Press of America.

CHAPTER 2

Academic Homecoming. Stories from the Field

Frans Kamsteeg

Abstract

Academics world-wide experience the daily consequences of the sell-out that neoliberal universities euphemistically frame as a combination of effectiveness, efficiency and excellence. In this contribution I use fiction, and in particular John Williams' recently rediscovered novel *Stoner*, to illustrate how painfully tangible these effects become in daily academic practice. The *Stoner* book shows the imbroglio of an aspiring American literature professor, whose career is presented as a symbol of the increasing academic depreciation of knowledge and Bildung. I argue that the literary quality of *Stoner* and other 'academic novels' can better than any sociological study convey the detrimental consequences of the unhappy marriage of ignorance, measurability and accountability that reigns today's universities. Sparked by an auto-ethnographic account of academic quality measurement I plea for maintaining what is still left of 'academic passion', hoping to prevent academia and its inhabitants from suffering the same tragic fate as many a protagonist in academic novels.

Keywords

public academic life – literature – belonging – quality – accountability

1   Introduction: on Academic Sell-out

Somewhere in the past, writes Robert Birnbaum, 'being a professional was ennobling [...presuming] a calling – a vocation – and a dedication to service' (2000, p. 225). Perhaps it is this Weberian and Humboldtian vocational ideal that makes university inhabitants generally feel 'at home', although feelings of unease and even alienation have entered the university over the last two decades, provoking what Nussbaum calls 'the silent crisis' (2010). Already in 1997 Bill Readings wrote his *University in Ruins* in which he ascertained that the university was rapidly handing over its autonomy to the market and its bureaucratic aligning, but recent struggles in African, North-American, and

European universities urgently put the global forces of marketisation, neoliberalisation, and the resulting alienation in the university back on the agenda again. In South Africa this alienation has taken a particularly articulated form. As Tabensky and Matthews (2015) explain, the South African higher education sector under apartheid ceased to be an inclusive 'home' and was transformed into an ambiguous place where students and staff were forcefully allocated and separated, thus gaining all the characteristics of a non-home. In 2015, ten years after a radical higher-education restructuring, the Rhodes-must-fall student protests in South African targeted not only the heritage of apartheid and colonisation of higher education institutions as such, but also questioned their 'colonised' curricula and institutional practices and their roots in European and global Northern canons. South African higher education then was taking stock of where it stood in terms of post-apartheid transformation. In all of the Afrikaner- and English-speaking universities students (sometimes supported by staff) were demanding to be finally freed from the symbols and practices of the not-so-recent past. The Rhodes-must-fall movement, that started at one of South Africa's internationally most prestigious universities, the University of Cape Town, was the starting-point of a stream of critical voices urging lower fees and a change in the academic set-up and governance structure of practically all institutions of higher education in the country (Booysen, 2016; Jansen, 2017; Ray, 2016). In most cases this meant that black and white students and staff claimed co-ownership of the institutions in which they felt unwelcome strangers because of the dominant institutional culture of whiteness inhibiting them from identifying with their places of study (Higgins, 2013; Jansen, 2009). The particular kinds and forms of knowledge that is privileged by these dominant cultures further deprived many students and staff of the possibility of feeling at home, a process that was only further exacerbated by the expanding neoliberal globalisation and governance at South Africa's universities after its democratic turn in 1994.

In the age of the 'consumer university' (Bauman & Donskis, 2013; see also Boutellier, 2015) this feeling of not-belonging and non-ownership, so evidently present in South Africa, is, however, widely shared in academia worldwide. In South Africa it is the apartheid-legacy and colonial institutional cultural trap that ignited the universities, while the same experience of expropriation and decolonialisation also became prominent in the 2015 protests in the Netherlands and other Western countries, including the USA. Staff and students rose against what is called 'the spirit of effectiveness, efficiency and accountability' governing present-day universities. Particularly academics from the humanities and social sciences severely criticise this neoliberal trend or 'fad', as Birnbaum already labelled it in 2000. Universities have turned from homes of 'gay science' into orphanages of knowledge, transforming all their inhabitants into market competitors in a rat race to produce knowledge (citations) and push knowledge consumers (students) through the pipeline of the knowledge economy jungle (Birnbaum, 1988, 2000; Gibbons 1994; Nussbaum, 2010; Noordegraaf & Schinkel, 2011). A typology of present-day universities by Paradeise & Thoenig (2013), for instance, reserves the label 'wannabes' for those universities ruled over by this kind of opportunistic utilitarianism regime, but it could just as easily be argued that this 'rationale' has affected and infected the full spectrum of institutions of higher learning, including those 'venerables'[1] that top the various international rankings, which supposedly measure their quality.

Without idealising any form of ivory tower academia, the passionate and joyful science Nietzsche describes – be it with some irony – in *The Gay Science* is governed by the 'will henceforth to question further, more deeply, severely, harshly, evilly, and quietly than one had previously questioned (2008, p. 7)'. Already in 1882 Nietzsche saw that this academic practice was ceasing 'to [...] a calculus of utility' (ibid., p. 201). He maintains that this 'utility' science can never represent the spirit of true science that 'must have originated in spite of the fact that the disutility and dangerousness of "the will to truth" or "truth at any price" is proved to it constantly' (ibid.). It is about time to acknowledge the importance for academics to reconfirm 'the importance of being earnest', as Nussbaum writes in her *Political Emotions* (2013), where she – building on Rawls – accentuates the key role to be played by (political) emotions, and particularly love and passion/compassion as the lubricants of society. In her view these fundamental emotions, first promoted in the family, are further taught at school, to – finally – fully develop in academia. Teaching critical freedom and the right to dissent create the circumstances for love and hence contribute to the promotion of the common good and the building of a sustainable and just society. To Nussbaum this just society rests upon the premise that it invites rather than coerces, which means that a critical spirit is leading, in which everything is subject to enquiry. It is this inquisitive and questioning mind that is to be taught at university – paired to an unconditional support of the inviolable principles of equality and justice, together fuelling love as the driving societal force. Hence public rituals, ceremonies, and stories, *as well as systems of education*, must be constructed on these fundamental values. Nussbaum invokes John Stuart Mill's inaugural Rector's Address at the University of St. Andrews to discuss the universities' contribution to this common good – in contrast to

---

[1] Paradeise & Thoenig (2013) for instance distinguish between 'top of the pile', 'wannabe', 'venerable', and 'missionary' institutions, with distinctive roles for management in each of them, as well as different views on the relation between research and education.

the pursuit of interest, valorisation, efficiency, output-effectiveness, and the corresponding accountability and audit frameworks (Nussbaum, 2013, p. 81; 82ff). Yet, preaching these values and principles today requires a high degree of civil courage, moral imagination, engaged scholarship, and empathy (cf. Ignatieff, 2013; De Waal, 2008). Public scholar and veteran Noam Chomsky is perhaps the most vocal defender of this plea in his *The Intellectuals and the State* (2014), already put forward in his early warning *The Death of American Universities* (1977). In both texts Chomsky builds on Max Weber's seminal *Science as a Vocation* (1946 [1919]) that promotes the love of teaching, that is, teaching to educate rather than teaching to test (cf. Biesta, 2016), to which I will come back in my discussion of academic citizenship at the end of this chapter. The plea that I will make there is built upon an exploration of how academic freedom and love of science is shaped and defended in world literature.

2 Literary Academic Champions Revisited

Perhaps the most compelling way of deepening the propositions of my introduction – and maybe even this volume as a whole – is by turning to literature, a point that is also made in the last section of Donskis' previous chapter. The most telling recent story about academia in this respect is John Williams' epic novel *Stoner* (2006 [1965]), a presently immensely popular book in the Western world. It is about a university professor (Stoner) whose love for English literature (which I take as a symbol for academic culture in general) remains unbroken despite the surrounding culture of an American university largely inhabited by mediocre people whose prime objective seems to be protecting the institutional order rather than academic standards. Stoner's story is that of an academic amateur – in the literal, positive sense of the word – who little by little becomes crushed by the small-minded micro politics that even compromises his most enlightened intellectual allies.

A Tragic Story
John Williams opens his book by telling the story of a university student from an impoverished farm who is struck to silence by a Shakespearean sonnet in his second year at an American Midwestern college, and subsequently decides to become a teacher in Medieval English literature himself, because his professor tells him so: 'you are in love, it's as simple as that' (p. 20). Stoner and his study friends discuss what they call the true nature of the university, which they decide to be 'The True, the Good, the Beautiful, just laying around the corner' (p. 29). For Stoner this is, however, not the beginning of a bright future.

Being a 'dreamer' in the words of one of his friends, it takes him a while to master the required teaching skills, but as soon as he starts believing that his own love of literature will bear fruit among his students, he gets entangled in the messiness of classroom demeanour, student apathy, and bureaucracy. After a brief but promising career as an assistant professor, he becomes a classic and tragic academic figure,[2] and gradually sinks into oblivion.

Williams' novel on the gloomy life of this academic loner and outsider recently became a bestseller, more than fifty years after its first edition in 1963. We can only guess why the book became so popular, but it is tempting to suggest it is because the text makes a passionate plea for the (academic) craftsmanship that Sennett (2008) maintains requires a re-appreciation of the skills and energy required for really good work, that is so in danger of being discredited in today's world. Although *Stoner* is most often lauded for its empathetic story of a man being misrecognised and belittled in his work (and by his wife for that matter), I believe it can also serve to draw some important lessons about 'the true nature of the University' (p. 29) and what makes for its quality, that almost metaphysical concept that is so hard to define, but that nevertheless 'for all practical purposes [...] really does exists' as Robert Pirsig argues in his classic *Zen and the Art of Motorcycle Maintenance* (1974, p. 187). This argument about academic quality is best illustrated when as a fresh university professor Stoner fails a graduate course student who is supervised by a colleague of his, because of his last-minute handing in of an incomplete, superficial, and partly plagiarised assignment. He qualifies this as proof of the student's 'laziness and dishonesty and ignorance', and advises him to consider leaving the university for the simple reason of not being entitled to have 'a place in a graduate program' (p. 147). Here Stoner uses the quality argument suggested by Pirsig (1974, p. 251) when he explains to the student that he simply did not produce the correct qualitative response to what an academic environment expected of him.

One could argue that what happened here was just an incident – after all for students in general internalising the academic habitus is time and energy consuming – yet the subsequent part of the story rather painfully shows the opposite: this student consciously refuses not only to revise his work but rather defiantly accuses Stoner of assessing him on the basis of unjustified criteria. When Stoner is later on required to be a member of the committee that has to examine the same student orally, it soon dawns on him that what just seemed a mere incident is turning into something far bigger than this. During the examination by Stoner it is the student's supervisor who changes the course of things. Instead of valuing Stoner for defending academic standards and

---

2   This is not how John Williams would see it (see page xii).

quality, his colleague becomes his opponent and tries to force him to accept the student's mediocrity by shrewdly guiding the student in his answers to Stoner's questions, while the two slightly intimidated other members – one being his old friend and the chairman of the committee – stay aloof, a choice that could well be considered to represent an attitude increasingly current in academia. Stoner, however, is not willing to budge an inch and relentlessly keeps questioning the student so that his disqualification becomes evident. The final verdict is postponed, but the student's supervisor assures his pupil that he has nothing to worry about.

After failing this Master's student in his course, and subsequently in his final exams, for an apparent lack of quality, Stoner refuses to think of accepting the position of department head, which is taken by the same colleague whose student he has failed. This is the part where from an academic perspective the story really becomes depressing. For it is only after the confrontational meeting that the chairman of the session tells his old friend Stoner that his opponent – the student's supervisor – will be the new head of the department. This is the moment they both realise that a point of no return has been passed. His friend tries to console Stoner with the remark that they (the university?) cannot keep 'this kind of student' out, to which Stoner objects that at least they can try, because 'it would be a disaster to let him [the student] loose in a classroom' (p. 167). The next day Stoner is threatened by his opponent with the charge of prejudice against the student during the exam, and even in the regular classes preceding the exam. In the end there are no charges, but for the next semester the new department's head removes him from all of his previous teaching responsibilities. Stoner then realises 'that is was possible that he might leave the University, that he might teach elsewhere' (p. 173), but his wife who is the last judge immediately rejects the idea: 'You should have thought of this before, of what it might lead to. A cripple. [...] Honestly, things are so important to you. What *difference* could it make?' (p. 174). The battle appears to have been totally lost when in the next semester the student triumphantly returns and has himself passed by a new examination committee installed by Stoner's adversary. For a while Stoner is the laughingstock of the campus, and subsequently he becomes a legend and campus character (p. 229). The shrewd machinations of his colleague using his power of chairman then results in Stoner keeping more and more to himself and slowly but surely marginalising himself from the academic community. A scandalous love affair with a student – movingly described in really high-quality language – decides his fate. He is given more and more classes to teach, in which he starts experimenting with unconventional teaching methods to challenge his students. The latter start to complain even more about him, as in class he often 'became so immersed in this subject that he seemed unaware of anything or anyone around him'. More isolated than ever, his life toddles on while teaching (for more than forty years) until he finally dies of cancer alone in his house with a pile of books next to him, one of which slips through his fingers in his last minutes on earth.

It is certainly remarkable that this moving story of a crushed academic in the depressing environment of a 'quiet' American university has become something of a slow-burn sensation. Nearly two decades after its author's death in 1994, *Stoner* hit Europe's bestseller lists, causing a stir in Britain, America, and the Netherlands. The unexpected and widespread reappraisal has earned the epithet 'the Stoner phenomenon', despite the fact that the novel was almost forgotten soon after its publication. Perhaps it was the wrong time for publishing a novel about this ordinary man, in a far from exciting environment, the university. Yet I believe the novel has a broader appeal. The idea on which *Stoner* is built, namely that reading literature – in this case a poem – can become a life-turning event that, moreover, stands as a symbol for the beauty and emotion that the academic endeavour can – or should – awaken today. I would like to believe that the fact that apparently there is a broad audience for this 'small' book means that there is still room for quality, beauty, and, by implication, for academia.

More Lessons from Academic Novels

Three other novels on academic life provide us with a somewhat different picture, yet they similarly present illuminating insights into current tendencies in our universities. John Kenneth Galbraith's *A Tenured Professor* (1990) chronicles Harvard professor Montgomery Marvin's rise to fame as a professor of economics who, as an academic teacher, keeps a low profile but who nevertheless is given tenure quite early in his career. While concerning himself with some rather unspectacular research projects, Marvin's extracurricular activities focus on becoming rich in a very short time. For that purpose, Marvin has developed a new formula – a stock forecasting model by means of which he and his wife can cash in on people's euphoria, greed, and, as they call it, dementia. Eventually, while everyone loses money in the stock market crash of October 1987, the Marvin couple makes a fortune. They decide to spend their money wisely, according to their liberal agenda. Intent on strictly observing the code of business ethics, they start to make use of the 'positive power of wealth' and embark on a life of philanthropy. They fund a number of chairs in peace studies to be established at, of all places, military academies. They also secure legislation by which companies are required to label their products according to the percentage of female executives employed by them. After they have launched several of their projects, their operations are increasingly considered un-American and officially put under surveillance. But no matter what happens, Marvin knows that he will be able to nourish his family, since he has been given tenure to promote a liberal agenda. As his old protector somewhat cynically reminds him: 'anyway you still have tenure. I hope you remember that I told you to get that first' (Galbraith, 1990, p. 197).

John Hiden's *Town and Gown* (2012) relates how probationary U.K. lecturer Eric Farnham tries to secure his future at a time of imminent university spending cuts. He does so by grasping the chance to win extra funding for his institution through cultivating a hard-nosed local businessman and his daughter. In doing so he comes into close contact with this man's ambitious, self-taught employee, Albert, a pairing that draws Eric into a punishing series of escapades and gives him a crash course in the shadier side of the city's entrepreneurial sector. This Albert, by contrast, takes to Eric's world like a duck to water. Just as Eric decides to retrace his steps in the face of the amorality implied by his town and gown business, Albert shows him that in fact the whole of academia is involved, and that he is the exception that proves the rule. The chilling story of a lecturer drawn into amorality/complicity by merging town and gown (symbols for academia and world, good and bad, heaven and earth, etc.) provides a grim picture of present-day academia, in a way that no university annual report will ever state, but that in its detailed minutiae of the main character's slow corruption of character is nevertheless hugely telling.

Robert Pirsig's classic *Zen and the Art of Motorcycle Maintenance*, by many considered both a cult book and a masterpiece, is about another academic hero and his quest for quality, a quest that even drives the protagonist of the story crazy. The book is about this nearly impossible to directly measure thing we call quality, which cannot be broken down into subjects and predicates. This is not because there is anything special about quality but rather because it is so simple, immediate, and direct (p. 25). Pirsig's book is written in the societally unsettling sixties and seventies, just like *Stoner*, and unlike the latter, was a hit in a time when students and other intellectuals raised their voices in an emotional and imaginative protest against the rationalist, differentiating, individualising, and domesticising consequences of modernity (see Margetts & Hood, 2010). It is quality as threatened by modernity that Pirsig tried to grasp and defend. Somewhere in the middle of the book (in chapter 20) his meticulous exploration of the quality concept comes down to the simple statement that 'quality is the response of an organism to its environment', which he then explains as the immediateness by which humans recognise quality in certain environments. Quality could also be described as the continuing stimulus that our environment puts upon us to create the world in which we live. Translated to the world of academia, it would mean that the university environment by implication/definition has, or should have, Pirsig's quality to create and foster the natural home for driving the intellectual passion for (new) knowledge and ideas. Quality à la Pirsig is academia's trademark, with universities as keepers of that quality where its practitioners are to feel at home, like fish in the water.

Galbraith's and Hiden's heroes, as well as Williams' figure of Stoner, put a number of important issues on the table. So, what is this academic passion Stoner stands for? How does this book display the qualities Martha Nussbaum's *Not for Profit* (2010) attributes to the humanities as core disciplines of the university project? Her main point stresses the idea that education is not for profit, but for democracy. In her view, the humanities represent a number of qualities that are unparalleled by any of the other sciences. These qualities are the following. First, they have the potential to educate students and help them become academic citizens of the world, who take societal responsibility on the basis of a thorough, emotionally grounded morality that is inclusive and diverse, as Nussbaum also, and more extensively, argues in her *Political Emotions* (2013). Second, the humanities can build this responsible academic citizenship through a Socratic pedagogy that values substantive arguments and imagination, which are not primarily driven by an economics-based view of the world. If we look at Stoner from this perspective, we see him almost desperately searching to 'infect' his students with the passion for academic knowledge that 'science' has awakened in himself, but which is systematically swept aside in an institutional setting that seems to be dominated by issues of power and interest, as well as disinterest for the kind of intrinsic quality that remains defenceless in a hostile – university – environment. To substantiate this argument, I include a personal story of such an environment, which, somewhat ironically, speaks of quality abundantly: the university examination committee.

3   An Autoethnographic Account from the Academy

Although the Stoner novel contains many more themes than academic passion, it is the love for knowledge losing out to mediocrity, self-interest, and institutional politics that stands out for me. Although my own academic environment in a Dutch medium-sized university also suffers from the above ills, I prefer telling a story – somewhere between realist, impressionist, and confessional (Van Maanen, 2011) – that revolves around excellence and quality. Universities world-wide compete in the various rankings; on their websites they usually quote the one in which their position is best. Much as what business corporations proclaim in their mission statements, universities refer to 'high-standard' education and 'world-class' research by 'excellent' scholars for whom quality and customer satisfaction go hand-in-hand in the production of knowledge and teaching performance. It is a common strategy to use a similar corporate language to sell the academic product on the market to as many clients as possible for the best price. Looking at the self-presentation of universities, the terminology unashamedly suggests we live in the age of the mass knowledge economy.

Quality has always been a prominent concept in the academic world. Periodically universities have to demonstrate their quality in quality assurance assessments by peers. Both research and teaching receive their share of what is considered a recurrent threat, upsetting university departments every five or six years. Until fairly recently, say 2000, the committees doing the hearings consisted of benevolent peers who assessed most research and teaching programmes accordingly, without asking for 'measurable indicators. However, in research, output, and citation, numbers nowadays figure prominently next to impact factors and acquired research subsidies. Teaching quality is measured by the presence and interlinkage of programme goals, assessment plans, learning objectives, peer-reviewed tests, exam analyses, and overall pass rates. The Dutch Ministry of Education has made local examination committees responsible for guaranteeing the required quality standards that are formally evaluated by the Netherlands Flemish Accreditation Organisation (NVAO).

As a member of the examination committee of my faculty, I have had the doubtful pleasure to be responsible for making teaching managers and teachers accountable by making them comply to a set of quality rules, that is, by providing them with the tools and parameters to provide the examination committee with sufficient hard data to demonstrate the required quality. University-wide, this has resulted, in the production of impenetrably densely written documents and overly complete forms that, not just seldom, lead to superficial box-ticking and numb reproduction of standard formulations by teaching staff, as well as to the production of abundant numbers of quality reports by admin staff. While this quality quest (or race) is experienced as massively burdensome by practically all who are involved in it – except perhaps the growing army of official quality keepers at all university levels – the story becomes outright tragic when we take a closer look at how this predicament impacts on students and their behaviour.

Students become increasingly focused on the exact content and requirements for them to pass their exams: number of pages to be read, assessment forms, mock exams, pass rate percentages, etc. Of course, there generally is still some intellectual interaction during teaching hours, but consuming behaviour becomes almost standard, particularly at undergraduate level. It is not exceptional any more that the examination committee spends complete sessions with teachers going through exam questions after complaints by students. The student's course evaluations increasingly tend to be critical of the testing: often tests do not live up to what the students had expected or, in market terminology, the product is not what they had 'ordered'. They become calculating consumers who want value for money, and teachers regularly accommodate these expectations and produce the goods ordered. This quality Catch-22 produces teachers desperately asking themselves what they can still ask from their students, while the latter enter a similarly desperate search to satisfy their teachers. Those teachers who do not comply are often faced with complaints, which the examination committee confronts them with. In this way, academic consumption and production take on the traits of a calculating game in which measuring numbers suggests the triumph of (pseudo) objectivity in which academics experience serious feelings of loss. The academy – and particularly its teaching – no longer feels like home, a place to feel in one's element. The irony is that, with all their regulating zeal, examination committees, as the quality gatekeepers, contribute to this very displacement and consequently even provoke academic sloppiness.

My involvement in this quality imbroglio at times produces strong feelings of muddling through and despondency. I think it can be said that the present-day consuming university (Bauman & Donskis, 2013; Donskis in this volume) with its quantitative and calculated understanding of quality is in danger of creating Stoner clones in larger numbers than we think. The town-and-gown dynamic described in this semi-confessional tale – like in the Hiden and Galbraith novels for that matter – leads universities to become instruments of a knowledge economy that turns an increasing segment of their academics into homeless and alienated people displaying the kind of behaviour that much resembles the desperate comportment that made reading *Stoner* so toe-curling.

4   Further Discussion: a Plea for the Public Academic

When our academic 'home' is lost in a world where 'nothing is personal, and everything business', we seem to have gradually entered the realm of *Liquid Modernity's* new Satan (Kattago, 2014, p. 151). Since it will force us to decline responsibility and remove the closeness between us and the Other, we enter a state of what Bauman & Donskis (2013; 2016) call *adiaphora*, moral blindness or numbness. As André Schwarz-Bart in his *The Last of the Just* dramatically argues, the latter must be resisted at all costs, even if there are only a few people left to do so.[3] Williams' *Stoner* is indeed the story of a single individual resisting and refusing to succumb to fatalism, cynicism, and reneging on quality in favour of fostering quality-based empathy and belonging instead (see also De Waal, 2008). We might translate this as an urgent call to create small but steadfast Gideon's tribes, consisting of Stoner-like figures, though hopefully a bit less helpless. More concretely we need to redefine and recreate our universities as 'homes' as I already suggested in the opening of this text. As environments for and communities of critical knowledge-seekers and science-lovers, universities must emanate and embody the kind of quality around academic principles, standards, and commitment that Pirsig advocates. If academics who swim against the tide-of-the-day, yet in the tide of tradition, form such 'islands of hope' or 'safe spaces', this may be to the benefit of democratic society, which in the now often proclaimed post-truth world is more needed than ever. The fruit of academic freedom in such environment bears the responsibility to work towards the development of academic citizenship. The university where I work bears in its name the word 'free'. Its tradition may not have always fostered academic freedom, but, when it is given new substance through the academic citizenship concept, its academics might well be seduced into taking on responsibility rather than just demonstrating accountability.

Some more words about this culture of accountability or about the so-called audit culture (Strathern, 2000; referred to in a public lecture by Michael Herzfeld, *The Devil in the Auditing*, 12 May 2015, Leiden). Auditors – including less than a few complicit academics, as I demonstrated in my autoethnographic piece – have taken over in terms of the definition of the future of universities, a future they define as being paved with numbers. Since in such a situation we are first and foremost consumers and only then, perhaps, citizens (Kattago, 2014, p. 4), Herzfeld urges us to fight this devil of neoliberalism – which in his view is neither neo nor liberal – that has taken over academia. I think I can join him there, but the question is how best to organise the fight.

Although I believe some auditing can be good for academics and academia, we should indeed reflect on how to 'wage this war'. Our preferred strategy as tenured staff could well be the Robin Hood approach, in which we form our own small bands of Stoners and 'fight' the system wherever it manifests itself by surprise and with playful acts of defiance. Whether such a 'guerrilla' can be won is an open question, but some battling might make us happier, perhaps more effective, and will certainly secure that we end professionally less

---

3   The title seems to refer to the Evangelist Matthew, whose 'For where two or three are gathered together in my name, there am I in the midst of them' (18:20) urges for an equally principled stance.

in despair than Stoner. We need spaces where we can indeed feel 'at home', so that we can play with our thoughts, share these with our students, and responsibly defend the value of this play by sharing it broadly – beyond the outlets that our auditors would like us to use.

As we have seen, academia has inspired writers to produce a number of literary novels, but they seldom present the places academics inhabit as really welcoming, 'homey' spaces. Other university novels than the ones I quoted hardly give a more favourable picture. Charlottes Brontë's *The Professor* (1994 [1856]) scarcely even pays any attention to the main character's profession. In John Coetzee's *Disgrace* (2000) literary professorship is even directly linked with moral weakness and professional boredom (though, admittedly, the novel doesn't really pretend to speak about universities). Rex Warner's *the Professor* (1938) provides a depressing description of the tragic fate of an academic professor accepting political responsibility. David Lodge's trilogy *Changing Places* (1975), *Small World* (1984) and *Nice Work* (1988) foreshadows the ever more reduced space academics experience for their calling. As noted above, John Hiden's *Town and Gown* depicts the nasty effects of sloppy scientists making common cause with local entrepreneurs, quite similar to the process John Kenneth Galbraith describes in his *A Tenured Professor* (1980), where Marvin Montgomery both tries to beat the university's tenure track system and use it for (his own) economic profit by making his scientific knowledge and skills subservient to this purpose. The university Williams depicts effectively dismantles any passion of 'true' and dedicated academics. Stoner's environment represents the type of soulless civilisation so gruesomely portrayed in Aldous Huxley's *Brave New World* (1932), is entirely devoid of the quality and values Pirsig's hero Phaedrus pursues in *Zen and the Art of Motorcycle Maintenance* (1979). If we group these literary representations – and there are definitively more – together the image arises of academia as a bound, even chained, sector that uncritically follows that latest fads and dictates from the hand that feeds it (Birnbaum, 2000), in a desperate attempt to survive at the cost of academic freedom (Higgins, 2013) and the loss of its critical voice in society.

What I have tried to argue in this piece is that universities should grant more space to the development of critical and informed knowledge and understanding – and particularly fight for the humanities as a valuable and unquestioned space in the university that is now increasingly squeezed out of the market-driven university. We need communities of learners (consisting of staff as well as students) that try to understand (*Verstehen*), and write about, how humans make sense (and nonsense) of the world they live in. In this endeavour some of us might want to follow Noam Chomsky's example of the public intellectual (the professor), whereas others prefer a less pro-fessing role and stay within the precincts of the university walls to teach, read, and write like Stoner, meanwhile educating young students in the love of knowledge and critical reflection. The latter rather live up to Ortega y Gasset's (1992 [1930]) now somewhat controversial view that doing science is indeed for the happy few, but that the university first and foremost is a place where students are being taught and learning takes place. This teaching (and learning) in Ortega's view takes place in what he calls the faculty of culture (broadly understood as multidisciplinary) that is to enlighten and provide broad (cultural) understanding of the world. If I understand him correctly this is in the end a plea for the broader liberal arts colleges that have recently become popular next to and opposed to the fast-growing mass-consumption universities. Although there is surely some elitist inclination in these colleges, they do represent the ideal that broad intellectual formation requires a serious study effort.

The humanities' emphasis on understanding and deconstructing – which has lost credibility under neoliberalism where the law of supply and demand has replaced the questions-answers pair – must regain its position of showing the way (*methodos*) in how we can acquire this knowledge: by asking questions, diving backstage and below the surface of first appearances and basic skills. Unlike Ortega y Gasset – who believed that doing science was eventually not for the majority of students – I think we owe our students more than half-hearted versions of science, research, and knowledge. Our present teaching and, consequently, learning are less and less the trial and error exercise of systematic doubt (in the broadest sense) but rather the testing of 'to be re-produced knowledge'. Hence teaching is increasingly considered a 'load' for university staff, standing in the way of serious research. Consequently, the attenuated current practice of teaching and research threatens the transgenerational continuity of both. As I noted in the beginning of this text, this transgenerational breach has become conspicuously visible in South Africa's present higher education sector, which is both wrestling with the spectre of its apartheid-framed institutional cultures (Jansen, 2009; Higgins, 2013; Steyn, 2001; Keet, 2015; Nkomo, 1992; Maré, 2015) and a transgressive, economistic, ominously called 'mode 2' (per)version of scientific knowledge (co-)production (Gibbons, 1994; see also Boutellier, 2015). The present call for scientific 'decolonisation' (cf. Mbembe, 2015) attempts to cover both misrepresentations of the knowledge-driven public mission of academia and its academics world-wide. Public intellectuals driven by this mission are now slowly standing up to adopt this post-colonial refusal to accept the simple and standard white middle-class male view of society and the market-driven instrumental rationale that mainstream science has adopted. It is time to embrace the goals of this movement and reinvigorate viable and robust humanities that provide safe spaces for the critical public academic practice as represented by Noam Chomsky, whose recently renewed 1977 message is now phrased *Because We Say So* (2015).

I would like to end with a final reflection taken from two Dutch writers. Philosopher Joke Hermsen in her *Melancholie van de Onrust* (2017, translation: Melancholy of Unrest) proposes a productive usage of the melancholic condition that so frequently affects us human beings these days. Melancholy can become productive when we allow room for it to develop without the pressure of chronological time. Extrapolating this idea to the field of education, she reminds us that the Greek *scholè* (our 'school') refers to rest, waiting, and idleness (p. 139). In present times, these meanings are not really considered to have positive connotations, but Meindert Flikkema's *Sense of Serving. Reconsidering the Role of Universities Now* (2016) shows that an academy that values the sense of synchronicity, place, heritage, and belonging may well enable the community of learners (or, why not, scholarly guilds, where learning through cooperation is valued, cf. Sennett 2012) to 'improve the human condition', for '*qui docet discit*: he who teaches learns' (Flikkema, 2016, pp. 180–181). The scholar-educator, as craftsperson in the sense described by Sennett, is committed to this goal and accepts what Gert Biesta (2016) calls the 'beautiful risk of education' – which essentially is a plea to skip the pressing structures of the teaching factory, to reduce the speed that the 'academic throughput' requires (Berg & Seeber, 2016; see also Wels in this volume), and instead to accept that students learn in unexpected and unanticipated ways. As Stoner would have it.

References

Bauman, Z., & Donskis, L. (2013). *Moral Blindness: The Loss of Sensitivity in Liquid Modernity.* Cambridge, Polity Press.

Bauman, Z., & Donskis, L. (2016). *Liquid Evil.* Cambridge, Polity Press.

Berg, M., & Seeber, B.K. (2016). *The Slow Professor. Challenging the Culture of Speed in the Academy.* Toronto, University of Toronto Press.

Biesta, G. (2016). *The Beautiful Risk of Education.* Abingdon, Taylor & Francis Ltd.

Birnbaum, R. (1988). *How Colleges Work: The Cybernetics of Academic Organization and Leadership.* San Francisco, Jossey-Bass.

Birnbaum, R. (2000). *Management Fads in Higher Education.* San Francisco, Jossey-Bass.

Booysen, S. (2016). *Fees Must Fall. Student Revolt, Decolonization and Governance in South Africa.* Johannesburg, Wits University Press.

Boutellier, H. (2015). *Het Seculiere Experiment. Hoe We van God Los Gingen Samenleven.* Amsterdam, Boom.

Brontë, C. (1994 [1856]). *The Professor.* Wordswore Editions.
Chomsky, N. (1977). Intellectuals and the State, *Huizinga Lecture*, Baarn, Het Wereldvenster.
Chomsky, N. (2014). The death of American universities. *Jacobin: A Magazine of Culture and Polemic.* Retrieved from: https://www.jacobinmag.com/2014/03/the-death-of-american-universities/.
Chomsky, N. (2015). *Because We Say So.* London, Penguin.
Coetzee, J.M. (2000). *Disgrace.* New York, Vintage.
De Waal, F. (2008). Putting the altruism back into altruism: The evolution of empathy. *Annual Review of Psychology* , 59, 279–300.
Flikkema, M. (ed.) (2016). *Sense of Serving. Reconsidering the Role of Universities Now.* Amsterdam, VU University Press.
Galbraith, J.K. (1990). *A Tenured Professor.* London, Houghton Mifflin Company.
Gibbons, M. (ed.). (1994). *The New Production of Knowledge: The Dynamics of Science and Research in Contemporary Societies.* London, Sage.
Hermsen, J.J. (2017). *Melancholie van de Onrust.* Rotterdam, Lemniscaat.
Herzfeld, M. (2015). *The Devil Is in the Auditing.* Public lecture University of Leiden, 12 May 2015.
Hidden, J. (2012). *Town and Gown.* Stoney Stanton, Indigo Dreams Publishing.
Higgins, J. (2013). *Academic Freedom in a Democratic South Africa. Essays and Interviews on Higher Education and the Humanities.* Johannesburg, Wits University Press.
Huxley, A. (1932). *Brave New World.* London, Chatto & Windus.
Ignatieff, M. (2013). *Civil Courage and The Moral Imagination.* Retrieved from https://openaccess.leidenuniv.nl/bitstream/handle/1887/51368/Cleveringarede2013boekje.pdf?sequence=1.
Jansen, J. (2009). *Knowledge in the Blood. Confronting Race and the Apartheid Past.* Stanford, Stanford University Press.
Jansen, J. (2017). *As by Fire. The End of the South African University.* Cape Town, Tafelberg.
Kattago, S. (2014). In the shadow of Antigone: Resisting moral blindness. *Journal of Political Power,* 7 (1), 149–154.
Keet, A. (2015). *Institutional Cultures/Environment.* Briefing paper prepared for the second national Higher Education Transformation Summit, 2015. Retrieved from http://www.justice.gov.za/commissions/FeesHET/docs/2015-HESummit-Annexure10.pdf.
Lodge, David (1975). *Changing Places: A Tale of Two Campuses.* London, Secker and Warburg.
Lodge, David (1984). *Small World: An Academic Romance.* London, Secker and Warburg.
Lodge, David (1988). *Nice Work.* London, Secker and Warburg.
Maré, G. (2015). *Declassified. Moving Beyond the Dead End of Race in South Africa.* Auckland Park, Johannesburg: Jacana.
Margetts, H., & Hood, C. (2010). *Paradoxes of Modernization: Unintended Consequences of Public Policy Reform.* Oxford: Oxford University Press.

Mbembe A. (2015). *Decolonizing Knowledge and the Question of the Archive.* Retrieved from http://www.staugustine.ac.za/sites/default/files/ctools/13.%20Mbembe%20-%20Decolonizing%20Knowledge...%20%282015%29.pdf.

Nietzsche, F. (2008 [1882]). *The Gay Science.* Cambridge, Cambridge University Press.

Nkomo, S. (1992). The emperor has no clothes: Rewriting 'Race in Organizations'. *The Academy of Management Review, 17* (93), 487–513.

Noordegraaf, M., & Schinkel, W. (2011). Professional capital contested: A bourdieusian analysis of conflicts between professionals and managers. *Comparative Sociology, 10* (1), 97–125.

Nussbaum, M.C. (2010). *Not for Profit. Why Democracy Needs the Humanities.* Princeton, Princeton, NJ, Princeton University Press.

Nussbaum, M.C. (2013). *Political Emotions. Why Love Matters for Justice.* Cambridge MA, Harvard University Press.

Ortega y Gasset, J. (1992 [1930]). *Mission of the University.* (La Misión de la Universidad, Buenos Aires). London, Transaction Publishers.

Paradeise, C., & Thoenig, J.C. (2013). Academic institutions in search of quality: local orders and global standards. *Organisation Studies, 34* (2), 189–218.

Pirsig, R.M. (1979[1974]). *Zen and the Art of Motorcycle Maintenance. An Inquiry into Values.* New York: Quill.

Ray, M. (2016). *Free Fall. Why South African Universities Are in a Race against Time.* Johannesberg, Bookstorm.

Sennett, R. (2008). *The Craftsman.* London, Penguin.

Sennett, R. (2012). *Together. The Rituals, Pleasures & Politics of Cooperation.* London, Penguin.

Steyn, M. (2001). *Whiteness Isn't What it Used to Be. White Identity in a Changing South Africa.* New York, SUNY Press.

Strathern, S. (2000). *Audit Cultures: Anthropological Studies in Accountability, Ethics, and the Academy.* New York, London: Routledge.

Tabensky, P., & Matthews, S. (2015). *Being at Home. Race, Institutional Culture and Transformation at South African Higher Education Institutions.* Pietermaritzburg, UKZN Press.

Van Maanen, J. (2011 [1988]) *Tales of the Field: On Writing Ethnography.* Chicago, Chicago University Press.

Vice, S. (2010). How do I live in this strange place? *Journal of Social Philosophy, 41,* 323–342.

Warner, R. (1938). *The Professor.* London, John Lane.

Weber, M. (1946 [1919]). Science as a vocation. In *From Max Weber: Essays in Sociology,* New York: Oxford University Press, 129–156.

Williams, J. (2006 [1965]). *Stoner.* New York Review Books Classics.

CHAPTER 3

Universities as Laboratories. Internationalisation and the Liquidity of National Learning

Stefano Bianchini

Abstract

This chapter explores circumstances and opportunities that mark the internationalisation of European Universities after the Cold War. It reports the results achieved by the European human capital strategy with a specific focus on the Erasmus mobility impact on young generations. It expands the analysis to transnational research and networks as modern methods of work for academic investigation. Then, the article highlights some crucial aspects of the debate on the social role of Higher Institutions, how disciplines should complement education, and University potentials implemented in support of their social engagement. Particular relevance is given to the internationalisation of Higher Education Institutions in years characterized by globalisation. By affecting national policies of education and research, its inputs contribute, in fact, to melt the homogenisation of cultures and languages promoted in the last two centuries. By contrast, this process generates tough resistances, which threaten the transnational education under construction. Subsequently, it is widening the gap between mobile and sedentary educated people. This may produce social conflicts with unpredictable impacts on how knowledge should be constructed, with the risk of stifling the role of Universities as laboratories of universal culture.

Keywords

internationalisation of education – Erasmus Programmes – mobility – transnational education

1   Introduction

The end of the Cold War gave new impetus to the idea of the university in Europe. By bulldozing the Iron Curtain, existing ideological and geographical borders were swept away. In this context, the universities, whose very word echoes with the 'universal' insight of science, erudition, and learning, had a tremendous opportunity to capture this momentum and invigorate their mission by promoting a new international dimension for their curricula, a scholarly cross-national networking, and a regular exchange of research outcomes and achievements.

Qualitatively and radically, this opportunity materialised with the progress of EU integration, its widening and deepening between 1992 and 2004. Diachronically, the extremes of this period go from the Maastricht Treaty (which established both the EU common currency and European citizenship) to the zenith of the integration process, well represented by the great enlargement eastward and the signing of the Constitutional treaty.

It is within this critical period of European strategic transformations that the EU member states convened on the need to give universities a 'great leap forward' in internationalisation by creating compatible diplomas, standards, and quality levels of education not only through a harmonisation of the architecture of higher educational institutions among the member states but also – and vitally important – through new forms of university interactions.

The Bologna process, which began in 1999, embodied this transnational effort. Not without discrepancies and harsh criticisms aimed at the increasing amount of bureaucracy, this process has radically transformed university structures and their teaching contents Europe-wide. A remarkable cross-national fertilisation has marked the EU (with limited results only in the United Kingdom), including most of its neighbouring countries, the Russian Federation, and, gradually, Central Asia. As a result, a European Higher Educational Area (EHEA) was established. By December 2015, it had encompassed 49 countries, far beyond the number of EU member states (and candidate or potential candidate countries), which is a confirmation that the advancement of research and knowledge increasingly depends on cooperation and exchanges across borders.

Basically, the implementation of such an ambitious design was structured according to a set of measures, among these:
- a three-cycle system of studies;
- mutually recognised and comparable degrees;
- scholarships for student mobility;
- teaching and research programmes aimed to encourage professor and staff mobility;
- a framework for joint programmes and new degrees, whose format can be based on joint, double, or multiple diplomas, implying different levels of mobility in all the subjects involved; and
- financial support for transnational networks for joint research projects.

The result is transnational educational and research partnerships that are key investments for building that *European* human capital, which will be fit to compete at the global level.

2 Building a European Human Capital: Some Data

Recent statistics issued by the European Commission in July 2014 offer a clear picture of the results achieved so far as a result of student mobility in Europe: the Erasmus Programme. Remarkably, 3 million students have enjoyed this programme since it was established in 1987–1988, and this interuniversity practice is intensifying. A recent study has recorded that, during one academic year alone, 2012–2013, 268,143 students went to another EU country for study or training. Of these, 61% were women, 67% were enrolled at the BA level, and 29% at the MA level. Of all students involved in the Erasmus Programme during the academic year 2012–2013, 79% took advantage of this opportunity to attend courses and pass exams, while 21% received a grant for a job placement in companies in another EU member state. Looking toward the future, EU investments in the new Erasmus plus Programme for the years 2014–2020 have been designed to award grants up to another 2 million higher education students.[1]

In consideration of these numbers and with the aim of measuring the impact of this programme on students' attitudes towards the process of European integration, the European Commission committed the 'Generation Europe Foundation' to carrying out a specific project, called EVA (Erasmus Voting Assessment), whose task was to investigate (1) the extent to which the Erasmus Programme has an impact on the EU feelings of the young generations involved in the Programme and (2) whether these feelings were also translated into voting behaviour. A very interesting report was published in July 2014 by the aforementioned Foundation, in cooperation with AEGEE and the International Exchange Erasmus Students' Network with two introductory remarks by the Commissioner Androulla Vassiliou and the EP member Doris Pack.

According to the survey results, collected and elaborated by the EVA research before the EP elections of 2014, 91% of respondents (aged 18–25) admitted to thinking of themselves as European citizens, and not just as a national of an EU member state, 'often (45%) or sometimes (46%)'. Compared with the Eurobarometer data of 2007 (which surveyed a young generation aged 15–24), the sense of closeness to European identity shown by university students was

---

[1] http://europa.eu/rapid/press-release_IP-14-821_en.htm.

steadfastly greater. In the Eurobarometer answers, in fact, only 54% of respondents think of themselves as European citizens often or sometimes.

Even more interesting is the difference in opinions that emerged between mobile and non-mobile students when requested to express what the EU meant for them. All 'positive' meanings related to the EU context were more appreciated by current or former Erasmus students than those who never studied in another country. In other words, a large majority was more likely to associate the idea of Europe with the ability to move within and across the borders of the member states; with the guarantee of a better future; with the protection of the rights of citizens, of peace, and a lasting economic situation; with the development of job opportunities; and even with the establishment of a European government.

It is worth stressing that particularly those aspects, which can be defined as 'political by nature', manifested the greatest distance in percentage between mobile and non-mobile students. As a result, the identification of the EU with lasting peace was appreciated by 40% of the former versus 29% of the latter. Similarly, the protection of citizens' rights attracted the support of 45% of the former versus 37% of the latter. Improvement in the EU's economic future was deeply rooted in the beliefs of the 41% of the mobile students versus 37% of non-mobile, and even the perspective of EU government involved identifying with the meaning of the EU by 34% of the mobile students versus 30% of the non-mobile. By contrast, a tiny percentage (between 10%–13%) of non-mobile students rather than those mobile (between 8% and 10%) was concerned about the risk of losing national identity and the influence of greater EU bureaucracy or expressed their Euroscepticism by believing that the EU was 'just a utopian project'. Furthermore, the feeling of EVA respondents about the future of the European Union was 73% optimistic and only 13% pessimistic. Considering the long-lasting impact of the EU crisis, which politically dates back to 2005 when the Constitutional treaty was rejected, and was later economically worsened because of the financial and sovereign debt crisis that began in 2008, this answer may sound quite surprising. And, in fact, EVA respondents showed a clear belief in the future of the EU, definitely more persuaded than the European population in general, whose optimism was contained to the 53% versus the 40% of pessimists, as the Eurobarometer recorded in 2014.

Even more interesting is the fact that the optimism of mobile students does not cast a shadow over their concerns – which still exist – about negative scenarios, mainly related to the risk of the deepening of the economic and financial crisis, social uncertainties, and the impact of future accessions.

In the end, the EVA research provided evidence about the level of information that mobile and non-mobile students have about EU institutions and the forthcoming EU parliamentary elections. Once again, the survey clarifies that current and past Erasmus students share a better knowledge of the mechanisms of the EP elections, the EU institutional framework, and how it works. Approximately 70% of them know that MEPs are elected in direct general elections by the European population. Although it might be surprising that 30% still believe that they are not elected by citizens, the percentage of 70% is significantly higher than the 50% recorded by the Eurobarometer in 2013 for young people of similar age (18–30). Significantly enough, 81% of students who in their past made use of an Erasmus mobility period voted in the EP elections in 2014: by contrast, the vote of those who were never abroad involved 7% fewer people, namely 74% of students.

It should also be noted that turnout in the EP elections in 2014 was 42.54%, while only 41% of the EVA-responding students who were using their mobility when the EP elections took place were likely to vote. In this case, however, the responsibility of the member states, the complexity of regulations, and/or a lack of support played a crucial role in obstructing the vote of young people during the period of mobility: as a result, 43% of the respondents who did not vote complained about the difficulties they had to face in order to be registered to vote, while 30% declared that they lacked the money to travel back to their polling station at home. Lack of information or commitment reached a much lower percentage, around 10% or even less.

To conclude, the EVA report stressed how respondents revealed 'a closer sense of identification with the EU, had a more positive outlook on its future, were more interested in participating, and indeed were more likely to vote during the European elections'.[2] In a sense, these figures also offer a transformative picture of the impact that a transnational, *nomadic* programme offered to students enrolled in the EU, like Erasmus, has on their behaviour, while they are still studying (Braidotti, 2011).

It is, however, interesting to note that this approach (and the mindset that stems from it) does not show a transitory character; on the contrary, it is likely to be confirmed once students approach the labour market. Recent available data state, in fact, that 5 years after graduation, unemployment among students who enjoyed an Erasmus grant was 23% lower than was the case of non-mobile students. The findings of broad-based research published in September 2014 under the title *The Erasmus Impact Study* not only confirmed the effectiveness of the programme in terms of employment opportunities but

---

2   *Erasmus voting Assessment Project Final Report*, Generation Europe Foundation: 2014, available at http://issuu.com/generationeurope/docs/evaproject_final_report_fordistribu/1?e=1430744/9429338, p. 35.

also provided crucial insights about the transversal competences that students acquire during their international experience: in particular, how deeply this experience marks their personality traits and attitudes in terms of tolerance, curiosity, adaptability, self-confidence, serenity, decisiveness in making decisions, and vigour in solving problems. In short, Erasmus vividly contributes to making young people more attracted by and more able to interact with a globalising world.[3]

This study was carried out for the European Commission by the Berlin CHE Consult (Centrum für Hochschulentwicklung) in partnership with the Brussels Education Services, the Compostela Group of Universities, and the Erasmus Student Network. Impressively, it surveyed nearly 79,000 mobile and non-mobile students, alumni, academic and non-academic staff, employers, and higher education institutions. The investigation stressed, among other things, that 93% of mobile students easily imagine their own future in another EU country (the percentage is 20% higher than that of non-mobile students) and 95% wish to work in international environments (versus 78% of non-mobile students). The *nomadic* inclination of Erasmus students is, in a sense, confirmed by the behaviour of alumni: 40% of them had changed country at least once after graduation, while only 22% of non-mobile students had.

Exploring the expectations and requirements of employers/entrepreneurs, the study emphasised that 92% of employers were looking for workers with the aforementioned transversal skills, well in addition to top knowledge in their field, when recruiting personnel. Furthermore, 64% of the employers noted in 2014 (versus 51% in 2006) how deeply the international background of graduates increased their own professional responsibility. Leadership as well is likely to emerge more effectively among Erasmus alumni: according to the data collected, 77% of them held positions with leadership components 10 years after graduation and 44% were more likely to be working as managers than non-mobile students.

Last, but not least, 'international love' has also played a relevant role in modifying lifestyles and behaviours in the EU context during, or because of, the Erasmus experience: in particular, the study noted an intensification of mixed couples, with 33% of alumni living with a partner of a different citizenship/nationality, while this percentage was much lower (13%) in the case of non-mobility students. In addition, 27% of Erasmus alumni declared they had met their current partner during their mobility period, and it has also

---

3 Erasmus Impact Study – Effects of mobility on the skills and employability of students and the internationalisation of higher education institutions, available at http://www.eubusiness.com/topics/education/erasmus-impact, European Commission: Brussels, 22 Sept. 2014.

been calculated that approximately one million babies were born under these circumstances.

3 Globalisation and the Underestimation of European University Internationalisation

Despite the broad and stimulating research conducted on students and alumni actively involved in mobility in the past few years, the study of the Erasmus impact on the academic and administrative staff of universities is regrettably less systematic and, to a large extent, poorer in terms of data and figures. Indeed, scrutiny needs to be expanded to broader dimensions in order to take in the impact of globalisation on the organisation of knowledge, how that knowledge is being disseminated, and to what extent it is receptive to the time-space compression that globalisation is intensifying (Szyszlo, 2016).

From this perspective, Erasmus mobility is just one component, although a crucially important one. University internationalisation, however, encompasses many activities, which include mobility of students, professors and staff, transnational curricula adaptations, joint research projects, joint teaching programme design and transnational (double, multiple, joint) degrees awarding, which have an obvious impact on the learning processes at home.

Furthermore, internationalisation as such has been widely discussed in academia, where a diverse terminology has emerged when referring to this process. Authors like Hans De Wit (2013, pp. 14–18) or Jane Knight (2008, pp. 19–22) have repeatedly emphasised a diachronic development of terms that focus primarily on one specific aspect of internationalisation, for instance, mobility or curricula-related ones – that is, from peace studies to global and international studies, from multiculturalism to intercultural education – or on national programmes in English for native students (particularly in economics).

Furthermore, in reconstructing the internationalisation dynamics, De Wit (2013, p. 22) stressed how deeply forms and accents have varied vis-à-vis historical periods and countries. In particular, he emphasised the focus on aid and cooperation for development that was promoted between the 1970s and the 1980s. Actually, this process began earlier – in the middle of the 1960s already – in the socialist countries that De Wit did not consider. Yugoslav and Soviet universities competed actively at the international level to attract the best students from the so-called 'Third World' by offering a wide spectrum of disciplines for their further education as a lever for promoting their own social systems worldwide. The Lumumba University in Moscow as well as the University of Belgrade (thanks to the Yugoslav non-alignment policy) were particularly active in this regard, and generations of African and Asian youngsters attended courses and learned the language before returning to their homelands.

True, most of the students of the Lumumba University in Moscow concentrated on their studies, remaining to a large extent isolated from the Soviet social context, but this was not the case in Yugoslavia, where the interaction with the local environment was much more dynamic and had a positive impact, even in terms of spreading knowledge of the Serbo-Croatian language internationally. It was not rare to meet alumni in China, the USA, or Libya, who were educated in Yugoslavia. Regrettably, the fall of communism and the violent dismemberment of Yugoslavia might be among the reasons why Western scholars have tended to downplay the relevance of this policy of international education that the socialist world had developed. Nevertheless, this experience explains to a large extent the background of interest and sensitivity of post-communist societies when it comes to raising their level of integration and internationalisation, as soon as the EU began to promote this policy.

This prospect began to mature, in reality, at the end of the 1980s when the European community moved to scholarship programme compatibilities and promoted the first mobility schemes. Drawing inspiration from an essay by Stefan Zweig (2014), who had suggested already in 1932 allowing students to spend one semester, or even a year, in a university abroad in order to know the contribution of other peoples to the innovation of techniques and the shared history of European civilisation (by combining – interestingly enough – the studies of humanities with the hard sciences), the Erasmus Programme was launched, giving a new perspective to the internationalisation of universities.

So, Zweig's dream began to be realised thanks to the recognition of the exams passed in another European university as part of the curriculum established at the home university. The issue quickly attracted the interest of scholars, and, particularly with the new millennium, the literature widely debated the role of globalisation on educational systems: Uwe Brandenburg and De Wit (2011); Felix Maringa and Nick Foskett (2010); Philip Altbach, Lis Reisberg and Laura Rumbley (2009); Peter Scott (2005); Ulrich Teichler (2004), and other scholars have extensively analysed academic competition at the global level. They have highlighted the increasing relevance of the Asian universities, in contexts previously dominated by the Anglo-American and Australian educational systems, and noted the multiplication of international ranking systems of universities, which has encouraged either a shifting of university commitments in terms of cross-border and offshore education, or emphasised powerful trends aimed at supporting tradable commodities, while meantime eroding the perception of education as a public good.

Curiously enough, however, all these studies have undermined the impact of internationalisation strategies on the process of EU integration. EU integration is definitely part and parcel of globalisation: therefore, its developments require filtering and contextualising in relation to the radical social and economic transformations that are challenging the primacy of USA education and its economy, thus granting a leading role to newly emerging countries as well, particularly the BRICS countries (Brazil, Russia, India, China, South Africa). Nevertheless, the Bologna process has a twofold goal: on the one hand, it aims to enhance the quality of education in order to compete globally; on the other, it aims to establish a European educational system *beyond* the member states dimension, since this effort is a crucial prerequisite for achieving the former. Successful steps in this direction have been taken already by involving the EHEA – as already noted – and a broader number of countries, from the Russian Federation to the Caucasus and Central Asia. Regrettably, this *European* dimension of the internationalisation of the universities is still underestimated in most of the international publications on the subject. There is no denying that the main reason for this appearance can be identified with the predominant role played by the Anglo-American educational system (their universities powerfully lead all international rankings), which remarkably influence the mental processing involved in the matter. Still, even the persistence in Europe of a nation-state political culture contributes to affecting – among other things – the study and the assessment of the Europeanisation of education.

Hans De Wit, in his stimulating edited report of 2013, recognised the transformative role of the Erasmus Programme, which started working in 1987–1988 when 3244 students took advantage of it and the EU member states were just 12. Furthermore, he concluded that, 25 years later in 2013, Erasmus had not only forged an 'Erasmus generation' of 3 million students in the meantime but had also significantly contributed to the reform of higher education in Europe, the introduction of the ECTS system, the development of the Bologna process, the implementation of inclusive policies towards East-Central European countries, and their prospective EU membership (carried out since 2004 and still under negotiation at least in South-Eastern Europe).

It should also be noted that over 52,600 academic scholars and university staff took advantage of this programme by visiting and monitoring other European universities in the academic year 2012–2013, offering additional seminars or lectures during their stay at the BA, MA, or PhD levels. EU figures also state that 500 practitioners, namely staff members from business environments, were invited to teach under the aegis of the opportunities offered by the programme, with a 20% increase in participation in comparison with the previous year, and a consistent improvement in learning outcomes in terms of the practical knowledge of students as well as their theoretical and academic education.

Consequently, the European Commission decided to expand the Erasmus Programme (renamed 'Erasmus plus') both financially and in terms of scope and targets for the period 2014–2020. Once again, some data would help here. In 2007–2013 the available budget was 3.1 billion euro. For the years 2014–2020 the budget was increased up to 15 billion euros, with the ambitious aim of supporting the mobility of 20% of the student population, namely an additional 5 million people. Meanwhile, the member states are now 28,[4] and the programme is also open to students from Turkey, Iceland, Norway, Lichtenstein, and Switzerland.

All that considered, De Wit concluded that the new 'Erasmus plus' project – with its stimuli for student mobility, together with the implementation of the internationalisation strategies of the higher education in Europe – 'is not a goal in itself but a means to enhance the quality of the educational experience and the international learning outcomes of the students'.[5]

Admittedly, however, such an assessment still sounds reticent, since it is powerless to highlight the *political implications* of the process of the internationalisation of the universities in the framework of the European integration. As said, this is in reality the most underestimated aspect in the current literature, which focuses on globalisation and its effects but lacks any investigation into how transnational higher education and culture contribute to building new political relations in Europe and radically change the social environment of European societies.

Indeed, student mobility is a key component of the EU internationalisation strategy of the universities, since it corresponds to a remarkable investment policy in human capital through younger generations. Nevertheless, a more comprehensive analysis of EU efforts in promoting this internationalisation is needed, since a new – and politically vital – role is going to be played by the universities as a decisive lever for the further integration of Europe.

4   The Potential of Universities, European Integration, and Its Critics

Looking from the perspective of internationalisation strategies, university life in Europe has radically changed in the last two decades.

---

4   Actually, they will drop to 27 when Brexit is finally implemented.
5   Hans De Wit (ed.), *An Introduction to the Higher Education Internationalisation*, Milan: Vita e Pensiero, 2013, p. 20.

Thanks to students, professors, and staff mobility, cross-border and transnational knowledge have increasingly marked both the broader understanding of the reality and the designing of the curricula, with a transformative impact particularly in the humanities and social sciences, which crucially forge a sense of citizenship. True, the flourishing of technologies, the progress in new discoveries in medicine, and research in the natural and applied sciences in general are quite used to easily crossing borders and acquiring new data and stimuli by expanding exchanges and cooperation. Scientists normally work in (international) teams, operate in highly competitive contexts, and the transfer of discoveries has rapid social effects in everyday life. Yet, it is also true that the cultural and social sciences are developing in a different environment, which – by contrast – suffers, to a large extent, from containments imposed by nation-state narratives.

We have mentioned that universities encompass, in the very name 'university,' the idea of the universality of knowledge. Nevertheless, most of the higher educational institutions were established in Europe after 1800, that is, when industrialisation and the national form of the state were affecting social developments in Europe. Educational policies, learning outcomes, and teaching methodologies were consistently adjusted. In fact, while 118 universities were established in Europe over seven centuries, between 1088 (University of Bologna's foundation) and the French Revolution, between 1800 and 1940 alone another 119 universities began their programmes and nearly 600 were founded after WWII. In other words, mass higher education has grown synchronically with industrialisation and the radical social transformations stemming from the increasing participation of the population at large in public affairs (in the sense of *res publica*) within the nation-state building process. Therefore, research and teaching activities have been primarily marked by a dual goal: on the one hand, to empower students with technical knowledge in order to prepare them for the world of work with solid competences, even by gradually transforming the universities into effective entrepreneurial players in support of the socioeconomic development of society. On the other hand, however, the universities have become a vector for a predominant interest in fostering the cultural *national* dimension through the study of *national* literatures, *national* histories, *national* histories of arts, *national* political and social sciences, etc. Lectures were held in *national* languages only (with rare exceptions), very few students attended courses in other countries (also because there were no-mechanisms of recognition), and the mobility of scholars was limited to some international events (conferences, seminars). As a result, knowledge was organised in such a way that recognition of the nation-state's solidification was presented as the final development of human society or, in short, the 'end of history'.

By contrast, all these aspects, in one way or another, have been challenged by the EU after the fall of the Berlin wall. Once the Iron Curtain came crashing down, the Schengen treaty was put into force, the perception of borders rapidly vanished, and the process of universities' internationalisation accelerated by including mobility policies, the Bologna process, the introduction of the three-cycles system, the compatibility of diplomas, the transformation of teaching methodologies, the growing relevance of transversal skills, long-life learning, job placement, the diversification of diplomas together with the encouraging carrying out joint programmes with joint, double, multiple degrees.

During the 1990s, radical transformations affected the higher educational system, and alternative suggestions were elaborated particularly in terms of methodological approaches. The vexed question of the relationship between the social sciences and the humanities, on the one hand, and the exact and applied sciences, on the other, quickly revived. In the United States, especially at Stanford, the 'Triple Helix Concept' was elaborated in order to give priority to a narrow link of universities, enterprises, and public administrations. The idea of an entrepreneurial university to serve the needs of industries, officials, and decision-makers was actively explained in terms of international competitiveness requirements, thereby leaving the social sciences and the humanities on the margins of the educational system, while the management of universities was understood to be restructured as a business, (Etkowitz 1993; Etkowitz & Leydesdorff, 1995; Ranga & Etkowits, 2013).

Meantime, the development of new communication systems and IT encouraged UNESCO (2005) to issue a report where a broader 'knowledge society' was envisaged by critically raising questions about both the 'hegemony of the techno-scientific model' in producing knowledge and the obstacles, at the local and global level, that mark the participation of a society in the broader global information society. A whole chapter was devoted to the role of institutions of higher education. In particular, serious concerns were expressed about the future of European universities, due to the huge expansion in attendance (massification of studies) and the decline in public founding. The latter resulted in an attempt to diversify the financial resources through a 'marketisation and commercialisation of educational services' to the detriment of the research dimension. In reaction, the report suggested considering the option of developing transnational university networks. Under these conditions, as was suggested, both research and teaching functions would be preserved. Moreover, connecting the universities through a variety of transnational disciplinary networks would avoid the risk of reducing institutions of higher education to a mere third level of the school system.

Even more stimulating was another UNESCO report (1996), which was revisited in 2013, and whose title was 'Learning: The Treasure Within'. Despite some criticism coming from the World Bank, the OECD, or some scholars like Bhola (1997), who were contented with a vision of education as 'profoundly humanistic... and less market driven', the Jacques Delors Commission (which wrote the document) introduced the lifelong-learning approach, by inviting both to rethink the challenges coming from information technologies and to develop learning approaches capable of respecting diversity. In particular, Delors suggested four main pillars for a more effective educational method. These pillars were articulated as follows: learning to know, learning to do, learning to be, and learning to live together. They offered an excellent reference framework, particularly for the internationalisation of the university programmes and joint/double/multiple degrees. Their combination, in reality, stimulates the exchange of knowledge at different levels, strengthens the link between research and teaching, as well as students' acquisition of what are known as 'transversal skills', including a greater independence and judgment due to the diversification of the learning experience through the mobility and the understanding of the variety of mindsets, histories, habits, and spirituality.

The Delors Report outlined a pioneering and very modern 'humanistic and integrated vision' of the learning process. However, when the Report was published in 1996, the neoliberal economic and utilitarian relationship between universities and business interests was the predominant (ideological) model, and the separation of disciplines was pursued with tenacity. Looking toward the future, however, this learning idea is doomed to lose its effectiveness, offering new room for the development of interdisciplinarity, and encouraging bridges between social sciences, humanities, and hard sciences.

Globalisation and interdependence, in reality, are already pushing in this direction: the recent success in fighting the Ebola virus epidemic in Africa blatantly showed that the medical search for a vaccine would not have eradicated the disease without the crucial support of anthropology, that is the ability (knowledge) to interact with the local mindset and beliefs.

As an additional confirmation, a recent article published in the online edition of *Nature*, with the forthright title 'Time for Social Sciences', clearly states that *'Governments that want the natural sciences to deliver more for society need to show greater commitment towards the social sciences and humanities'*.[6] The key argument developed in the article refers exactly to the inclusion of social,

---

6 http://www.nature.com/news/time-for-the-social-sciences-1.16621?WT.ec_id=NATURE-20141225.

economic, and cultural factors in the physical, chemical, medical, biological, and environmental research features, otherwise 'a great deal of cultural creativity will be wasted'. Severely critical of the government of the United Kingdom for lacking any understanding of this commitment, the article stresses the relevance of inclusivity in the research of the natural sciences if their goal is to produce knowledge not only for the benefit of the society but also for the development of a 'capacity of understanding' the society (as well as to be understood by) in order to make the society receptive to innovations and able to accept and use them.

As the historian of economics Alexander Gerschenkron (1962) emphasised in the early 1960s in his seminal comparative study on the prerequisites for the economic take-off, a cultural predisposition in support of development and change is an unquestionable and decisive factor for success. Interdisciplinarity is, therefore, an additional, crucial component for the internationalisation of the universities and the transnational qualification of their programmes.

Consequently, how to achieve this qualification methodologically and improve human capital so as to be able to face the challenges of the increasing complexity and interdependence of our societies depends to a large extent on the ability to work in teams and operate through networks. Furthermore, the data included in the reports of the European Commission that were illustrated at the beginning of this chapter highlight very well how this is already furthering the construction of a transnational and networking-based human capital.

5 Networking and Post Nation-State Perspectives. Opportunities and Reserve

In this context, marked by interdependence and globalisation, networking is a crucial lever of change. Networking is a method of working, a scheme to make transnational cooperation and interdisciplinarity a habit for the scholarly world. Admittedly, not everybody in academia welcomes this approach, which is highly demanding, as it requires *flexibility* and a fluent multilingual attitude in order to teach, communicate at the scientific level, write projects and reports, publish, and be evaluated. Moreover, administrative mentalities either in the various ministries or in the universities often fear loss of control over the implementation of programmes and research activities, are therefore reluctant to apply flexible rules when, by contrast, they are crucially relevant for the smooth functioning of international cooperation. Still, networking has been increasingly embraced by a large part of the academic world, including the humanities and social sciences, which traditionally are disciplinary spheres more used to working individually.[7]

Networking, in fact, has been vitally stimulated by the call for applications by the European Commission for scholars, students, and staff. In order to stimulate cross-national fertilisation, the proposals for research projects as well as educational, training, life-long programmes, opportunities for placement, etc., are to be structured on the basis of transnational teams and multiple partnerships when inviting submissions for financing. This requirement is not just a façade, since implementation of the projects has to be conceived starting with the applications and, then, carried out by strictly following a rationale based on active transnational forms of cooperation. Consequently, in order to make the networks work, the mobility of participants with different background and discipline approaches becomes inevitable. As a result, transnational networks, interdisciplinarity, and mobility are integrated as crucial factors that enable Europeans to meet and share institutions, economic interests, a legal framework, habits, ways of conducts, behaviours, cultures, and friendship.

Networking also provides a vital opportunity to encourage scholars and students to cope with a plurality of angles and to look at the world through a variety of lenses. Alternative narratives have therefore identified unexpected room for matching: the public discussions that followed have paved the way either to 'discover' the *métis* nature of European cultures or to build a framework of understanding of often quite opposing memories, leading to potential co-ownerships of memories. In this context, pluralities and singularities appear in a new light and the interaction of contacts and interests (that networks enhance) will define an effective framework for spreading trust and empathy across mental and physical borders.

In this way, through networking and mobility, different levels of *métissages* may take place, generating a number of implications, from social to economic and cultural dimensions. The web of relationships that will be established has so far proved to be capable of reinforcing cooperation in the future, producing ideas for harmonising differentiated societies, and ultimately promoting a shared, European sense of belonging.

Indeed, networking and mobility are not a peculiar 'invention' of EU institutions. European history has developed multi-layered networks over the centuries. Diasporic populations, travellers, explorers, intellectuals, artists,

---

7 Compare Jennifer Streeter, *Networking in academia*, in EMBO Reports, Nov. 2014, 15 (11), pp. 1109–1112, available at https://www.ncbi.nlm.nih.gov/pmc/articles/PMC4253483 and the conference report of Marta Zampa, et al., *'What's in it for us?' Six dyadic networking strategies in academia*, in Studies in Communication Sciences, 2015, 1 (15), pp. 158–160.

merchants, and migrants (from Jews to Germans, from Roma to Greeks, from Armenians to Italians, just to mention a few examples) repeatedly and severely marked the reshaping of European societies, strengthening their *métissages* in a plurality of forms. The circulation of ideas, the expansion of trade, and the development of transportation networks (from canal networks to railways on up to low-cost flights in more recent times) have powerfully contributed to reinforcing the process of cross-national fertilisation.

True, educational policies, promoted both by nationalism as ideology (despite the heterogeneity of its interpretations) and the nation-state building praxis since the French revolution, have systematically undermined the role of transnational networks and mobility within Europe. Concentrating their efforts on convincing people of their own 'uniqueness and homogeneity' in language, culture, history, and the arts, the national political cultures (however perceived) have transformed the humanities, and social and cultural studies into authoritative vectors of group identification, into tools for measuring loyalties, and into forms of legally and socially bound in-out relationships. Their separation from other disciplines has been applied according to the idea that the natural sciences in particular are the most reliable, trustworthy, and 'neutral'. Prominent scholars, like Gellner (1984) or Anderson (1991), have extensively analysed these phenomena and the role of the 'clergy of the nation' ascribed to the humanities only.

For at least two centuries the national political culture promoted educational systems by disregarding the extent and itineraries through which these *métissages* have been linking Europe. As a result, it has deeply affected the perception of 'otherness'. Therefore, conflicting narratives were nurtured and alternative memories constructed, while avoiding confusing effects with exact disciplines, that are allegedly considered to be not 'contaminated' by political ideologies (Cohen, 2001).

Instead, the EU integration framework offers an unprecedented space for contesting these opposing national narratives. Potentially, it will help in reconsidering the legacy of European knowledge as being the result of intense and multi-layered interactions. These stem from diasporic experiences, mobility, mutual contacts, and *métissages*, that is, factors that pave the way to a post-nation state cultural understanding. Therefore, the development of EU integration may generate a constructive context for building confidence and empathy across borders, making transnational cooperation, interdisciplinarity, and the use of multilingualism routine. For all these reasons, the founding fathers of the EU believed that this approach would better guarantee peace and development, as well as a more effective competitiveness for EU member states on the global level.

Applying networking, interdisciplinarity, and mobility as working methods to higher educational institutions is not only consistent with such a rationale but also challenges the existing system of teaching. In this way, the internationalisation of universities takes on a new appearance, since it goes far beyond the international dissemination of scientific discoveries or the 'traditional' knowledge of other cultures on the basis of national interpretative criteria. By overcoming those current obsolescent approaches to knowledge, which are inadequate in the face of globalisation, the 'new' internationalisation encourages – through intense exchanges – a *métis* education, a transnational syncretism in terms of knowledge and lifestyles, as well as a nomadism of relationships, which are generating a *new* European culture, juxtaposed to the national ones.

Universities (as well as school systems) may represent a vibrant lever in this process of change, although not always aware of it, or willing to implement it, even when they are allowed to do so. Networking, mobility, and the Bologna process spread powerfully when the implementation of the Schengen treaty, the EU enlargement eastward, and low-cost flights converged. Under these circumstances, the time-space compression accelerated by IT connections was simultaneously the cause and the consequence of wide national shocks. I have stressed in other papers that the Schengen treaty is a revolutionary agreement, since it challenges one of the key pillars of Westphalian state sovereignty, that is, state control over a fixed population (Bianchini, 2015). Moreover, EU enlargement since 2004 and the intense low-cost flow of people have made visible the effects of a growing circulation of citizens. This freedom of movement within the Schengen area is a consistent implementation of one of the four freedoms of the EU.

In other words, a new educational policy is precipitating the gradual liquefaction (Bauman, 2000) of the existing learning process, which has remained trapped under national criteria restrictions for a long time. The mechanisms of mobility, networking, and exams/diploma compatibilities are creating radically new learning contexts. Multinational classes are growing in number and, even when this is not the case, faculty mobility is encouraging a cultural nomadism of students and the staff. Multilingualism is becoming a vital skill for communication between teachers and students, among students, and between teachers and staff for accomplishing administrative needs. This process is challenging the language homogenisation that characterised higher educational institutions until the fall of the Berlin wall.

Since then, a twofold language process has taken place. On the one hand, multilingualism has been encouraged by the EU as a prerequisite for participating in communitarian institutions, in training and educational programmes, as well as a fact stemming from the multinational peculiarity of classes. On the other hand, English has begun to play a predominant role in a number of international teaching programmes.

This development came with EU enlargement eastward, when the traditional two-sided relationship was replaced by multiple cooperation. Indeed, the process accelerated at the turn of the millennium when the EU was still only made up of a few member states and the Cold War was over. However, in the case of bilateral agreements between universities, leading for example to co-*tutelles* in PhD programmes or to double diplomas on specific disciplines aimed at enhancing the mutual exchange of knowledge, languages other than English are being used even today in the implementation of learning activities.

Nevertheless, a new phenomenon has emerged with the spread of English as the lingua franca in EU universities' international programmes. It is about the materialisation of a sort of 'EU or communitarian English', which is structurally different from the language spoken in the United Kingdom, mainly because it is a vehicle of communication for non-mother tongue individuals and, to a certain extent, because influenced by the communitarian terminology in use in Brussels, then disseminated in the member states. Because of these characteristics, the 'EU or communitarian English' is a language without literature, without poetry, therefore without the emotional sphere that marks national languages. In short, it is a product incompatible with any primordialist vision of a political society, far beyond the hopes and the dreams of Herder, Fichte, and the activists of anti-enlightened romantic nationalism.

As is well known, the identification of a nation with a language and its literature is rooted both in the ethnic and civic understanding of the nation, despite their own differences in approaches. It is enough to cite Mazzini or Wilson for confirmation that the literary language has been considered a benchmark of a nation, despite the tangible difficulty in defining what a language is. In any case, and consistent with this belief, the standardisation of national languages has been imposed by nation-state governments for amalgamation needs, marking the educational system in-depth, from primary schools to universities for at least two centuries.

Currently, however, the internationalisation of European universities is promoting a societal transformation of cultural elites, following a trajectory open to new frontiers in human relations. Determined by the multilingual education of mobile young generations, in a context where 'communitarian (not literary) English' is playing a predominant role anyhow, cultural nomadism is crucially contributing to the deconstruction of previous achievements in terms of social identification of a group. Consistent with an increasingly interdependent world, with the requirements of transnational markets and corporations, with the process of globalisation, the internationalisation of higher education in

Europe – based on mobility, networking, diploma compatibilities, multilingualism, and communitarian English – is generating a transnational European élite acquainted with operating in contexts marked by diversities, heterogeneity, and a plurality of narratives.

This does not imply the end of literary English or national literary languages. Their construction in fact never eradicated pre-existing vernacular literatures anyway, which are still alive in poetry, movies, songs, and theatrical performances. Simply, there is little basis even to imagine such a cultural decline in the foreseeable future. On the contrary, 'not literary' English is becoming an additional achievement for transnational European culture. The success of its use across borders lies in juxtaposing it with current national languages and literatures, enhancing the potential produced by facilitated exchanges.

Moreover, the EU multi-language strategy (with English as a 'working language') is not the unique tool aimed at breeding new transnational elites. A crucial role will be increasingly played by curricula cooperation and the transnational awarding of diplomas, especially when combined with the mobility of students, teachers, and staff. This convergence of internationalising actions in the implementation of degree programmes will have a potent impact on both nation-state fusion and the awareness that identities are multiple, rather than 'unique and distinct' for each people.

Actually, the relationship between nation-state and national identity is intimately connected, like two sides of the same coin. The whole process of nation-state building has been promoted and carried out in Europe on the assumption that *one* dominant (and homogenising) identity is the strengthening factor of the collective sense of belonging, supposedly based on *one* language, *one* territory, *one* culture, *one* common history, a direct/mutual recognition between ruled and rulers, a shared economic system of interests, etc.

By contrast, universities' *joint* programmes generate a radically new educational environment. By attracting students and a faculty from different countries, by developing multiple forms of mobility, and awarding double, multiple or joint diplomas, a set of transversal skills flows in the teaching arrangement. As a result, disciplinary in-depth learning takes place in a context where students and scholars meet in a greater familiarity of otherness. Their interaction creates the best conditions for establishing a mutual knowledge, which involves habits, lifestyles, and an exchange of information about the variety of their countries of origin. In this way, trust is enhanced, empathy promoted, and diversities accepted as a norm, rather than a menace.

Consequently, the fluidity of the relationships that are produced goes far beyond the limits of the nation-state political culture, where neighbours are often seen as enemies or potential enemies, and diversities a factor of 'cultural contamination', which threatens the identity of the group. Instead, this fluidity is a great investment for peace and security, since studying and working together for two or more years increases the social permeability of the people involved and strengthens their networking capabilities. Cross-cultural adaptability skills and cross-disciplinary integration are, in fact, crucially relevant for young generations that are prospectively expected to act in a globalised world. In addition, the friendship relationships that they are able to establish meanwhile comprise an additional investment in terms of transnational networks that may prospectively operate in a number of fields, from business to politics, from arts to sciences.

6 Internationalisation of Universities, Social Fluidity, and Resistance to Change

Ulrich Beck focused his thoughts on the need to build a *cosmopolitan* Europe (Beck & Grande, 2014). In fact, the strategies so far implemented in order to encourage the internationalisation of universities' curricula, mobility, research, and networking comprise a vital opportunity to establish a transnational society, based on interdisciplinary knowledge, which is simultaneously a pivotal lever for EU *cosmopolitanism*.

This prospective education is strictly connected with the scholarly development of research networks: the knowledge thus produced generates additional effects, beyond the universities' campuses in different social contexts. With the mobility of students, scholars, and staff, a plurality of bridges is established not only within the EU but also, broadly speaking, with all the countries involved at least in the EHEA. Studying and/or researching together encourages the preservation of dialogue and friendship, even in historical contexts where bilateral relations between states are contentious.

The involvement, for example, of the Russian federation in the EHEA is extremely important. Underestimating its desire for cooperation at the scholarly level by reducing funds or diluting the participation of Russian higher institutions in EU programmes as a consequence of mutual economic and political sanctions during a contingent political dispute is not only meaningless but may also lead to unpredictable negative consequences. Recent cultural and educational decisions of the European Commission are not encouraging in this regard. Luckily, however, not all doors were closed and cooperation with Russian universities has remained not only desirable but also possible.

In addition, mobility produces additional effects on the surroundings of the university campuses since local population and local economic activities have to cope with the needs and demands of a melting-pot- and highly educated society, whose aspirations include the respect of different religious prescriptions, food requirements, communication languages, wide internet access, entertainment, etc. As a result, the life of local communities faces new transformations and, in this respect, a broader 'educational dimension' stems from international programmes. Leaving classrooms, meeting local populations, and transferring knowledge to social and economic environments powerfully contribute toward reducing the still widespread negative perceptions of 'otherness' by assigning positive values to the movements of people and cultural syncretism. In other words, the internationalisation of university programmes can generate inclusive social feelings.

Recently, as a consequence of the major flow of migrants and asylum seekers from Africa and the Near East, the internationalisation of universities has manifested a new potential. That is, it has helped inclusiveness by offering opportunity to study to young people, while encouraging the local population to see the phenomenon with a different eye than that of racism, xenophobia, antisemitism, and anti-Islamic fears. Moreover, the presence of a growing community of students who are from mixed marriages or second-generation migrants, and possess multilingual skills can bridge the gap between the local and the global, making *métissages* and neo-nomadism gradually accepted.

Admittedly, governments, political parties, and social movements do not always welcome this challenge. Some of them, not necessarily right-wing oriented, like to appeal to emotions in order to attract consensus or mobilise voters to support them. Very often, when radical transformations are taking place, a sense of anxiety and reticence spreads within the society. This 'vulnerability' generates fear. Fear, in turn, encourages the rejection of changes among individuals; as a result, under these circumstances, sectors of public opinion fall into the trap of racism, xenophobia, antisemitism, and ethnic cleansing demands under the presumption that they are effective tools to restore group solidarity and the sense of security of the community (or nation). These phenomena are well known; they have been extensively studied and explain very well as the reason why wars occurred in Yugoslavia, Moldavia, and the Caucasus. In recent times, they shed light on what the sources are that incite racist waves in the EU member states, particularly the old ones, from Italy to the United Kingdom, from Denmark to Finland. Similar feelings are at the origin of the statements expressed by the leaderships of the 'Visegrad four' and the Baltic countries against the quota distribution of migrants and asylum seekers.

By contrast, the internationalisation of the universities represents an opportunity to promote an opposite cultural approach in terms of public engagement, educational skills, and socialisation.

At the same time, however, the reform of higher education is still under the constraints of EU member states legislation, their national political cultures, and systems. Additional limitations are produced by neoliberal ideology, business approaches, and the way disciplines are studied, particularly the humanities and social sciences, as they traditionally define the civic education of new generations. Not surprisingly, they are often excluded from the hard science curricula. As a result, the technical education of students is not complemented by an understanding of the environment where they are expected to work.[8]

In a nutshell, a coherent implementation of university internationalisation is obstructed by a number of factors, which are generated partially by the powerful opposition of administrative bodies and partially by hostility against intercultural relations. Both phenomena are not only a mental product but also a consequence of the rooted polarisation between the global and the local.

Notwithstanding public statements and commitments, in particular those agreed and signed at the EHEA Ministerial Conference of Bucharest of April 26–27, 2012, little has been achieved since. Lots of words have flowed in support of academic and professional recognition, learning mobility, international openness, European qualification frameworks, and interdisciplinarity. Furthermore, 47 Ministers responsible for higher education in the European Higher Education Area concurred in encouraging *higher education institutions to further develop joint programmes and degrees as part of a wider EHEA approach. We will examine national rules and practices relating to joint programmes and degrees as a way to dismantle obstacles to cooperation and mobility embedded in national contexts*.[9]

The subsequent Conference of Yerevan, convened on May 14–15, 2015, recognised the negative impact of the bureaucratic approach on the common educational area and promised 'to give new impetus to the cooperation'. The signatory ministries made the commitment to review national legislation, remove obstacles to prior learning, and, therefore, facilitate the access to higher education programmes. In addition, they adopted special measures for joint

---

8   However, the exclusivist approached to curricula is increasingly contested. For example, the Colorado School of Mines has introduced studies in foreign languages, history, music, literature, and public affairs in the belief that 'Mines is not all about science and technology'. The Council of Europe in 2016 produced an important document: '*Competences for Democratic Culture. Living together as equals in culturally diverse democratic societies*', where the inclusion of social sciences and humanities in hard sciences curricula is strongly recommended. See https://rm.coe.int/16806ccc07.

9   http://www.ehea.info.

degree programmes, stating that, if an agency is carrying out an evaluation of accreditation of the entire joint programme, *'the result is to be accepted in all EHEA countries'*.[10] How much of these assertions will be implemented remains to be seen. Potentially, however, they are an important step forward in overcoming the limitations encoded in most national legislation, which is still inadequate for facing the challenges of joint programmes and degrees, making the process of harmonisation slow to develop. Persistent national requirements, often mutually conflicting, make curriculum design and programme management a problematic exercise, if not a hazard.

In Italy, for example, obsolete 'tables of the classes of BA or MA programmes' cannot seriously be applied to international programmes and even less so 'imposed' on partners, particularly in cases like Austria, whose accreditation process implies that all partners offer at home a number of courses with the same learning outcomes and similar syllabi. Moreover, the accreditation process in Italy is valid for only one year, and every year a systematic submission of paperwork and a strict respect of quantitative criteria (that often change) prior to the beginning of lectures are required. On the contrary, in Lithuania the accreditation process, which is to be reformed soon, begins when the programme is under way, and only after a long qualitative process, led by an international commission, is accreditation awarded for a maximum of 6 years. Under these circumstances, the rules for adapting or modifying teaching plans during the implementation of the programme are often mutually conflicting and, if amendments to programme regulations are not carefully studied, adjustments may lead to an undesirable loss of accreditation in one of the partner countries.

Similarly, the list of career opportunities is recognised differently; it may happen that some professional profiles, which are normally included in the prospective educational goals of the programme in a partner country, are rejected in another one.

Additional difficulties revolve around the willingness of scholars to teach in a language other than their mother tongue. Basically, older generations are more reluctant than the younger ones. Moreover, some universities encompass this commitment within the regular obligations of the teacher. Others, instead, offer an economic incentive, whose amount varies considerably according to

---

10 See the *European Approach for Quality Assurance of Joint Programmes*, which was draft in October 2014 and then approved by EHEA Ministers in May 2015 during the Yerevan Conference. The document is available at the following address: https://www.eqar.eu/fileadmin/documents/bologna/02_European_Approach_QA_of_Joint_Programmes_v1_0.pdf.

the circumstances. As a result, this behaviour becomes an issue when joint programmes need to be established between universities that apply different policies in this regard.

Therefore, carrying out a joint programme depends to a large extent on the degree of adaptability of the universities, which in turn rests on the *individual willingness* of the partners and scholars, on the level of flexibility of the administrative personnel, on the ability of the university officials to interact with the ministry and sometimes even to influence the interpretation of rules.

7   Conclusion

At the beginning of this article, I reported on the results achieved by the European human capital strategy. Erasmus mobility is still one of the most relevant success factors. I went on to elaborate on the political-cultural impact of this EU operation, which led to the establishment of EHEA, joint programmes and degrees, networking research teams, and so on.

By contrast, but not surprisingly, in the midst of the European crisis of governance, while facing asylum seekers and migration flow, the Slovak Presidency of the EU suggested in November 2016 to cut 50% of the Erasmus Programme budget for the years 2017–2020, down from the € 200 million proposed by the EU Commission to € 100 million.

The desire to annihilate such a successful programme patently stems from the fear that nationalist elites might be replaced, prospectively, by cosmopolitan, integrated, transnational, and nomadic European elites, which are educated through mobility, networking, and interdisciplinarity. Manipulating unscrupulously the unsettled issue of the migrant distribution across the EU and merging it with the fear of recent terrorist attacks, the Slovak proposal – albeit temporarily rejected – is a powerful indicator that EU integration is far from being consolidated.

Furthermore, Slovakia is not alone in this behaviour. For example, the Italian government has considered the possibility of establishing a threshold for the mobility expenses of all public administrations. Since state universities are considered public administration after the 2010 university reform, this proposal, if implemented, will affect the options of professors in spending the miserable amount they individually receive every year for their research activities. Treating, in fact, the Italian universities in the same way as the post offices, the aim of the state's policy is to obstruct one of the key international activities of academic researchers. Simultaneously, the newly established accreditation agency pretends to assess quantitatively their research production, by influencing salary awards and their eligibility in the national commissions for career advancements (regardless of their disciplines expertise).

Under these circumstances, it is evident that the internationalisation of the universities (as well as their autonomy) is seriously threatened. Reluctance to make the international activities of the higher institutions work is intensifying both within ministries and the administration of the same universities.

Furthermore, the legal fragility of the EU framework for university convergence is acutely being challenged. Despite magniloquent statements and some crucial cornerstones represented by the Erasmus Programme, the Bologna process, networking, and interdisciplinarity as methodologies, the EU still lacks a set of norms regulating the transnational joint structure of programmes, their accreditation, and quality assurance strategies. Leaving these tasks to the negotiating capacity of the member states, which are politically reluctant, administratively inflexible or, sometimes, just slow in harmonising their higher education policies has made the implementation and the management of joint programmes a deeply frustrating exercise and, in some cases, nearly 'mission impossible'. Under the new circumstances of the populist drift emphasised by Brexit, which was basically produced by a rejection of people mobility although not necessarily directed against the academic world, the delay in the harmonisation of university policies may generate a wide educational failure, able to affect negatively the aforementioned cornerstones. The collapse of the integrative sentiment within the EU has strengthened the belief that the centralisation of powers and the homogenisation of rules, according to national and local attitudes, are the most effective ways to guarantee control over education. Attempts to design regulations that return international programmes to national or even (local) university rules are prospectively increasing the parochialism of educational programmes. Instead of recognising the wealth stemming from multiple transnational cooperation, which requires negotiation with partners and administrative flexibility according to the needs of each programme, the trend is to homologate what cannot (and should not) be homologated.

Subsequently, the fear of flexibility is not only a peculiarity of governments. It is crucially embodied in public administrations, including those of universities with their own political presidia. This is not yet a generalised behaviour, but it is a trend: a growing trend. The prospective implications of this behaviour are easy to understand compared to the quality of teaching activities and the international education of young generations. Actually, the international education risks are fading gradually.

An additional detrimental factor that may affect the transformative role of international education is strictly connected to the increasing gap between the global elite (whose education is still in progress) and the persistence of local, parochial understandings of reality. This aspect is connected to the reasons why national governments have slowed down the development of international strategies of education. In fact, as is said, joint programmes (in their own wide variety of forms) are training a mobile, multilingual, *métis*, neo-nomadic, and transnational elite. Its inner closeness is reinforced by its ability to handle both new communication systems and the new geography of connections that the Internet and low-cost flights are radically transforming. Their contribution to space-time compression annihilates distances and borders, making urban centres and far away cities from rural areas closer. In this context, part of the population is going to be trained in order to face the challenges of integration and globalisation, while another part, often monolingual and sedentary, remains excluded. This cultural disparity is already polarizing the global and the local understandings of real life. Consequences are visible not only and not so much between generations, but mostly between differently educated people and/or between people who had divergent opportunities to access knowledge and a career.

It is among those lacking adequate tools to interpret social changes that emotional reactions against interculturalism, or phenomena like racism and xenophobia, have greater chances of being nurtured. In other words, an essential human 'reserve' is mentally disposed to follow exclusive political strategies, even if they are unable to govern the fluidity of the changes of our world. Paradoxically, the mix of feelings of rejection and intolerance, insecurity and uncertainty that characterise such guidance is not only culturally fragile but has a *transnational* character. It crosses borders, can easily be identified in a plurality of countries, and recently has been seeking some sort of convergence even within the European Parliament, despite their demands for strict national cohesion, the emphasis on territory and sovereignty, and the critiques of integration and globalisation. This polarisation is very dangerous because it paves the way for radical clashes, to severe cultural incompatibility within European societies, with unpredictable repercussions for the EU future.

This is the context where universities are expected to play an innovative role, far beyond any attempt at restricting their training mission within the limits of vocational or national schemes. In other words, they have a tremendous task ahead. They need to enhance the education of a new elite, spread critical thinking so it extends beyond classrooms and influences society by establishing a more dynamic relationship with the school system.

The world is changing and higher educational institutions cannot relinquish their responsibilities and *raison d'être* under these circumstances. Joint programmes currently represent the most intense opportunity for re-launching a leading role for the universities, producing synergies across the borders, not only in the interest of EU integration, but more broadly, in order to expand knowledge, trust, and empathy among people. The aftermath of these actions, either teaching or research network findings are to be shared with a broader community. In this context the relationship between universities and schools may prospectively play a crucial role.

We are living in a global, increasingly comprehensive society. New generations need tools to facilitate their job in intercultural environments, multi-skill acquisitions, and a strong interdisciplinary sensitivity. It is increasingly inadequate to contain knowledge within separate boxes, despite the resistance of academia, which still concentrates its efforts on protecting the priority of disciplines in the identification of teaching programmes, PhD studies, even in the selection of scholars. On the contrary, the same flow that is eroding borders and nations is melting disciplinary rigidity. Any act of knowledge, decision, information, analysis, reconstruction of events, etc., requires a comprehensive approach, able to grasp the complexity of implications that, at different levels, may affect our increasingly multifaceted societies. Consequently, a leading elite is expected to develop an interdisciplinary methodology and an interdisciplinary sensitivity, because educated accordingly. At the same time, in order to soften the global/local gap mentioned above, transnational educational systems should promote interdisciplinary approaches, plurality of angles, and subject contents both in LLL programmes, in the schools, and in the media.

To conclude, universities do control a decisive lever for EU integration, peace, trust, and empathy in our societies. They have an obvious *social engagement* in terms of building knowledge and matching the needs of the times. Joint programmes are the next, crucial step to be implemented, in combination with networking, mobility, interdisciplinarity, research, multilingualism, and transversal skills.

Despite resistance at the national and local level, the academic world cannot spend time remembering a supposed 'golden age' of early national university organisation. On the contrary, it is expected to face the challenges of globalisation and world transformation. It is expected to show the courage of innovation, to break down obsolescent and centralised rules, expand flexibility in the forms and quality of teaching, produce new synergies for society, and cope with the reorganisation of human life and its relationships according to the quick changes imposed by space-time compression. Nation-state fusion is, in this context, unavoidable. It is for governments and public administrations to decide whether it is more fruitful to govern the change or to resist it. For their own nature as centres for producing knowledge, it is a must for universities to confront the new and act transnationally. Otherwise, they lose their role and *raison d'être*.

References

Altbach, P., Reisberg, L., & Rumbley, L. (2009). *Trends in Global Higher Education: Tracking an Academic Revolution*. Paris, UNESCO.

Anderson, B. (1991). *Imagined Communities*. London, Verso.

Bauman, Z. (2000). *Liquid Modernity*. Cambridge, Polity press.

Beck, U., & Grande, E. (2014). *Cosmopolitan Europe*. Cambridge: Polity Press.

Bhola, H.S. (1997). Adult education policy projections in the Delors report. *Prospects*, 27 (2), 207–222.

Bianchini S. (2015). Yugoslav and EU decline. The dynamics of dissolution and sovereignty reframed, In Jensen, J., & Miszlivetz, F. (eds.), *Reframing Europe's Future. Challenges and Failures of the European Construction*, Abingdon-New York, Routledge, 160–178.

Braidotti, R. (2011). *Nomadic Theory. The Portable Rosi Braidotti*. New York, Columbia University Press.

Brandenburg U., & De Wit, H. (2011). The end of internationalisation. *International Higher Education*, 62, 15–17.

Cohen, B.R. (2001). Science and humanities, across two cultures and into science studies. *Endeavour*, 25 (1), 8–12.

De Wit, H. (ed.) (2013). *An Introduction to The Higher Education Internationalisation*. Milan, Vita e Pensiero.

Etkowitz, H. (1993). Innovation in innovation: The triple helix of university-industry-government relations. *Social Science Information, 42*, 293–338.

Etkowitz, H., & Leydesdorff, L. (1995). The triple helix: university – industry – government relations: A laboratory for knowledge-based economic development. *EASST Review, 14*, 14–19.

Gellner, E. (1984). *Nations and Nationalisms*. Oxford, Basil Blackwell.

Gerschenkron, A. (1962). *Economic Backwardness in Historical Perspective*. Cambridge, Harvard University Press.

Knight, J. (2008). *Higher Education in Turmoil. The Changing World of Internationalisation*. Rotterdam, Taipei, Sense Publishers.

Maringa, F., & Foskett, N. (2010) (eds.), *Globalisation and Internationalisation of Higher Education. Theoretical, Strategic and Management Perspectives*. London, Bloomsbury Publishing.

Ranga, M., & Etkowitz, H. (2013). Triple helix systems: An analytical framework for innovation policy and practice in the knowledge society. *Industry and Higher Education*, (4), 237–262.

Scott, P. (2005). The Global Dimension: internationalising higher education, In Khemj, B., & De Wit, H. (eds.). *Internationalisation in Higher Education: European Responses to the Global Perspective*. Amsterdam, European Association for International Education and the European Higher Education Society (EAIR).

Streeter, J. (2014). Networking in academia, in *EMBO Reports*, November 2014, 15 (11), 1109–1112 retrieved from https://www.ncbi.nlm.nih.gov/pmc/articles/PMC4253483.

Szyszlo, P. (2016). Internationalisation strategies for the global knowledge society. *Canadian Bureau for International Education (CBIE)-Bureau canadien de l'éducation internationale (BCEI)*, CBIE PhD Research Series.

Teichler, U. (2004). The changing debate on internationalisation of higher education. *Higher Education*, 48, 5–26.

UNESCO. (1996). *Learning: The Treasure Within*. Retrieved from https://unesdoc.unesco.org/ark:/48223/pf0000109590.

Zweig, S. (2014). *Tempo e mondo. Solo gli uomini muoiono, mai le idee. Conferenze e saggi 1914–1940*. Prato, Piano. B. (eds.).

Further Readings

Council of Europe. (2016). *Competences for Democratic Culture. Living Together as Equals in Culturally Diverse Democratic Societies*, Strasburg. Retrieved from https://rm.coe.int/16806ccc07.

Delors Commission. (1996). *Learning: The Treasure Within*, Delors Commission Report to UNESCO of the International Commission on Education for the 21st century. Paris, UNESCO.

European Commission. (2014). *Erasmus Impact Study – Effects of Mobility on the Skills and Employability of Students and the Internationalisation of Higher Education Institutions*. Retrieved from http://www.eubusiness.com/topics/education/erasmus-impact.

Generation Europe Foundation. (2014). *Erasmus voting Assessment Project Final Report*. Retrieved from http://issuu.com/generationeurope/docs/evaproject_final_report_fordistribu/1?e=1430744/9429338, p. 35.

Labrie, N., Amati, R., Camerini, A.L., Zampa, M., & Zanini, C. (2015). What's in it for us? Six dyadic networking strategies in academia. *Studies in Communication Sciences*, 15 (1), 158–160.

Sobhi, T., & Cougoureux, M. (2013). *Revisiting Learning: The Treasure Within. Assessing the Influence of the 1996 Delors Report*. Paris, UNESCO.

UNESCO. (2015). *International Bibliographic Database on Higher Education*. Paris, The International Association of Universities.

UNESCO. (2005). *Towards Knowledge Societies*, Paris, UNESCO.

CHAPTER 4

Liberal Arts to the Rescue of the Bachelor's Degree in Europe

Samuel Abrahám

Abstract

The purpose of this chapter is to demonstrate the importance of the liberal arts model as the most suitable to fulfil the potential of Bachelor studies, as well as argue that the moral element as part of any quality education will be crucial for the future challenges that Europe faces. One of the aims of the European Union educational policy has been coordination and synchronisation of its diverse systems, in order to promote student and academic exchanges and diploma recognition. This became particularly poignant after the fall of communist regimes in 1989 when a great diversity of university systems existed across the continent. The Bologna Declaration signed in 1998 introduced a 'credit system' where each course taught at any university would be easily transferable to another university in another country. This has been hailed as great success, but it has not materialised in its envisioned potential. The reformed undergraduate education, refurbished through the liberal arts model, would assure not only education with depth and breadth but also the moral aptitude and the cognitive capacity of students, enabling them to confront an uncertain future. The Bologna Declaration of 1999 allowed the Bachelor's-Master's division; it is time, this paper argues, to allow the Bachelor's stage to fulfil its full potential.

Keywords

liberal arts – future – Europe – morality – education

1   Introduction

Educational institutions have globally become immensely important and seem to be always in some kind of crisis. And even during a temporary calm, academia seems to be either recovering from or heading toward a crisis – financial, structural, or existential. These institutions have grown in size and number as demand for university education has grown exponentially during the last fifty years. In fact, schools are, as Ivan Illich (1970) reminds us, the most universal institutions – more than any church or industry – transcending geographic and ideological boundaries, embracing every country in the world (p. 44). They devour huge chunks of national budgets and are deemed by politicians to be a tool to make their country competitive, innovative, and modern. The more educated its population, the more likely is a society to be perceived as potentially prosperous. The concern about the state and status of educational systems always provides an excuse for government intervention. And politicians feel obliged 'to solve' these crises with some long-needed reform, innovative plans, and periodic restructuring. Thus, educators either complain that the interference by government is too intrusive or that it neglects their needs and demands. Sometimes it seems that the best scenario is to leave this rather conservative and mighty educational apparatus on its own, leaving its structure intact while enjoying state funding. And yet they are never to be left alone because every society and its educational sector are locked together to face an uncertain future and to deal with the purpose, direction, and costs of their universities and various research institutes.

As in every state sector that demands funds, be it industry, the defence sector, healthcare, culture, or schools, the crucial question is priorities. In the case of higher education in Europe, it is a faculty's research potential and publications that represent the most prestigious part of academia. The others, the students, seem to be at the service of university administrators and educators, and not vice versa. Historically, this is an anomaly that requires explanation and demands correction. The reasons for the current status seem simple. Universal literacy and huge increases in the number of university students require a mammoth effort for administrators to balance their task to maintain high university rankings while expanding the number of students in order to receive state funding. Often quality suffers from the pressure of quantity, and the biggest loss is suffered by the undergraduate sector where students can be mass-lectured and mass-examined. Such massification of undergraduate education does not influence the ranking of a university much, and, hence, there is little incentive to concentrate on the status of students' learning. Rather, priority is given to the quality of research, publications, and PhD programmes. Not surprisingly, even at prestigious European universities, it often seems that an undergraduate student is just a number to justify the research status and existence of a professoriate. The attempt to deal with the *status quo* on the European level has mixed results and requires much rethinking and reform.

The European Union is an ideal supranational institution that offers a huge opportunity for centrally initiated changes in the form of standardisation, approximation, and in the variety of innovative educational models. Besides alleviating the discrepancies of national educational structures, Brussels thinks that there is an urgency to make Europe competitive vis-à-vis the USA and other non-European countries. The last major educational reform was instituted through the Bologna Declaration signed in 1999, which, among other things, initiated the creation and Europe-wide implementation of the Bachelor's degree. Yet this major structural reform was not followed up by the necessary debate among educators about the nature and content of the newly created Bachelor's stage, or about the purpose and structure of higher education in the 21th century. This debate about a new strategy has been badly needed considering the immense increase in the number of undergraduate students. In addition, with the implementation of the Bologna Declaration, seemingly much has been reformed but, in reality, very little has changed because universities are by nature conservative institutions and have managed to preserve the old departmental structure as a sort of 'national defence' against 'supranational intrusion' from Brussels. The least affected by the reform was the undergraduate studies' content, structure, and process of education; and the narrow specialisation of studies within single subject departments have remained intact.

The three-year-long Bachelor's degree has been introduced as one segment of the Bologna Declaration to replace, along with the Master's degree, the old five-year-long programmes of studies. It has been in a state of crisis ever since. The reasons are manifold and the purpose of this chapter is to point out the background and the causes of the dismal state of the undergraduate studies in Europe today. It will cover the historical aspect of higher education and explain why Europe has neglected its own tradition of *Bildung* that was instrumental in the formation of educational systems in Europe in the early nineteenth century. Next, this chapter will describe the existing models of Liberal Arts education in Europe. It will also propose a way to reform the Bachelor's degree, offering structural changes in order to make it meaningful and useful for millions of high school graduates entering universities throughout Europe. It will be argued that the preservation of the current status of the Bachelor's degree would cause a decline in the quality of education, increase the costs, and eventually undermine its operation in numerous countries. Paradoxically, it is a return to the Liberal Arts educational model, originating in Europe centuries ago, that can offer restoration of the position of the undergraduate degree as a suitable preparation for further postgraduate studies. In addition, it would prepare students for the occupations gradually unfolding during the twenty-first century. The liberal arts model stresses not only the content of what is studied but also the structure of classes as well as the method of teaching and learning where primary focus is on students' cognitive competence and, importantly, moral stance.

2 The *Status Quo* of the Bachelor's Degree in Europe

One of the aims of the European Union's educational policy has been the coordination and synchronization of its diverse systems in order to promote student and academic exchanges and diploma recognition. This became particularly urgent immediately after the fall of communist regimes in 1989 when a great diversity of university systems existed across the continent. Although each country preserves sovereignty over its accreditation process and the shape, size, and number of its universities, the interest of all has been to allow students and academics to participate in exchanges and cooperation. In order to achieve this, the main provision of the Bologna Declaration signed in 1999 by all EU ministers of education was the introduction of a so-called 'European Higher Education Area', which primarily allowed a 'credit transfer system' where each course taught at one university would be transferable to another university in the same or another country.[1] This led to an explosion of student exchanges where millions of students within Europe receive a stipend to spend a semester or year of their study at another university abroad. This has for years been hailed as the greatest success of the Bologna process and was particularly beneficial for young scholars and PhD students in expanding their knowledge, establishing contacts, and enhancing their research. Scientists from former communist countries could work with their Western colleagues using sophisticated equipment not available in their home institutions. Scholars from social studies and the humanities could enrich and compare their research during extended trips, workshops, and conferences. The EU has been providing generous travel and research funding for these academic activities. This has been arguably one of the most positive developments of European integration.

Another aim of the Bologna Declarations was the division of university studies into Bachelor's and Master's degrees as the Declaration divided the old five-year-long education and PhD studies into undergraduate and graduate cycles.[2] Allegedly, the division was only a last-minute decision amidst tense

---

[1] Information on the Bologna Process and its evolution is found on the website, http://ec.europa.eu/education/policy/higher-education/bologna-process_en.

[2] The text of the Bologna Declaration is found on https://www.eurashe.eu/library/modernising-phe/Bologna_1999_Bologna-Declaration.pdf.

negotiations.[3] The reason for this division was to differentiate undergraduate and graduate studies, the same as it has been the case in Anglo-Saxon countries, and in particular to be compatible with the USA system. Also, the old five-year degree seemed too long for certain professional studies and for job training. In theory, a Bachelor's degree could be a terminal degree as has been the case in Anglo-Saxon countries. However, there, the Bachelor's degree has a different structure and traditionally lasts four years in contrast to the three-year-long degree that has been a standard in Europe.

The division into Bachelor's and Master's studies in Europe could have been of great benefit to students if the focus and purpose of the two had been clearly delineated. For example, if the first degree offered more general education, cognitive competence and training in so-called 'intellectual skills', while the Master's degree offered a professional degree, or a preparation for PhD studies. This reform has never happened. The politicians signing the Bologna Declaration created the division, but it was not followed by a sufficiently broad discussion among educators about the content and purpose of the two degrees. regrettably, as of now, in the overwhelming number of institutions of higher learning there is no difference between the current Bachelor's degree and the previous first three years of study of a five-year-long programmes. The old system has remained intact, and that is the source of substantial tension. Students start to specialise from day one of their Bachelor's studies and cannot depart from this path without starting their studies all over again. After graduating, they continue in the same field of study, usually at the same department, for another two years to complete a Master's degree. And this is currently considered at many European universities as a redundant arrangement obliging administrators to organise an extra Bachelor's thesis for each student and an extra graduation, which, understandably, is deemed costly and time-consuming.

The functioning of the Bachelor's degree has been problematic because it is spread and compartmentalised along the thousands of specialised departments. The old design of departmental division has survived intact, undermining the whole system. To undo this, as will be argued later, would require restructuring the departmental division and that would mean a major reform of the European university system. Suffice it to say that with respect to the Bachelor's degree the survival of departmental divisions is an anachronism. As Stanley Katz (1996) argues: 'The current departmental structure has outlived the rapid increase of information and knowledge ... [T]he departmental structure of today's research universities is largely an artefact of branches of

---

[3] Personal communication with Milan Ftáčnik, then Minister of Education of Slovakia and the signatory of the Bologna Declaration.

knowledge that seemed distinct at the turn of the [nineteenth] century but have remained distinct only for reasons of academic and administrative convenience' (p. 84). This prevailing anachronism of departmental division is, as will be explained later, particularly damaging for the current status of the Bachelor's degree.

Paradoxically, if this inherently flawed design survives permanently, the introduction of a Bachelor's degree in Europe will seem redundant and will be tolerated only as a structural imposition through the Bologna process. The Bachelor's stage has already been considered a failure by many prominent educators, who consider it as an enforced division that goes against tradition and even against common sense. It is often viewed as incomplete university studies to be finished with a Master's degree. Some countries even contemplate ending the division and returning to the five-year-long degree.

The mechanical division of studies is not the only major problem of the Bachelor's degree. There are several others that will need to be addressed during any reform of higher education in Europe. One is the role and relationship of student and teacher; the other is the latter's institutional affiliation and personal attachment. As Ernest L. Boyer (1996) stresses, in Europe an old German tradition prevails, 'with its emphasis not on the student but on the professoriate; not on general but on specialised education; not on loyalty to the campus but on loyalty to the guild' (p. 145). Indeed, in the age of narrow specialisation and the unwritten rule of 'publish or perish', teachers focus predominantly on research and publishing and consider teaching often as a necessary burden. The doyen of liberal arts education in Europe, Hans Adriaansen (2017), points out, with some vexation, the current status of university teachers who 'have shifted their focus from teaching to research, which is, in fact, a form of goal displacement similar to the shift bankers have made from clients to bonuses' (p. 29).[4] Those most affected by this trend of lectures-exams and the research-publishing academic (vicious) cycle are undergraduate students who come less and less in contact with their research-driven professors who often ignore and disdain their teaching responsibilities.

Another and related problem of the Bachelor's degree today is that undergraduate students are not instructed and trained to acquire the intellectual skills so important for further studies, research, and employment prospects in a systematic way. The reason is that European universities, mostly state-funded, select as many Bachelor's students as possible because their state financing depends on the sheer number of students admitted. What, and how, teaching

---

4 In Europe it is often called 'Liberal Arts and Sciences' in order to stress that liberal arts should contain sciences, as historically they always did. I will use the term 'Liberal Arts'.

is done, and what a student learns, seems secondary to ministries of education and thus not a priority for universities. In addition, the academic ranking of the universities is not dependent on quality of teaching and time dedicated to Bachelor's students but on a number of publications, level of research, and the prominence of professors. This arrangement has a positive effect on PhD students, partially on Master's students, but is definitely harmful to undergraduate students. Even the most prestigious European universities that boast top academics, scientific research, and excellent MA and PhD programmes, offer predominantly mass Bachelor's programmes. In such an environment, even excellent lecturers would not have enough time to provide feedback on student work, with hundreds of students in a lecture course. Besides, at large research universities, professors would surely prefer scholarly discussion with their postgraduate students who specialise in the same field and not with Bachelor's students. In addition, if there are large classes, it is common to hold only multiple-choice tests at the end of the semester, or one major paper with little supervision or feedback. Teaching assistants from among the PhD and even Master's students are beneficial but do not compensate for the expertise of professors who are, however, usually not available to their students on a regular basis. In many post-communist countries, there still exists an oral exam practice where the students are questioned randomly, often at the whim of the examiner. All these are most unfortunate educational practices in Europe that need to be addressed and corrected.

Another issue is the importance and proportional weight of the humanities, social and natural sciences, and vocational studies. Universities in Europe are under political pressure to prepare their graduates for employment, and hence natural science and vocational education enjoy a great advantage with respect to funding over the humanities and social sciences. This, of course, is a global trend, but in Europe there is little discussion about what this shift implies. Universities offer fixed, specialised programmes and are often presented as job-training centres. And yet, paradoxically, as Stanley Katz comments: 'Post-industrial economies place little value on the retention of specialised knowledge but instead emphasise basic numeracy and literacy (including computer literacy). The situation strikes me as a tremendous opportunity for a humanist to claim more space and time in the undergraduate curriculum...' (p. 82). Still, there is little debate among either academics or politicians about what the purpose of a university in contemporary society is, or what should be the role of the humanities in our turbulent and crisis-ridden societies. A suggestion that a university graduate, as a result of their studies, should become a responsible citizen would be considered an inapt, even tactless, intrusion into the private realm of an individual. University education today is considered a sacred right that no one is going to alter and diminish in any major way. In fact, if there is any change it will be rather toward shifting more resources to research and development, to natural sciences, or to vocational education. Indeed, if university studies are considered merely as job preparation programmes, the cognitive and ethical element of humanist studies will be deemed by many to be a wasteful inheritance from the past. This is an alarming prospect not only for higher education but also for the condition of democracy in Europe.

It is in this area of making the Bachelor's degree meaningful that Liberal Arts studies can provide substantial improvement. But, before we discuss how Liberal Arts could make Bachelor's degrees in Europe self-contained, meaningful, and overall beneficial, it is important to examine first the nature and purpose of education in our time and look at historical developments that show how the old European tradition of *Artes Liberales* and *Bildung* was displaced and replaced with narrow specialisation, preference for vocational training, and why academic studies have led to the gradual marginalisation of humanities.

3   Education

Each epoch views education differently, reflecting social and political conditions, and the priorities and concerns specific to it. Curriculum in the first universities was divided between theology and *Artes Liberales*, the latter to acquire broad knowledge in philosophy and natural sciences as well as to master the art of disputation. Later, liberal education added 'three philosophies' – natural, moral, and metaphysical – to provide students with comprehensive education, moral foundation and the intellectual skills of writing, oratory, and scholarship (Kimball 1996, p. 16). It had been believed that the knowledge and the skills were worthy in themselves, although they would also prepare for professional training. In other words, such an education was considered to represent the ends, constituting a meaningful and good life, and not the means to it.

Many educators today question such spiritual and moral dimensions of education, stressing, instead, the priority of mastering a certain field of study or being skilled in a professional subject, for example law, medicine or business. They see the old concept of education as something redundant in today's technology-driven, fast-advancing, and changing societies. There is nothing wrong with the old way, but there is simply no time today, they argue, for such a noble but old-fashioned endeavour as searching for 'the good life'. Educators, students, and politicians increasingly perceive universities as a vehicle to secure employment, financial security, and professional prestige. Education in this perspective becomes a commodity, a means to an end, not an end in itself.

Hence, those aspects of education that do not fit this 'modern' end are deemed superfluous. And, the result is disastrous. Today one can spend five years studying at university, obtaining Bachelor's and Master's degrees even in the social sciences, let alone the natural sciences, without taking a single course dealing with history or covering any moral, spiritual, or artistic dimension that formed the humanistic tradition in Western civilisation. And yet, it is so important for the intellectual, cognitive, and moral development of a young individual to study these subjects. It provides a base for life-long learning, independence of thinking, and a moral foundation to face up to the challenges presented by currently diminishing solidarity, economic disparities, or political radicalisation. At the moment, humanistic and moral aspects are absent during Bachelor's studies, and there are wide ranging negative consequences to this development. Let us explore the background and value of this type of education.[5]

The original purpose of education has not become obsolete with the rise of modernity and technology. On the contrary, as we witness how obstinately politicians, intellectuals, and scholars approach contemporary moral and ethical dilemmas and problems, there is a need to offer education that contains moral and philosophical dimension. John Henry Cardinal Newman, in his *The Scope and Nature of University Education* (1852), explores the purpose of education when he states: 'I am asked what is the end of university education, and of the liberal or philosophical knowledge which I conceive it to impart: I answer, that … it has a very tangible, real, and sufficient end, though the end cannot be divided from that knowledge itself'. And then adds his famous conclusion: 'Knowledge is capable of being its own end' (p. 83). Hence, for him education and knowledge are intertwined, both having a moral and ethical base without which knowledge is just something cunning and education encyclopaedic and shallow. Newman's words may sound old-fashioned, lofty, and redundant, but they gain a new meaning in today's crisis-ridden, radicalising world, plagued with political corruption and looming environmental disaster. Knowledge 'capable of being its own end' feels like a sanctuary of sanity and decency in a world of legitimised vulgarity, a world where an ever more overbearing advertising industry dictates the tastes and trends to the same young people who should be able to resist this attack on their senses and sensibilities. The absence of these ideals is most vividly exposed as many politicians, public figures, and religious leaders who call for justice, tolerance, and moderation are in despair facing the crowds of those who cannot distinguish these terms from the calls

---

[5] In the past, secondary school education provided comprehensive courses in philosophy, history, and art as well as improved skills in critical thinking, writing, and oral presentation. While that may have been true in the past, data indicate an erosion of this kind of learning at the secondary level.

of injustice, bigotry, and uncontrolled rage invoked and instigated by populists and racists. The struggle for the moral foundation of our societies is not what is said by the elite but what is being heard and understood by the population. Thus, an educated individual as invoked by Cardinal Newman is and will be the crucial barrier facing populists and bigots.

One often hears that knowledge of virtues and vices are to be acquired at home, through spiritual guidance rather than during university studies. Although partially valid, there are at least two objections to this claim. First, the traditional institutions of family, church, and civil society have weakened in our post-industrial, fragmented world facing trendy and ephemeral standards, religious radicalisation, and the clash of identities politics. Second, it is increasingly difficult to hold onto one's own value-system while facing a world that is changing so fast, and is becoming more complex and divided. No wonder that the beginning of twenty-first century has seen an increase in the number of populist and radical nationalist movements. They are able to exploit the confusion and fears of people who are unable to digest and make sense of social, economic, and political turmoil. Even in Western societies, an increasing number of people turn to fraudulent and obscurantist political preachers who promise safety, protection, and final victory of whatever bigoted and selfish cause. One remedy for these ills – even one that is not fool-proof, as will be argued – is good education, open to questioning prevailing stereotypes and clichés, encouraging criticism of one's own society if the latter fails to meet the high moral standards known and cultivated – with varying success – for millennia. Such an education cannot just be a means to some end but must be an end in itself for young people if they are to recognise truth from lie, hoax, and deception.

The philosopher Isaiah Berlin quotes in one of his interviews how an old philosophy professor commenced his philosophy class:

> All of you, gentlemen [sic – ed.], will have different careers – some of you will be lawyers, some of you will be soldiers, some will be doctors and engineers, some will be government servants, some will be landowners or politicians. Let me tell you at once that nothing I say during these lectures will be of the slightest use to you in any of the fields in which you will attempt to exercise your skills. But one thing I can promise you: if you continue with this course of lectures to the end, you will always be able to know when men are talking rot.

This suggests how relevant the knowledge of philosophy is for young students studying a variety of subjects. Berlin adds to this: 'One of the effects of philosophy, if it is properly taught, is the ability to see through political rhetoric, bad arguments, deception, *fumisterie*, verbal fog, emotional blackmail and every kind of chicanery and disguise. It can sharpen critical faculty a very great deal' (Jahanbegloo 1991, p. 29). It should be added, and Berlin would surely agree, that critical faculty is also sharpened through study of literature, art, and history.

The contrast between the critical education so necessary for recognising the 'rot' and the conduct of contemporary Bachelor's level of education is staggering. What defines and dominates the vast majority of European undergraduate studies after the introduction of the Bologna Declaration is still narrow specialisation, fixed programmes from day one, and a limited scope of courses all provided by a single department. As Boyer (1996) argues, 'The tendency of the disciplines has been to isolate themselves from one another, with academic departments becoming political bases, not centres of intellectual quests' (p. 149). Large departments having hundreds of students but, surprisingly, even small departments, lack space, time, and often the will needed to refine intellectual skills and train critical thinking through conversation, argumentation, and disputation among students and with their teacher. Boyer (1996) and Adriaansen (2017) both lament the retreat of the teaching profession, the key aspect of university life. It is worth quoting both:

> The simple truth is that almost all of us are where we are today because of the inspiration of an inspired teacher. Yet, on far too many campuses, it is deemed better for a professor to deliver a paper at the Hyatt in Chicago than to teach undergraduates back home. And it's really sad the way we speak of research 'opportunities' and teaching 'load'.
> BOYER 1996, p. 151

Teaching at university colleges[6] requires a special kind of teacher: teachers who understand that the chance that one of their students will win the Nobel Prize is much bigger than that they themselves will end up as Nobel laureates. University colleges need teachers whose pride lies in the career of their students (Adriaansen 2017, p. 30). It is often argued that a heavy 'teaching load' comes at the expense of 'research opportunities'. Indeed, good teaching requires more hours spent talking to students, and providing feedback on their papers, but should not scholarly life also include sharing one's knowledge and experience with students? Is not teaching a meaningful application of one's research?

A Bachelor's degree student graduating from a narrow study department often enters a graduate programme without acquiring intellectual skills and

---

6 The third part of this chapter explains the concept of 'University College'.

broad academic competence. He or she continues to study in a narrow field of specialisation and research while not having been better equipped to properly comprehend and analyse the complexities of social and moral dilemmas facing their societies. The German language has two fitting expressions related to this issue. One is *Bildung*, an old term based on conceptions of education by Herder, Hegel, and von Humboldt. It is related to the above description of the Liberal Arts model in which research is closely connected with teaching, stressing also students' free choice in shaping their educational path. According to *Bildung*, the ultimate aim of education is also self-knowledge. In parallel with the Liberal Arts, *Bildung* includes a moral dimension because, as previously argued, it 'includes the ability to engage in immanent critique of one's society, challenging it to actualise its own highest ideals' (Eldridge). The other German term is *Fachidiot* referring to narrow specialisation in a single discipline where scholars are unable to connect dots with other subject studies and remain ignorant of the social conditions surrounding them. If students versed in *Bildung* are able to resist the siren call of populism, bigotry, and 'saviours' of various ilk, *Fachidioten* are, at best, oblivious to the social compact around them and, at worst, lacking any moral and social bearing; therefore, they are easily swayed and even become supportive of extremists, chauvinists, and tyrants of this world.

So what kind of Bachelor's degree is needed for in the twenty-first century? On the one hand, there is a need for specialisation in certain field or subject areas but that should follow after undergraduate students have mastered subjects enhancing their cognitive skills and moral outlook. The main aim of the Bachelor's stage should be to deepen and broaden various aspects of knowledge, and to cultivate critical abilities enabling one to defend one's moral position. In fact, all these skills and the acquisition of a moral compass provide students with the tools to be innovative, discerning, and creative in those specialised fields studied in post-graduate studies. Educator and former President of Harvard University, Derek Bok (1986), discusses the importance of 'critical education' that creates an autonomous individual, necessary for any society, at any period. He claims that, 'A critical mind, free of dogma but nourished by humane values, may be the most important product of education in a changing, fragmented society' (p. 47). There is no doubt that it is an undergraduate education that is most suitable for inculcating critical knowledge. The young mind between the ages of seventeen and twenty-one is mature enough and prone to certain ideals without worrying about immediate mundane needs. Such an idealistic mind still perceives its well-being and being good as closely connected vessels. The timing seems to be crucial. In fact, later in life there may rarely be a chance for a majority of citizens to reflect objectively and openly about the complex web of the world's predicaments. Stanley Katz (1996) stresses the importance of instilling critical education at a certain age: 'It is my conviction that undergraduate education often serves as the last and the best chance post-secondary students have to broaden their intellectual horizons and to prepare for the great demands that society will place on them. In addition, undergraduate education provides the best circumstances in which democratic values can be inculcated or reinforced' (p. 79).

It is a broad Liberal Arts education that provides the best opportunity for a young mind to expand its intellectual horizons and to internalise democratic values. It is superior to even such studies as philosophy, sociology, psychology, or political science, which predominantly contain the study within their own disciplines, and any interdisciplinary component is absent or minimal. Liberal Arts studies contain elements of disciplines and enhance the content of their curriculum with a specific structure of seminar studies and comprehensive teaching methods that focus on student-based learning rather than lecture-type teaching common in other programmes. It is simply not enough to digest relevant bodies of knowledge through texts and lecture because at the current rate of change that knowledge is likely to be obsolete within the next few years. Liberal Arts prepare students to adapt, adjust, and keep on learning through a process of teaching in which this transformation and internalisation of knowledge takes place. The triad of content, structure, and process, or as Adriaansen (2017) calls it 'programme, scale and pedagogy' (p. 28), together represent a combination conducive to quality learning that equips students for further scholarly studies as well as professional or vocational studies. It also prepares students for employment thanks to critical thinking and intellectual skills. It is not surprising that numerous corporate CEOs see the long-term value of Liberal Arts education, understanding that they benefit from having employees who can 'think, write and present' (Yarmolinsky 1996, p. 134; Adriaansen 2017, p. 30).[7]

4   Liberal Arts as an Opportunity for Europe

The second half of this chapter will describe the historical foundation of this model and a short history of the reintroduction of Liberal Arts to Europe as well as articulate the reasons why Europe should embrace it for its undergraduate

---

7 Even engineers need intellectual skills for the modern economy. As Schneider (2005) observes: 'Engineers and technology employees also need strong communication and collaborative skills; knowledge of social, global, and diversity issues; ethical reasoning; and the ability to integrate these different kinds of knowledge with engineering solutions' (p. 65).

studies. Finally, it will offer a few Liberal Arts models – from modest small-scale ones to a more radical comprehensive one that could be utilised for such reform and transformation of universities in the future.

Liberal Arts education, and the concept of *Bildung* already mentioned, are concepts of education that, in the course of the nineteenth century were replaced in Europe by rigid departmental structures, gradually moving toward narrow specialisation and, above all, toward an emphasis on research. This model has prevailed at the vast majority of European universities and continues to the present. Paradoxically, this focus on research evolved at German universities that claimed *Bildung* as their foundation but prioritising only the research component rather than acquiring the self-knowledge devised by von Humboldt who stressed both. He also believed 'that teachers and learners are jointly doing research and that it is this form of jointly acquiring knowledge that defines university education' (Adriaansen, 2017).

A much older concept than *Bildung* is *Artes Liberales*. It originated from a combination of two streams of the Ancient Greek approach to education. One was Plato's (1955) search for the truth through philosophy; the other was Socrates' stress on rhetoric, ethics, and virtue. The former was thought to be an instrument for acquiring knowledge, and the latter was a path how to become a better and virtuous human being (Zakaria 2015, pp. 42–44). These two streams were the foundation of what evolved into the seven Liberal Arts of the *Trivium* and the *Quadrivium* that, as mentioned above, later evolved into Liberal Arts programmes in early modern Europe.

The Liberal Arts model moved to the United States in the seventeenth century and evolved and survives there to the present day. There are today around five hundred private colleges that are mostly residential, and about half of them are relatively small Liberal Arts colleges. Almost exclusively, Liberal Arts studies in the USA are undergraduate four-year-long programmes.[8] Even the most famous so-called Ivy League universities in the USA have undergraduate programmes based on the Liberal Arts model.[9] It is far from being a rigid model and has been evolving continuously with respect to the content of subjects and method of study, as historian Bruce Kimball argues (Kimball 1996, pp. 22–26). Hence, it is a flexible model of education with respect to the content, as long as it emphasises the methods of learning and teaching.

---

8 There are a few exceptions, for example the Master's Degree in Liberal Arts at The New School for Social Research of New York. Usually, the argument is that it offers a broader perspective to students who had narrow specialisation during the Bachelor's stage.
9 The Ivy League Universities are considered Brown, Columbia, Dartmouth, Harvard, Princeton, Yale, and the University of Pennsylvania.

The Liberal Arts studies were introduced in Central Europe after the fall of Communist regimes and in the Netherlands, also in the 1990s.[10] Initially, they all had a strong American connection either through personal ties or through institutional initiatives.[11] In 1996, the Education Leadership Program, on the initiative of Julie Johnson Kidd of The Endeavor Foundation, started a network, *Artes Liberales,* in order to promote Liberal Arts in post-communist Central and Eastern Europe. This lasted for five years.[12] From this initiative later emerged Liberal Arts programmes at Warsaw University taking the name *Artes Liberales* and later, in 2006, the *Bratislava International School of Liberal Arts* (BISLA), based in Slovakia. Almost parallel to *Artes Liberales* in Central Europe, the Dutch professor of Sociology, Hans Adriaansen, after involvement with Liberal Arts at Smith College in the USA, singlehandedly initiated the introduction of this model in the Netherlands. The first so-called university college at Utrecht University under his leadership was created in 1998 and since then there have been ten such programmes in that country. There are several other Liberal Arts programmes, the fastest growing number is in the UK and there are a few such programmes also in Germany.[13] More than twenty European Liberal Arts programmes collaborate through the European Consortium of

---

10   There have been several Liberal Arts colleges previously but they had been accredited in the USA and have not been part of the European educational system simply because there was no Bachelor's Degree before the Bologna Declaration. They are excellent private, rather expensive, institutions and only marginally cooperate with their European partners. They are *American University of Athens, American University of Paris, John Cabot University of Rome, Franklin University in Lugano,* and *Webster University* in Vienna; in the 1990s the *American University of Bulgaria* was established.

11   *Vitautas Magnus University* in Kaunas, Lithuania, was initiated as a restored university in that city in 1989. It was financially supported by Lithuanian émigrés in the USA and unofficially based on a Liberal Arts model.

12   The Founding members of *Artes Liberales* in 1996 were Samuel Abrahám (Slovakia), Jerzy Axer (Poland), Cesar Birzea (Romania), Serhiv Ivaniuk (Ukraine), Peteris Lakis (Latvia), Rein Raud (Estonia), Jan Sokol (Czech Republic), and Julia Stefanova (Bulgaria). The USA was represented by the Director of the Educational Leadership Program (ELP), Nicholas Farnham and his associate Professor Adam Yarmolinsky. The Educational Leadership Program was an activity that existed within the Christian A. Johnson Endeavor Foundation of New York, now renamed as The Endeavor Foundation. The goal of the ELP initiative in Europe was to bring an understanding of the Liberal Arts curricular approach and pedagogy to Central and Eastern Europe and the former Soviet States after the collapse of the Soviet Union.

13   See the list of various Liberal Arts programmes in Europe at the web page of The European Consortium of Liberal Arts and Sciences (ECOLAS) www.ecolas.eu a network based in Bratislava, Slovakia.

Liberal Arts and Sciences (ECOLAS), cooperating to shape, define and advance Liberal Arts in Europe.[14]

The introduction of Liberal Arts studies encountered substantial difficulties in Europe. It has been either unknown or viewed with suspicion, even disdain among many European educators. There are several reasons for this unfortunate reception. One is that it is incorrectly perceived as a USA import unfit for the European educational scene. The other is that it is a model in sharp contrast to current early specialisation at European universities. Liberal Arts is wrongly perceived as an '"anything goes"-programme, which, particularly in times of economic crisis, wouldn't help students to get a decent job' (Adriaansen 2017, pp. 29–30). Still, other sceptics view it is a small, somehow elitist programme, unfit for large-scale undergraduate education in Europe. Furthermore, it has been difficult to accredit Liberal Arts studies in an environment of fixed single-subject programmes because numerous national accreditation committees find it difficult to incorporate a complex and multifaceted programme such as Liberal Arts studies.

And yet, if the Bachelor's degree is to become a meaningful and useful component of the European higher educational system, and not perceived as an unwanted child enforced via the Bologna Declaration by politicians and 'Brussels', Liberal Arts programmes should be embraced wholeheartedly. Several reasons for this have been mentioned above; suffice it to say that undergraduate education, by incorporating a Liberal Arts model, would gain in several respects. First of all, these would be student-based and broad competence-based programmes that would replace the early narrow specialisation prevailing today. Second, students would be able to search for a specialisation gradually and could declare a major that best fits their abilities and preferences after two or three semesters of study. This would result in much smaller student dropout rates than is currently common throughout Europe. Third, the focus on intellectual development and curiosity, critical thinking, and effective communication is not a guarantee but it is conducive to the aims of educating citizens willing to sustain the common good in a civil society (Boetsch et al. 2017, p. 6). Fourth, students studying a variety of subjects, as well as taking common core courses of rhetoric, ethics, and methodology, would be able to cultivate critical thinking. Fifth, liberal arts would make the Bachelor's stage potentially a terminal degree giving students the choice of whether to continue in a more

---

14   ECOLAS – the initiative of Hans Adriaansen and Samuel Abrahám in 2009 and later joined by Laurent Boetsch – is based at BISLA in Bratislava, Slovakia, and has been lately supported by The Endeavor Foundation (USA) that has supported and promoted Liberal Arts in Europe since 1996.

advanced programme, or to enter a variety of jobs in industry, services, and management.

Before reviewing various available models of Liberal Arts studies, it is important to assess what represents a Liberal Arts programme and what only bears its name without fulfilling the basic preconditions of such studies. It is complicated by the fact that there are not *one* but *many* models of Liberal Arts. Still, there are several minimal standards that need to be met. It was stated above that the key to any of its definitions is the presence of three essential elements that differentiate it from the traditional, narrow specialisation, departmentally based, lecture-exam model of undergraduate education. The basic preconditions of Liberal Arts are diversity of content, limited scale of institution, and small classes, as well as a specific type of pedagogy. The programme or content must contain a wide range of courses from the humanities and the social sciences as well as the natural sciences.[15] All these are necessary in order to attain what Derek Bok (1986) calls competency-based skills. Among them are so-called 'soft skills' that develop effective communication, improve analytical abilities, and strengthen problem-solving capacities. And then there are social and ethical skills enabling the student to make value judgments, improve facility in social interaction, achieve an understanding of the relationship between the individual and his or her environment, develop awareness and understanding of the contemporary world, and, finally, develop an understanding of and sensitivity towards the arts and a knowledge of the humanities (Bok 1986, p. 60).

There is one controversial caveat that should be stated clearly about the Liberal Arts: mastering the competency-based skills does not assure that a student becomes automatically a good citizen, as the countless mission statements of Liberal Arts institutions claim. No education can assure that. Liberal Arts allow students to differentiate between good and evil, to detect and analyse the intent and motive of peoples' action. It does not inculcate virtue. Turning again to Cardinal Newman (1958) who points out that:

> Knowledge is one thing, virtue another; good sense is not conscience, refinement is not humility ... Philosophy, however enlightened, however profound, gives no command over the passions, no influential motives,

---

15   It is common in Europe to call this programme 'Liberal Arts and Sciences' in order to stress the fact that natural sciences have been part of *artes liberales* since the beginning and still hold their place. However, there are several programmes within the Liberal Arts, both in Europe and the USA, that do not contain natural sciences yet, thanks to the structure of the institutions and pedagogical process, as well as the great variety of course and co-curricular activities, these programmes are still part of Liberal Arts.

> no vivifying principles. Liberal education makes not the Christian, not the Catholic, but the gentleman (sic; eds.). It is well to be a gentleman, it is well to have a cultivated intellect, a delicate taste, a candid, equitable, dispassionate mind, a noble and courteous bearing in the conduct of life – these are the connatural qualities of a large knowledge ... still, I repeat, they are no guarantee for sanctity or even for conscientiousness, they may attach to the man of the world, to the profligate, to the heartless ... (p. 99).

It is important to acknowledge the limitation of even the best education. How students utilise this knowledge is up to their judgment and moral profile, and one must hope that it will lead him or her to become a decent citizen. Human nature is unpredictable and human *Eros*, as understood by the Ancient Greeks, and as Socrates reminds us while facing Calicles in the dialogue *Gorgias*, is the most difficult energy of all to navigate in the right direction. As Plato (1955) elaborates in *The Republic*, it is a duty towards oneself and towards one's society for a philosopher to become an educator in order to navigate the energy of young people to become virtuous human beings. To give this up would undermine one's own moral duty and betray young peoples' cognitive and moral potential. None of this is currently the goal of university education. It is the ambition of Liberal Arts education to do its best to help students to mature intellectually and become good citizens.

5 Current Liberal Arts Models in Europe

There are several models of Liberal Arts education that could be currently or gradually implemented by private institutions or state-funded universities in Europe. Some are small-scale and independent while the others are larger and based within large universities. There is a model that represents a radical solution for every undergraduate student and its introduction would literally cause an educational revolution and comprehensive restructuring of universities.

There are three models of Liberal Arts programmes operating in Europe – independent colleges, university colleges, and medium size universities embracing some aspects of Liberal Arts. The first two models offer education predominantly in English in order to assure a wide international body of students, whereas, the third model might vary in the language of instruction. Being grafted onto still-uncharted and often unfriendly territory, it is important to list both positive aspects but also some risks to what the foundation of Liberal Arts programmes encompasses.

The independent colleges are the most similar to the small colleges in the USA. These have state accreditation in their domiciled country and have also some USA accreditation.[16] There are advantages and disadvantages to this model. The advantage is that there is no state interference shaping the programme and the colleges are free to create a model suitable for their mission adjusting to social and political conditions of the country in which they are based. There are a small number of students in seminar-type classes, and a good student-teacher ratio allows a tutorial system in which teachers closely supervise their tutees. Not having postgraduate programmes, the academic and social interaction between teacher and students is quite intensive. The disadvantage is that because of its small size, an independent college provides only a limited number of courses and majors. However, the intensity of study and the focus on social and intellectual skills compensates for a limited choice of programmes. One has to add that it tends to be rather a costly programme because such a college must fulfil all, often copious, bureaucratic requirements of ministries of education and accreditation bodies.[17]

The Liberal Arts scheme that has the largest potential to expand in Europe and that started in the Netherlands in 1998 is the University College (UC) model. It is a unit within a major university, having its own faculty and residences for students. In addition, the funding usually comes from the state distributed through the home university. Location could be either within a campus of the founding university, or geographically distant, connected only institutionally. The advantage of this model is that a UC can draw on the resources of a larger university and share space and social setting. It is an intensive programme for up to 600 students with core courses, a unique curriculum, and seminar-type classes.

Overall, the benefit to the home university is the presence of an excellent undergraduate programme that has a positive effect on faculty outside the UC itself. It seems that if the government is willing to support UCs, the benefit is substantial as is the case in the Netherlands where already ten universities have established UCs. It is a model worth emulating because it provides student-based learning and a relatively large choice of courses while students master intellectual and social skills. In addition, the close interaction between

---

16   There are three such colleges: *Bratislava International School of Liberal Arts* (Slovakia), *European Humanities University* (Lithuania), and the *European College of Liberal Arts* (ECLA), in Berlin, Germany (currently part of Bard College, thus Bard College Berlin).

17   The answer would be to increase the fees, but that would preclude admission of variety of students from multiple backgrounds. Besides, student fees in Europe are mostly low or non-existent. Thus, high fees would make these colleges, although providing thorough Liberal Arts education, not really very competitive, to say the least.

teachers and students, and core courses related to ethics, political theory and arts, in addition to extracurricular activities and community services are all conducive to educating students to obtain a more comprehensive education than regular students who study solely narrow subjects in a particular field. The disadvantage of the UC model might be the dependence on the home university's supervision and administration. The danger to the existence of the UC might be a change of leadership at the home university. A new rector might not view a UC as favourably as his or her predecessor and this might endanger the Liberal Arts programme because costs per student at the UC are higher than within the home university.[18] Furthermore, finances are directed usually through the rector's office and this can cause a strain on funding.

The third model introduces some elements of Liberal Arts into the entire curriculum and method of teaching at established, medium-size universities. The set-up preserves the original, departmental structure while offering certain core courses common in a Liberal Arts setting. Students are encouraged to select courses from different departments in order to assure diversity in their curriculum. The size of classes might still be larger than what a Liberal Arts model recommends, because to divide the whole university into small classes while preserving students in individual departments would be financially unfeasible. There are some programmes that offer a traditional lecture-exam model but alter the course approach by introducing, for example, problem-based learning as opposed to the traditional lecture-exam model. This model is offered at some universities in the UK and Germany (Boetsch et al. 2017, pp. 21–30). It has a chance of expanding to some other countries where there is an effort to improve the quality of teaching and learning and to break the massification of lecture halls and the impersonal approach of undergraduate study. This laudable effort is, however, only a partial solution to improve undergraduate education. It can turn into only a formal reform of the educational model, focusing on a variety of offered courses, but only minimally adjusting the size of classes or the pedagogy. In addition, there would be constant tension between various departments 'feeling the ownership of students'. Thus, a multidisciplinary curriculum for students might be considered by a department to be at the expense of their full-fledged single discipline curriculum. Moreover, the great advantage that a student in a regular Liberal Arts programme does not declare the major immediately after entrance is lost in this model where students apply to departmental mono-disciplinary studies. This early specialisation is really not compensated for by the offer of a variety of core courses or courses from other

---

18   The Liberal Arts Program in the *New Bulgarian University* was terminated by a new rector who had not the passion, or understanding, for Liberal Arts as had his predecessor.

disciplines throughout the course of study. Finally, the pedagogical methods of teachers from various departments would not assure the commitment of teachers to the Liberal Arts pedagogy (Boetsch et al, p. 32). Hence, such partial reform must be constantly monitored, negotiated, and often imposed on the departments or otherwise the whole scheme can become rather costly and ineffective if such a model is devoid of a refined pedagogy and stresses competency-based skills.

All three models exist and function in different countries in Europe and through cooperation and exchange of experience they try to improve their individual models.[19] The University College model is dominant in the Netherlands, whereas, the third model of implementing some aspects of Liberal Arts is gaining some popularity in the UK and Germany. Finally, the opportunity for creating independent Liberal Arts colleges in Europe is quite limited because it must be supported by private donors and there is no tradition similar to the USA where, starting in seventeenth century, either private donors, religious orders, or various churches founded so-called residential colleges.[20] Hence, the Liberal Arts models, as they presently exist in Europe, have a limited scope and involve only a fraction of undergraduate students. However, the quality of graduates from these models is much higher than from other schools and, for that reason, they are in great demand by graduate schools or employers. Also, they are the living proof that undergraduate education in Europe can be of the highest quality.

6 New Revolutionary Model

There is another model that could affect the entire educational system in Europe and, as mentioned, would mean a revolution in education. The scheme is radical yet relatively simple: first, to transform entire universities into university colleges and, then, at the college level, students would obtain an intensive and versatile Liberal Arts education. Needless to say, it would provoke resistance from several quarters, especially from the academic community that is by nature conservative. Thus, such a large-scale reform of the whole university

---

19 There were several common projects among European Liberal Arts programmes. First, one to establish ECOLAS (2010–2012) and another called BLASTER (2015–2017) to cooperate in three areas: teaching training, undergraduate research, and quality standards. See www.ecolas.eu.

20 Currently, in the USA, there are no new colleges being founded. On the contrary, some are having great difficulty surviving.

model could only be the result of a broad, Europe-wide discussion and political action on the scale of a New Bologna Declaration.

One might ask why such a radical reform is necessary. Well, if politicians, educators and employers want Europe to become innovative yet tolerant, prosperous yet having an educated class able to resist the anti-democratic forces currently on the rise, then education, and in particular, the undergraduate education must play an important role. And this reform has a chance only if it is based on the Liberal Arts model because only this type of study leads to cognitive competence and civic responsibility able to confront the challenges of the twenty-first century. The reform is also needed because at present each student has to face a most difficult choice of selecting one narrow departmental study out of many hundreds. 'For students at the age of 17 choosing one specific programme out of so many possibilities is more than just a challenge: it is almost impossible' (Adriaansen, 2017). Hence, the current system is not only unfair and difficult for students but it is also costly for the state that derives no benefit from a student who does not finish a degree. The reform might be complicated, maybe expensive, but it would significantly enhance the undergraduate study experience and would affect millions of students.

The transformation of the Bachelor's degree would be revolutionary yet would utilise existing models, structures, and philosophies. There would be a major change in the structure of the *whole* university and in the process of teaching. The first change would be structural – students would be admitted to university colleges and not to individual departments; the second would require a radical change in the role of the teacher in relation to students. Pedagogy would have to be altered from the current lecture-exam pattern to pedagogy aiming at student-centred learning; and, third, it would also require a review of the current obsession where the ranking of universities is solely based on the quality of research and not also on the quality of students' education. Student-centred teaching would thus be of the same importance as research. Finally, the most affected would be the departments that would lose a large number of students to colleges.

The most radical step would be to remove Bachelor's studies from the narrow discipline of departments and, instead, place undergraduate students into different university colleges. Division into a collegiate structure would actually imitate an old Oxbridge model of colleges still existing at the two great English universities, and at many large universities in the USA and Canada. Students entering a college within a large university would first study, and make choices and changes without committing themselves to a single departmental programme. Students at the same college would eventually disperse into a variety of subject areas, yet they would share a common core and a variety of different courses, as well as a common social experience. The college setting allows students, who are generally more interested in solving and understanding different kinds of problems, to choose from a variety of courses offered by different departments. Furthermore, a college setting would be conducive to the creation of a community of scholars and students that would mutually benefit from academic and social interaction.

Another major change instituted by the new scheme would relate to the respective roles of teachers and students. Each college would have to have an adequate number of full-time professors with diverse academic backgrounds in order to offer tutorial services to students on their path to discovering new areas of study. Universities would have to improve both academic prestige and financially reward teaching, which would become a highly respected profession again. Currently, a young academic after finishing PhD enters the teaching profession with little teaching experience and hardly any pedagogical preparation. To reverse this trend, each teacher would be required to go through teachers' training in order to succeed in student-based programmes. Not surprisingly, all three existing Liberal Arts models in Europe are forming teaching centres that provide assistance and guidance for their teachers.

The new model would also involve introduction of undergraduate research as an integral part of collegiate education. It would require dramatic changes in the way research is currently valued at major universities. In their quest for prestige and funding, researchers working within a narrow discipline are often more attached to their fellow scholars from across the globe than to their home institution. Undergraduate students are the last to be asked to participate in their professors' research. The transformation of universities into colleges would not diminish the importance of research. It would only have to be slightly re-oriented by becoming an integral part of the pedagogy and of each college activity. Involving students in their research, professors would not only create crucial bonds with their students, they might also gain insights into how best to communicate the results of their research to a wider public.[21] One should add that this model would also have a positive effect on professors whose research is generally enhanced if combined with teaching in an interdisciplinary environment.

---

[21] Undergraduate research is also focus of current Liberal Arts schools cooperating in this area. See the booklet 'Current Undergraduate Research in Liberal Arts and Sciences' (CURLAS) produced by Warwick University (UK) and University College Roosevelt (the Netherlands) as part of the BLASTER project that involved cooperation in three areas – teaching training, quality standard, and undergraduate research www.ecolas.eu.

The new model would certainly weaken departments because they would see it as undermining their long-established privileged position. The departments in their silos of disciplines might be the toughest source of resistance to this scheme. As Katz (1996) remarked with some chagrin: 'If the academic department is not the enemy of knowledge, it is almost certainly the foe of pedagogical reform' (p. 85). The university college transformation, one should stress, would not abolish departments themselves, for they would remain available to Master's and PhD students while also serving the colleges with a variety of courses. What would change is the end of departmental monopoly over Bachelor's degrees as is universal throughout Europe today.

7 Challenges

The transformation of universities into colleges, to be sure, would require much research, debate, and preparation before it would be accepted by educators and politicians to replace the current departmental structure. The key question underlying the debate would revolve around the question: Whom does the university serve first, students or faculty? The current research-driven university setting heavily favours the professoriate, while the Liberal Arts perspective sees undergraduate students as equally important stakeholders in higher learning. It is the better academic results of students, as evident by the graduate school placement of Liberal Arts graduates that would legitimise the division into colleges, the enhanced status of teaching, and undergraduate research. Furthermore, high retention rates, already familiar among the existing Liberal Arts models, would be financially significant. And yet the change would be difficult. The leap might be, at the beginning, too radical for the rather conservative environment of universities.

The major hurdle to overcome, one that deserves some attention, is the question of costs. On the surface a collegiate setting, small classes, a tutorial system and large numbers of contact hours would demand much greater costs in comparison to massive classes and the lecture-exams model where hundreds of students are free to attend lectures during the semester and then pass the final exam or submit one long paper. Indeed, as Yarmolinsky (1996) claims, 'The central economic fact about liberal education is that its core processes consume as much labour as they did before the Industrial Revolution' (p. 126). However, Adriaansen (2017) argues that costs might not be higher; they might even decrease. He calculated that, for example, the University of Utrecht with 18,000 undergraduate students could be divided into 30 colleges with 600 students each. And the costs should not be higher than the same number of students currently divided into 44 separate departments with multiple academic and non-academic staff (p. 30).

Another objection to this radical change might be more mundane for it would mean for professors a different division of labour, more balance between teaching and research responsibilities. Indeed, teaching in a Liberal Arts setting is pleasant but quite time consuming, often challenging while reading multiple assignments, providing feedback, leaving ample time for tutorials as well as preparing joint undergraduate research projects. All in all, in the eyes of the scholar seeking 'research opportunities', all these 'teaching loads' would come at the expense of delivering another paper at a conference in a Hyatt somewhere in Europe. However, an alternative is the current situation, which often leads to what Murray Sperber et al. (2005) describe as a 'non-aggression pact' between faculty and students:

> Because the former believe that they must spend most of their time doing research, and the latter often prefer to pass their time having fun, a mutual nonaggression pact occurs with each side agreeing not to impinge on the other. The glue that keeps the pact intact is grade inflation: easy A's for merely acceptable work and B's for mediocre work (p. 138).

One can object that it is not the common experience, and surely there are many conscientious teachers who do not practice this 'non-aggression pact' with their students. Yet, one can argue that the current system at large research universities is predisposed to such an arrangement and leads to a manifestly debased relationship and to a negative influence on the student's future.[22]

Whatever the resistance to this new model, if implemented, it would constitute a major, positive change in the educational system. It would take several decades to realise and if it is to succeed, it would have to be a political and Europe-wide decision. Although the educational establishment today feels some crisis, the solution is not seen in reforming the Bachelor's degree but in having more students, research funding, and state of the art facilities. That is neither a solution nor is it sustainable. Pondering the future, Adriaansen (2017)

---

22 I was told by one of my former students, who is doing a Master's degree in philosophy at a prestigious university, that her teacher took her long paper and immediately handed it back without opening it, telling her smiling: 'you have an A'. She was supposed to be delighted. Having a Liberal Arts experience as an undergraduate, she was offended.

might be right, arguing that, 'unless universities go "collegiate", they will have trouble to survive' (p. 30).

Fortunately, thanks to Liberal Arts education, there is a recipe for major improvements in the European educational system. It is a matter of convincing politicians and educators that the European Bachelor's degree must be reformed. Parents must be informed that there is great disparity in the quality of higher education. For all high school graduates in Europe there is great opportunity and advantage in what Adriaansen (2017) called a Dutch Mix: a combination of the Liberal Arts model in combination with a collegiate division of the university. As often in history, the Dutch are at the forefront of educational reform. For the sake of the future of European education, those who care about quality undergraduate education must cooperate and reform the current university structure of hundreds of departments where seventeen- and eighteen-year-olds are slotted in the silos of one of the thousand departments.

8 Conclusion

All the praise of the Liberal Arts model, some could retort, is just lobbying for a change that is not that necessary. What is at stake, however? For one, complacency is always dangerous – the challenges facing the twenty-first century seem much more urgent than they were even a decade ago. Something has snapped in the Western political and economic model, and there is no clear path of development. Events are not moving upwards and to stability, rather they are in a state of frenzy, and the outcome is unknown. Universities – at the forefront of innovation, depositories of the greatest minds – can and must help face up to moral, political, and environmental crises that sooner or later, in the course of this century, Europe and the globe will have to confront. There will be great pressure on these institutions of higher learning to respond to emerging intellectual, political, and social needs. We can witness already that vocational training, in opposition to academic studies, has become ever more dominant, being prioritised by receiving the greatest amount of funding. Yet, with demographic, environmental, and, eventually, with political and economic crises, the challenges looming ahead are not short-term but medium- and long-term; and neither their magnitude, nor solutions to them, are yet known. Our current solutions are not sufficient to meet these future challenges. To be ready for these unknown crises, what is needed is an educated a younger generation that has the capacity, skills, and a sense of moral obligation to solve and to improve the conditions that they will inherit from the previous generation, including our generations who are heftily contributing to the future malaise.

The universities for centuries helped to find solutions but at times also remained complacent, silent, and even, collaborated with the powers to be. The reformed undergraduate education, enriched through the liberal arts, would, under the right circumstances, assure the moral aptitude and the cognitive capacity of students, enabling them to confront an uncertain future. If successful, the future scholars, artists, and intellectuals would not be at the tail of, but would be at the head of political developments. The challenges in the past were in many ways very different from the challenges of the future. It is a truism to state that the scientific revolution and technology enhances as well as endangers our existence, and that the solutions remain within us humans. The ancient philosophers taught us that human nature has not changed neither will the difficulties to navigate it in the right direction diminish. We need new Socrateses to confront the *Eros* of smart, smug, and hot-tempered modern Calicleses. Liberal Arts education seems an old remedy for new challenges. The reason is not some miraculous property of such an educational model but rather its flexibility, its ability to adjust, learn from the past, and bring to the surface the best of human potentials.

The Bologna Declaration of 1999 made the Bachelor's-Master's division possible; it is time to allow the Bachelor's stage to fulfil its full potential. Universities owe that to the societies that finance them and protect them 'as *partly-protected* spaces in which the extension and deepening of understanding takes priority over any more immediate or instrumental purposes' (Collini 2017, p. 233). They also owe it to the current and future generations of students who will sustain universities and who will be able to keep the planet safe for the future. Let us finish with the words of Julie J. Kidd who for two decades has been supporting the revival of Liberal Arts in Europe. She wrote the following about the USA, but it is equally valid for Europe:

> The healthy emotional, ethical, and intellectual development of our young people should be our first priority. Failure to focus on these key issues obviously does not emanate from venal motives, but rather, I believe, from a lack of recognition of the seriousness and depth of the ever-growing malaise around us. If we do not take time to address these issues collectively, we will be jeopardising not only the well-being of our nation but also the future of our children and, indeed, of our planet.
>
> KIDD, 2005, p. 206

References

Adriaansen, H.P.M. (2017). The international university college: A Dutch lesson. *THINK -The HEAD Foundation Digest*, 27–30.

Adriaansen, H.P.M. (2017). The future of Dutch mix (Public lecture, The Hague, October 24, 2017). Retrieved from http://www.ecolas.eu/eng/wp-content/uploads/2017/12/LEZING-24-OKTOBER-ed.pdf.

Boetsch, L., Bali, V. & Schreel, L. (Eds.) (2017). *Guide to Emerging Liberal Arts and Sciences Practices in the EU*. Retrieved from http://www.ecolas.eu/eng/wp-content/uploads/2017/11/Handbook-final-BLASTER.pdf.

Bok, D. (1986). *Higher Learning*. Cambridge, Harvard University Press.

Boyer, E.L. (1996). The student as scholar. In Farnham, N.H. & Yarmolinsky, A. (Eds.). *Rethinking Liberal Education*. Oxford: Oxford University Press, 145–155.

Collini, S. (2017). Speaking of Universities. Michael Eldridge: *The German Bildung Tradition*. Retrieved from http://www.philosophy.uncc.edu/mleldrid/SAAP/USC/pbt1.html.

Illich, I. (1970). *Deschooling Society*. London, Harrow Books.

Jahanbegloo R. (1991). *Conversations with Isaiah Berlin*. London, Halborn.

Katz, S.N. (1996). Restructuring for the Twenty-First Century. In Farnham, N.H. & Yarmolinsky, A. (Eds.), *Rethinking Liberal Education*. (77–90). Oxford: Oxford University Press.

Kidd, J.J. (2005). It is only a port of call: Reflections on the state of higher education. In Hersh, R. & Merrow, J. (Eds.). *Declining by Degrees: Higher Education at Risk* (195–207). New York, Palgrave Macmillan.

Kimball, B. (1996). A historical perspective. In Farnham, N.H. & Yarmolinsky, A. (Eds.) *Rethinking Liberal Education*. (11–35). Oxford, Oxford University Press.

Newman J.H. (1958). *The Scope and Nature of University Education*. New York, E.P. Dutton& Co.

Plato (1955). *Gorgias*. New York, The Bobbs-Merril Co.

Schneider, C.G. (2005). Liberal education: Slip-sliding away? In Hersh, R. & and Merrow, J. (Eds.), *Declining by Degrees: Higher Education at Risk* (61–76). New York, Palgrave Macmillan.

Sperber, M., Hersh, R., Merrow, J. & Wolfe, T. (2005). How undergraduate education become college lite – and a personal apology. In Hersh, R. & and Merrow, J. (Eds.), *Declining by Degrees: Higher Education at Risk* (131–143). New York, Palgrave Macmillan.

Yarmolinsky, A. (1996). Constraints and opportunities. In Farnham, N.H. & Yarmolinsky, A. (Eds.) *Rethinking Liberal Education* (125–143). Oxford, Oxford University Press,

Zakaria, F. (2015). *In Defence of Liberal Education*. New York, W.W. Norton.

Web-based Sources

Bologna Declaration. Retrieved from https://www.eurashe.eu/library/modernising-phe/Bologna_1999_Bologna-Declaration.pdf.

Information on the Bologna Process and its evolution. Retrieved from http://ec.europa.eu/education/policy/higher-education/bologna-process_en.

CHAPTER 5

Academia in the Fast Lane vs. Organisational Ethnography and the Logic of Slow Food

Harry Wels

Abstract

The chapter entails a reflexive, autoethnographic approach to think through some of the perceived developments in global academia, especially in terms of time and workload in the light of demands of academia, past and present. The author takes empirical data and substantiations from his own teaching experiences in the Netherlands and frames a cautious hope for a future of academia on the metaphor of the slow-food movement which was started in Italy in the mid-1980s.

Keywords

slow science – academic teaching – work pressure – freedom

∴

> Every book is a form of quiet gratitude – to the ideas, people, and encounters that formed it.
>
> DONSKIS, 2013, p. 94

∵

1   Introduction

Working in academia is by many staff members perceived as a 'rat race'[1,2] resulting in perceptions of overload and work pressure (for the Netherlands,

---

[1] www.huffingtonpost.com/vicki-abeles/education-stress_b_5341256.html, accessed 28 October 2016.
[2] http://theconversation.com/cracks-in-the-ivory-tower-is-academias-culture-sustainable-8294, accessed 28 October 2016.

see FNV, 2017³), indicating that it is all about how fast one can get students through a curriculum and how fast one can publish and 'show results' in career competition with others. These are all aspects of the corporatisation of the university (cf. Reading, 1996; Ginsberg, 2011). The question is whether this is a 'bad' thing for the academic project (see for a balanced analysis of what slow and fast means for issues of inequality and power, Martell, 2014), or more specifically, for critical intellectual growth and development, which is arguably the driving goal or project of the academy (cf. Moshman, 2003)? In other words, is this kind of acceleration in academia something to be worried about or should we actually allow for a 'temporal autonomy' (Vostal, 2016) of academia, that is, everybody decides for her or himself? In this chapter I will argue that in a generalised way, intellectual development needs time to mature and therefore this acceleration is threatening the academic project to say the least, if not destroying it completely. I will argue metaphorically that like 'fast food', 'fast academia' is not intellectually healthy, no matter how tasty it might be considered at first bite (cf. Berg & Seeber, 2016; Mountz et al., 2015). I take organisational ethnography as my example and metaphor for 'slow science', as that is the research I have been involved in throughout my own academic life. I further take inspiration from the slow food movement as others have done, with the proverbial snail as its logo (ibid.).

The slow food movement started in 2009 in Italy and its symbol became the snail.⁴ The movement started as a contestation of the junk and fast food industry. It has been actually part of a worldwide movement of slow,⁵ actually rather fast, in which 'slow' has also been applied to other spheres of life like parenting, reading, and sex (Honoré, 2004). Bauman and Donskis (2013) use the *logic* of the slow food movement as a metaphor for what ordinary life in academia should be, a logic 'of deliberate thought, *unhurried creativity*, and measured existence' (Bauman & Donskis, 2013, p. 136, italics added); they make a plea for universities to be facilitators of 'intellectual slow food' (ibid., p. 137). 'Slow', not in the sense of dull, stodgy, dispassionate, or apathetic, all words belonging to the same family of 'slow', but rather living up to the example of that other animal that reminds us of slow, the turtle. '(I)n Native American lore, turtles remind us of the pace at which natures grows. Seedlings don't turn into trees

---

3   Some selected results from this report to substantiate the claim of 'work pressure' among academic staff (in the Netherlands): 66% of the 2546 respondents say that they can never finish their work; 78% structurally work during weekends and evenings; 53% work during holidays; 45% continue to work during illness.
4   www.slowfood.com/about-us/our-philosophy/, accessed 23 June 2016.
5   www.slowfood.com/about-us/our-philosophy/ →'slow food world-wide'.

in a week. Sod only becomes grass after months of tending. Damaged nerves don't recover, sometimes, for months.[6] Intellectual development could be added to these examples that need time to mature, 'marinate', to stay close to the discourse of the slow food movement, and become full grown and growing. But instead, in their argument, universities have become and follow 'a logic of quick results and achievements' (Bauman & Donskis, 2013, p. 136), a university with an intellectualism that opens the doors to a 'consuming university' (the title of the chapter, 131–167); universities have chosen the fast lane.

In Michael Foley's (2012) wonderfully entertaining but at the same time beautifully reflexive book on 'the ordinary' and the lessons we could take from 'the [literary] champions of everyday life' like Marcel Proust, James Joyce, and the like, he describes how Western culture has embraced a quantitative approach to time 'in units extending forward and backward' (Foley, 2012, p. 137), instead of an approach that takes into account how we experience time, which is not through measuring it but through 'feeling' (p. 137) it as a process. A maybe surprising but I think relevant example of this 'feeling' in the context of (organisational) ethnographic fieldwork in relation to time, and one that we can probably all relate to at some stage, is boredom. '(F)or the bored person, time seems to stand still', while 'for a person totally absorbed… time almost ceases' (Raposa in Toohey, 2011, p. 20). In boredom one has to wait for time to pass, it 'is never an easy emotion to tolerate', but at the same time boredom 'has always had this curious connection with *creativity*' and it allows 'you to be yourself' (Toohey, 2011, p. 186, italics added). In ethnographic fieldwork, or 'Deep Hanging Out' as Clifford Geertz (1998) translated and coined the term, in whatever contexts, there are always and inevitably times of boredom (I can attest to that after 30 years of fieldwork experiences). 'Boredom and lethargy are often experienced by ethnographers in the field but much less written about. Ethnographers are prone to write about moments of action. As a result, they often give the impression of their fieldwork as a series of exiting events. In most fieldwork there is indeed conflict, joking, and activity. Nonetheless, much of what many witness in their field research is low-energy, slow and, quite frankly, boring'.[7] And in the context of 'slow' we need that boredom like nothing else, as Kets de Vries (2014, p. 2) observes: 'I suggest that doing nothing and being bored can be

---

6   www.psychologytoday.com/blog/is-no-fairy-tale/201111/why-slow-is-good-lessons-turtle, accessed 28 October 2016.
7   http://aissr.uva.nl/research/externally-funded-projects/sites/content13/ethnography-27-29-august/sessions/sessions.html#anker-f-boredom-and-lethargy-in-ethnography-marguerite-van-den-berg, accessed 28 October 2016.

invaluable to the creative process. In our present networked society, introspection and reflection have become lost arts (...) (D)oing nothing is a great way to induce states of mind that nurture our imagination (...) Seemingly inactive states of mind can be an incubation period for future bursts of creativity (...) (U)nconscious thought processes can generate novel ideas and solutions more effectively than a conscious focus on problem solving'.

This boredom though has not only got to do with time but also with the content of ethnographic fieldwork. Ethnography, and organisational ethnography for that matter, focuses on the everyday of ordinary life (Ybema et al., 2009). Ethnography is considered a methodological approach (O'Reilly, 2012), a practice (Pink, 2009), an interpretive assemblage (Yanow & Schwartz-Shea, 2015), a writing skill (Clifford & Marcus, 1986), that asks for a combination of a particular form of boredom with the mundane, the banal, the unimaginative on the one hand and intellectual creativity to make analytical sense of it on the other. 'Doing ethnography' according to Geertz (1973) refers to 'fieldwork' and 'being there' (Watson, 1999; Borneman & Hammoudi, 2009), but at the same time to the writing of the ethnography (Brettell, 1993). Boredom is a quintessential aspect of 'doing ethnography', both in the field and in writing. Fieldwork and writing in ethnography should not be seen as two different consecutive phases in the process of doing ethnography, but as two aspects of the same process, 'doing ethnography', in which there is writing during fieldwork (of field notes, reflexive notes, diaries, and capturing everyday life) and fieldwork in the writing (reliving, interpreting, reflecting, and returning to the fieldwork (notes) time and again). Boredom is integral to this process as doing ethnography requires of the researcher to wait for things to happen, or not, which latter can be just as significant, in the field and behind the computer; time stands still and the ethnographer waits, anticipates, but is not the initiating agent of the everyday life that s/he is trying to grasp, capture and understand. S/he is also not waiting for spectacular things to happen but to experience the 'boring' routines of the everyday in organisational life; things that hardly anyone notices as they are so common and familiar, that for anyone else belong in and dissolve into the uninteresting and boring background of organisational life. Like a monotonous noise that you forget about, don't hear any longer, until it stops, and then you realise that is was there all along, but it had become so familiar that it did not require any special attention anymore: it ceased to remain explicit. It is the creativity of the organisational ethnographer to interpret boredom and 'make (...) the familiar strange' (Ybema & Kamsteeg, 2009, pp. 101–119), to make the monotonous explicit, to bring the background to life, to describe and analyse how the unconscious everyday shapes and directs organisational life as we know it; to make boredom exciting.

Organisational ethnography is a process of the *longue durée*, a slow science. Not only because once you (dare to) label yourself as an ethnographer after so many years of experience in fieldwork, it also takes a long process to learn and acquire the skills that an ethnographer needs: 'doing ethnography' requires a pedagogy that 'takes time' and sees time as an ally instead of as an opponent that has to be conquered and beaten, time that marinates and matures 'doing ethnography', like in slow food (therefore the word 'marinate' seems so appropriate). In what the university has become there seems no room left for this pedagogy that embraces and cherishes time, that asks of students and researchers alike to immerse themselves for a longer period of time in the field and the everyday at home or abroad, that asks for craftsmanship and a guild-like set up of apprenticeship, a pedagogy that gives and allows for time instead of taking it by clocking and measuring only research outputs: 'how will we form the next generation of European intellectual and politicians if young people will never have an opportunity to experience what a non-vulgar, non-pragmatic, non-instrumentalised university is like' (Bauman & Donskis, 2013, p. 139).

In this chapter I present a personal case study of how students struggle with organisational ethnography as a topic, standing for all the slow sciences, in the current 'corporatisation of academia' (Alvesson, 2013b). I will do that in a style that will use a combination of Bauman and Donskis' book (2013) and Geppert and Hollinshead article (2017) as its example, respectively as a (heated) conversation – between me and the readership of this book – and basing myself on my own subjective experiences in mainly Dutch, and to a lesser extent South African,[8] higher education. All this takes place in a context that I sometimes experience as coming close to what Geppert and Hollinshead (2017, p. 9) write that 'the bottom line is sustained by the spreading of the belief that no employee is good enough, no venture is good enough and no action is good enough'. This has resulted in this essay, which has some characteristics of a lampoon in its positioning vis-à-vis what the university, also thanks to me,[9] may have become.

---

[8] My research has been located in South and southern Africa since the mid-1980s, with an emphasis on South Africa since the second half of the 1990s. All this research and the ensuing publications are very much part of my intellectual development over the years and shine through strongly in my professional identity.

[9] Please don't get me wrong, I am no saint and I have been part and parcel of this process that I now critique: 'the dismantling was accomplished with our own hands, the hands of academics... We are all accomplices in that accomplishment: even those few among us who felt like protesting and never gathered the courage and determination to stop the rot' (Bauman & Donskis, 2013, p. 140).

2 Teaching Organisational Culture and Ethnography at a Dutch University

After many years teaching in an international Master's programme, I am asked to give a course on organisational culture and ethnography for second year Bachelor's students. This course has never been a problematic one for students at all, most of them usually pass. The course has a very basic structure: 13 lectures, including a final Question and Answer session, 115 minutes each. I prescribe two books, one of 236 pages from cover to cover, including content pages, bibliography, and index, and a second one 337 pages long. The first book (Alvesson, 2013a) is a theoretical one trying to argue for a particular approach to understanding organisational culture and change: a book in its second edition, with two new additional chapters. The second one (Jansen, 2009) is an organisational ethnography of a cultural change process at a South African organisation. The first one has been used in this course before (but in a first edition); the second one is new.

The lectures take the students through all the chapters, and for pedagogical reasons made explicit and elaborated upon during the opening lecture, without the use of Power Point and also not providing summaries of the books. The teaching is very much in the spirit of a 'reflexive pedagogy' (cf. Harling Stalker & Pridmore, 2009): contextualising the two books intellectually and ethnographically and trying to challenge students to reflect on their own positionality in relation to the two books and the social and cultural realities these two books try to represent and understand. During *every* lecture I tell them about the exam at the end of the course and give them one or two questions that I could ask in the exam. I tell them that everybody can pass the exam as I will ask them to reproduce the academic texts that are discussed during the lectures for some 60–70% of the questions and 30–40% of the questions will be about interpretation of the texts. At the end of the course I have given the students at least some 13–15 examples of possible exam questions (which I did not ask in the actual exam, as I told them).

Originally 310 students registered for this course (registration list at Study Secretariat). The university bookshop sold 74 copies of the more theoretical book of Mats Alvesson, which is now a second edition with two added chapters compared to the first edition, and 103 copies of the organisational ethnography of Jonathan Jansen (personal communication with the university bookshop). During the lectures I always combine chapters of the two books so as to mix and juxtapose the more theoretical understanding of organisational culture and change with the more ethnographic and empirically orientated case study from South Africa. The people from the bookshop tell me that they ordered extra copies of the organisational ethnography twice, as they were 'overwhelmed' by the number of copies sold, still, sales by far do not exceed half of the number of registered students.

There are two lectures a week, one on Tuesdays from 9 am till 10:45 am and a second one on Thursdays, from 1:30 pm till 2:45 pm. The lecture halls are big enough to host all 310 students. The opening lecture is attended by an (optimistically) estimated 100–120 students. From the second lecture onward attendance drops to between 45–65 students. The lecture on Tuesday attracts the smallest number of students. The ones that come to all the lectures I start to recognise and know by name, and I enjoy giving the lectures and the interaction with these 'hard core' students.

Towards the end of the lectures and the course, I receive from the administration the list of students that have registered for the exam, 298. Because of the large number there are quite some logistics involved and the exam is held in a convention centre in Amsterdam in order to be able to host that many exam students (together with other exams from other faculties of our university). Furthermore, because of the large numbers I only deliver the right number of exams and paper to write on and for the rest the logistics around and during the exam are taken care of by people from an employment agency. It is appreciated if you, as lecturer, show your face at the beginning of the exam, which I do. I recognise the regular attendees of the lectures and wish them well. I see more people though that I have never seen before, but whom I equally wish good luck with their exam. It results in a 31% pass rate (Study secretariat).

The resit of the exam (second and last opportunity) is a couple of weeks later and 166 students register for this second attempt. After some five to seven emails from students requesting an extra Q&A session before the resit, I organise what they ask for. I prepare myself well and organise three sub-sessions of half an hour based on the first letter of their surnames (A-H, I-P, Q-Z) in order to give every student that comes the attention he or she deserves. I post all this information on Black Board and every student receives an individual email with this information. At the actual session, eight students show up. The resit has a pass rate of 23% (personal communication with the Study secretariat). I anticipate protests as now all the students that have failed have to take the exam next year. I receive some three emails, but that is it. One of them asking if I will use the same literature next year. From the answers to the exam questions, I can clearly notice that many students just haven't read the books at all.

This is what happened during the academic year 2015–2016 (and repeated itself in 2016–2017 and 2017–2018). The coordinator of this Bachelor's programme has asked me if I am prepared to give the course again next year, which I happily agreed to. The evaluation of the course is filled in by 72 students and is very positive about my enthusiasm during lectures, but rates the exam as suboptimal. The scores for these items were below average, especially on the items 18, 19, and 23, respectively asking to rate: 'I knew clearly in advance what to expect in the exam; the exam was a good indicator of what I had learned in this course; overall rating of the exam'. Actually, and ironically, the very items for the evaluation reproduce the arguments I try to raise below! On the whole, the graph of the evaluation showed that this course was below the average university score, except for that one item out of 20, 'encouraged to think about the material', which scored way above average (this was not only mimicked in 2016–2017 and 2017–2018 but also led to an even more devastating graph below the average university score).

Similar stories come to me from colleagues from other Dutch universities and from other disciplines, and also internationally. I hear similar stories, but usually only informally and after a drink or two, which is of course 'subjective' and cannot be taken into consideration as it is not 'official' and 'too ordinary and everyday'. But ethnographic fieldworkers know better than to just shuffle this information aside as 'irrelevant'.

It seems clear that at least part of what might be happening here is that taking time to read and study is under severe threat for students. I would like to take that observation up later in the chapter but first want to flag and briefly mention that in this personal example a lot of critical issues with regard to what is happening in higher education around the world seems to come together. First of all, the McDonaldisation and massification of higher education (Parker & Jary, 1995; Altbach et al., 2009; Rossi, 2010), which implies that students in academia are treated like particles in a process of industrial rationalisation and commodification. Its flipside is that students start to behave like consumers in a restaurant and leave what they don't like and generally behave like 'clients with demands' (cf. Hayes & Wynyard, 2006).[10] The rationalisation of universities as 'businesses' furthermore encourages students to see academia more as an extension of their earlier primary and secondary school experiences than as institutions that foster independent and critical thinking. It seems that as a result we should conclude that critical thinking is on the decrease.[11] Important to note here, also to come back to taking (slow) time to read (and study), is the observation that '(t)here is a necessary connection between critical thinking and skilled reading and writing' and 'if I know that

---

10   See also: http://time.com/108311/how-american-universities-are-ripping-off-your-education/, accessed 28 October 2016.

11   www.criticalthinking.org/pages/the-state-of-critical-thinking-today/523, accessed 28 October 2016.

what I am reading is difficult for me to understand, I intentionally *slow* down'.[12] Which brings us back to the question I would like to raise in the context of my argument in this chapter: What has (students') reading to do with the logic of slow food?

3   Reading as Waiting

A stereotypical story that is often told by Europeans that have visited the African continent is that 'Europeans may have the clock, but Africans have the time'. One could interpret this as that Europeans know how to *measure* time, but have lost touch with *experiencing* time.[13] It is a common complaint in our global societies that we don't find time to read anymore.[14] If we are to believe what people say, they would love to read more, but they simply don't find or have time for it. The paradox is the following: When we *measure* time, we can't find it to read books; when we read books, we *experience* time and find it. This counts for literature and popular books, and it also counts for ethnographies: when we try to find measured time, that is, the *clock*, to read a voluminous (organisational) ethnography we will never read it; if we read an (organisational) ethnography we will experience *time* and we will find the time to read. The logic of the slow food movement can be recognised here: If we constrict food in our clock driven existence, we will end up with fast food; if we experience time, we will end up as adherents of the movement and apply it metaphorically to our way of life, including our reading habits. That is to say, reading and allowing ourselves to experience time in the process, reading and requiring students to read books for their courses can become a conscious act of resistance to the further McDonaldisation of higher education.

But in our factory-like approach to higher education (cf. Parker & Jary, 1995), reading books is probably considered as inefficient a suggestion as writing books in the Dutch context. Nowadays Dutch academics are pressured to write articles for 'high impact' journals and not devote time to writing books.

---

12   Ibid., emphasis added.
13   Disclaimer: This is not in any way meant to essentialise differences between 'European' and 'African' perceptions of time, so often rhetorically used to rationalise European power and privilege and legitimise racism.
14   See for instance: https://medium.com/@hughmcguire/why-can-t-we-read-anymore-503c 38c131fe#.5khrm16mc; https://www.theguardian.com/commentisfree/2014/oct/29/love-reading-dont-have-time-stop-excuses; http://www.forbes.com/sites/jordanshapiro/2014 /05/13/kids-dont-read-books-because-parents-dont-read-books/#67c334334faa, all accessed 18 August 2016.

In annual reviews it is literally easier to score credit points with journal articles than with publishing a book. If you speak to academics informally during their ordinary everyday life, they might tell you that they do not even find time to keep up with the new *journal* articles that appear in their field, let alone *books*. Often, they tell you with a certain sense of pride and professionalism that their phone has 'an app' that 'alerts' them to new articles in their field with a title or an abstract. Because of the numbers of journal articles being published, they admit that they usually do not proceed beyond the alert but still consider themselves on top of their discipline by just being alerted to new articles without ever reading them in full. Maybe there are colleagues who will officially challenge this gross generalisation, but my combination of 'auto-ethnography' (Ellis, 2004) and 'at-home ethnography' (Alvesson, 2009) can substantiate this claim with countless anecdotes, examples, and other (organisational) ethnographic details that I have taken from my everyday academic life for more than 25 years.

Part of intellectual slow food is slow reading,[15] for which there is no longer sufficient time in academia. Together with the increasing *pressures to write* and publish articles (often replacing books) is the *lack of time and patience to read* texts from start to finish or from cover to cover. It should be noted of course that because all academics are so pressured to publish articles, the tsunami of articles that are actually published is staggering and there is no way that anyone can ever read them all, or even keep up with new literatures, let alone to intellectually reflect on the contents. This occurs all the more so in a context in which academic credibility and status is measured in numbers of article citations and not in the numbers of pages, articles, and books you read, nor the possible impact of reading contents and combinations of thought.

Experiences and examples from another angle: Facilitating Post-Graduate Supervision[16] courses in South Africa for many years, we agree time and again with our South African colleagues from various universities across the country, and from different disciplines, how reading is at the heart of building a

---

15   See www.slowmovement.com/slow_books.php (accessed 9 August 2016); www.slow-bookmovement.com (accessed 9 August 2016). The 'slow book manifesto' argues that only particular books count as 'slow books': they insist on literature. 'Blog posts won't, of course, but neither will newspaper pieces or even magazine articles. Also excluded: non-literary books (www.theatlantic.com/entertainment/archive/2012/03/a-slow-books-manifesto/254884/) (accessed (9 August 2016).

16   See for more information on this project: http://postgraduatesupervision.net/, accessed 31 May 2018.

scholarly identity for post-graduate students. No matter the almost unanimous agreement on the importance of reading for developing a scholarly identity, when we talk as academic colleagues, staff members amongst ourselves, about our own (academic) reading behaviour, most of us have to admit that we hardly if ever read articles or books from beginning to end anymore ourselves. Many of us usually read efficiently what parts we need for our own writing and the quotes we want to use in our publications or what we have to read in terms of students' work, which usually leaves hardly any time to read anything else, let alone in full. This pressure to live up to this kind of academic efficiency and so-called 'professionalism' leaves nothing to chance; we cannot be surprised anymore by what we read. We know what we want for our own writing and how to judge students' work. Reading (academic texts) has become equally instrumentalised to our writing and protocolised in terms of our assessments of students' work; the fulfilment of reading is gone.

Let me make it personal and talk to you, my colleague, through the text of this essay: when were you last intellectually 'blown away' by an unexpected article or a book; when was it that you (nearly) forgot about yourself, and time for that matter, because you were so absorbed in the reading that you felt as if having entered a parallel universe; when has a book altered your 'course in life' or academic thinking again; when was it that you felt awkward that the final pages were in sight and you actually loathed the moment that you would have finished the reading; when was the last time that you were 'taken over' by a text; when last was reading sensational; when was *not finishing* the text not an option that crossed your mind?

No matter how fast you read, when you read complete texts, you enter the domain of 'slow'; in reading complete texts there is some sort of appreciation for 'fully' getting to know something instead of in fragments, and of giving opportunity to an author to present and convince you as a reader of their argument. 'Full(y)' is probably a better word to use in this context than 'complete': You can finish your quantity of food *completely*, but in the logic of slow food it is not about finishing quantities, but about food that is 'full' of taste, with a connotation of being 'rich' in satisfying a variety of taste buds. This is how a text should taste, 'full' and 'rich'; it is not about quantity, but about the sensation and experience of fulfilment (what is in a word). 'Fulfilment' leads to being able to tell about the experience, the texts, with confidence and conviction; fulfilment facilitates reproduction of texts and main arguments.

One of my observations during courses was that students find it increasingly problematic to 'reproduce' or 'learn' texts by heart. In the time-consuming world we live in, there is no way that you can read a text and be able to reproduce what you have read first time. Harkening back to my course on Organisational Culture and Ethnography I described above: from the very first lecture onward I told my students that 70% of the exam questions would consist of questions that asked of you to 'just' reproduce. Furthermore, I told them that in marking the exams, we would grant more points to those answers that stayed closest to the texts in the books. Students told me that university education shouldn't be about reproducing texts. I tried to counter this by saying that in every professional field you should be able to reproduce standard, although temporary, 'truths' of the discipline, and that in a face-to-face conversation with a fellow-professional on a particular topic that relates to your expertise, you cannot constantly rely on or refer to Google (or any other digital search device). Fulfilment leads to the ability to reproduce, like a poet who is saturated with reading and composing words, can recite texts *ad libitum*. Reading to the full and again and again is something that is close to the ideals of the slow food movement: local, everyday (staple) and seasonal produce comes back again and again and year in year out and can be recognised, reproduced, and recited by every cook and connoisseur.[17]

'Slow' connotes strongly with waiting and patience. In reading it is waiting for a plot to unfold, an argument to develop, and patience to reach the climax of the argument, the results of the reasoning. Patience and waiting are key ingredients of liminality (Sutton et al., 2011, p. 30; Schweizer, 2008, p. 112), a concept initially coined by Van Gennep in 1909 but broadly popularised by the late anthropologist Victor Turner (1920–1983) (1967, pp. 93–111) to denote the middle phase of a ritual process, in which an individual undergoes a transition from the one stage, phase, or position, into another one. Classic examples being puberty rites amongst various ethnicities around the world where females go into the first phase as girls and exit in the third phase as women. Or males go in as boys and exit as men. In the middle second phase 'individuals are understood to be "no longer" and simultaneously also "not yet"' (Wels et al., 2011, p. 1). In Turner's own words, 'neither here nor there; they are betwixt and between the positions assigned and arrayed by law, custom, convention, and ceremonial' (Turner 1969, p. 95); people (im)patiently await series of Deleuzian becomings. This is what reading and time is all about; it is a liminal phase of becomings, a liminal phase in which the reader awaits what next intellectual becomings will befall him or her. To read asks for patience, but it

---

[17] This is not to say that 'truths' are once and for all or cast in stone. On the contrary even, academic 'truths' change and meander over time and are always in processes of Deleuzean 'becomings'.

also develops patience in therapeutic ways;[18] reading is an antidote to instantaneous living as seems to be propagated by the current time and age, and which the corporate university has embraced as its mantra. Diplomas must be produced in no time. This no longer allows for the creativity that experiencing time and a sense of boredom seems to generate. Reading as 'a temporary liberation from the economics of time-is-money, as a brief respite from the haste of modern life, as a meditative temporal space in which one might have unexpected intuitions and fortuitous insights' (Schweizer, 2008, p. 2) does not fit academic life or thinking any more. In the current time and age there is no time for waiting in academia, which paradoxically has led to a certain level of indifference, a lack of attention in the way that the French activist and philosopher Simone Weil spoke about it, when she suggested that waiting 'must be relearned as a form of attention' (in ibid., p. 2). 'Attention waits' (Blanchot in ibid., p. 89). Then waiting through reading 'can be a rewarding experience' indeed (ibid., p. 126) and lead to intellectual creativity.

Students, at least the ones that followed my second year Bachelor's course on Organisational Culture and Ethnography (OC&E), based on the figures on the number of books being bought and by the number of students who passed two exams primarily geared towards checking how well the two books were read and could be reproduced as a result, seemed to have no time or patience to take this time to read or to wait and enter the liminal phase that is crucial to intellectual becomings. Might it have to do with the sense that students, fellow academics, and other people worldwide often complain or have a stereotyped idea that academic texts are 'boring'?[19] And boring in a way that they do not suspect that this could lead to creativity (see above)? I can see the point that academics write boring texts. I read them myself sometimes as well. But in organisational ethnography, in 'doing ethnography', writing in an attractive way is considered as important as the presentation of the data and its analysis. The best organisational ethnographies are sometimes real 'page turners'. Read Timothy Pachirat's (2011) *Every Twelve Seconds* about organisational processes in slaughterhouses in the United States, and I promise you, you will not stop reading before the book is finished. There are more organisational ethnographies like that, one of them being one of the two books I prescribed for

---

18   https://www.daveursillo.com/7-unconventional-ways-to-develop-patience/, accessed 11 August 2016.

19   www.theguardian.com/education/2007/sep/04/highereducation.news. Response: http://onewaystreet.typepad.com/one_way_street/2007/09/academic-writin.html. https://pathsonwater.com/2015/03/25/dear-authors-why-are-academic-texts-so-boring/, all accessed 11 August 2016.

my course OC&E, Jonathan Jansen's (2009) moving account of eight years of having been the first-ever black dean of the Faculty of Education at the University of Pretoria:[20] an organisational ethnography of which students asked me at some stage if it was 'really an academic text'. When I asked them what brought them to ask that question, they answered that they had to cry while reading it, and that this had, they tell me, never happened to them before with an academic text. Was reading Jansen's organisational ethnography worth the waiting? Was the imagined boredom of reading a book from cover to cover resulting in attention? I actually interpret my almost, if not completely, obsessive reading of books from cover to cover as one of my most explicit acts of resisting the cult of speed in academia, an 'ethical choice' (Berg & Seeber, 2016, p. 59), where '(s)lowing down is about asserting the importance of contemplation, connectedness, fruition, and complexity' (ibid., p. 57). Shouldn't reading, in the spirit of the logic of the slow food movement, not be made more explicit as an integral part of 'doing ethnography' and doing scientific and intellectual work in general? Reading as an act of resistance to the 'rat race'?

4 Doing Organisational Ethnography as Metaphorical *Habitus*

Almost any reader will realise that the question with which I ended the previous section is strictly a rhetorical one, with only one answer possible, YES! When Brettell (1993) edited her book and referred in the title to 'read(ing)', she did not mean to say that reading should be part of 'doing ethnography'. She reflected on what happens if people read what has been written about their everyday lives: Do they recognise themselves in the text; do they agree with how their lives are represented by a (relative) outsider ethnographer. In other words, it is an edited volume on the politics of representation. This is the general trend in the debates, discussions, and conversations about 'doing ethnography', that the concept of reading is not contextualised and problematised enough in the literature on 'doing ethnography', is too much taken for granted, too much taken in the direction of the topic under research, and is not applied to the reading habits of the ethnographer him or herself. The kind of reading I have been trying to argue for in this essay is about the *experience* of reading (as related to time and fulfilment) and its beneficial effects on ethnographic creativity and intellectualism, and how this time-consuming activity of reading 'thick books', full of 'thick descriptions' (cf. Geertz, 1973) is worth the waiting and the effort. Or even more strongly put: to me slow reading is crucial for

---

20 The University of Pretoria is, in terms of the apartheid system of divided categorisations, a historically white and Afrikaans-speaking university.

developing and sustaining a level of intellectualism that a university education in my perspective should offer to students and that should be the preferred *habitus* (cf. Bourdieu, 1984[21]) of academic staff. Given the 'corporatisation of the university', the *habitus* that is 'guiding' (see definition in note 60) academics now is 'the fast lane' as described and pointed out above. 'Doing (organisational) ethnography' in the way I argue for can be seen as a counter movement to this 'fast lane' *habitus*, while at the same time suggesting a concrete alternative *habitus*. The alternative *habitus* would then be to slow down and go slow on intellectual development, to go slow on reading, to go slow on writing, to go slow on the academic project as a whole; go slow in order to fast-track intellectual development and critical thinking; universities facilitating a *habitus* that takes 'doing ethnography' as its metaphor and example for 'slow science' following in the spoor and logic of the 'slow food' movement.

As this book is dedicated to the memory our dear Leonidas Donskis, I would like to end, as I started, with one of his inspiring aphorisms, although this time slightly adapted for reasons of fit: 'In death a friend extended my life – by redrafting the cartography of my thoughts and by becoming the subject of my [chapter]' (Donskis, 2013, p. 104).[22]

References

Altbach, Ph.G., Reisberg, L., & Rumbley, L.E. (2009). Trends in global higher education: Tracking an academic revolution, A report prepared for the UNESCO 2009 World Conference on Higher Education, retrieved from https://s3.amazonaws.com/academia.edu.documents/30910755/Altbach__Reisberg__Rumbley_Tracking_an_Academic_Revolution__UNESCO_2009.pdf?AWSAccessKeyId=AKIAIWOWYYGZ2Y53UL3A&Expires=1527766860&Signature=cse%2BogfbYyKiZKgzJ6Dd%2BosQ1vY%3D&response-content-disposition=inline%3B%20filename%3DTrends_in_global_higher_education_Tracki.pdf, (31 May 2018).

Alvesson, M. (2009). At-home ethnography: Struggling with closeness and closure. In Ybema, S., Yanow, D., Wels, H., & Kamsteeg, F. (eds.) *Organizational Ethnography. Studying the Complexities of Everyday Life* (156–174). Los Angeles, London, Sage Publications.

---

21   Bourdieu's *habitus* is probably most clearly put by Wacquant (2005) (cited in Navarro, 2006, p. 16) as 'the way society becomes deposited in persons in the form of lasting dispositions, or trained capacities and structured propensities to think, feel and act in determinant ways, which then guide them' (http://www.powercube.net/other-forms-of-power/bourdieu-and-habitus/, accessed 18 August 2016).

22   The exact citation is 'In death a friend extended my life – by redrafting the cartography of my thoughts and by becoming the subject of my *new book*' (italics added)

Alvesson, M. (2013a). *Understanding Organizational Culture.* Los Angeles, London, Sage Publications, Second Edition.

Alvesson, M. (2013b). *The Triumph of Emptiness. Consumption, Higher Education, and Work Organization.* Oxford, Oxford University Press.

Bauman, Z., & Donskis, L. (2013). *Moral Blindness: The Loss of Sensitivity in Liquid Modernity.* Cambridge, Polity Press.

Berg, M., & Seeber, B.K. (2016). *The Slow Professor. Challenging the Culture of Speed in the Academy.* Toronto, University of Toronto Press.

Borneman, J., & Hammoudi, A. (eds.) (2009). *Being there. The Fieldwork Encounter and the Making of Truth.* Berkeley, University of California Press.

Bourdieu, P. (1984). *Distinction: A Social Critique of the Judgement of Taste.* London, Routledge.

Brettell, C.B. (ed.) (1993). *When They Read What We Write: The Politics of Ethnography.* Westport, Bergin & Garvey.

Clifford, J., & Marcus, G.E. (1986). *Writing Culture: The Poetics and Politics of Ethnography.* Berkeley, University of California Press.

Donskis, L. (2013). *A Small Map of Experience. Reflections & Aphorisms* (translated from Lithuanian by Karla Gruodis). Toronto, Berkeley, Guernica.

Ellis, C. (2004). *The Ethnographic I. A Methodological Novel about Autoethnography.* Walnut Creek, New York: Altamira Press.

FNV (2017). Rapport Werkdruk in Universiteiten, (Report on Work Pressure in Universities). Retrieved from www.fnv.nl/site/nieuws/webassistent/Annika-Heerekop/werkdruk-medewerkers-universiteiten-ongezond-hoog-3/onderzoek werkdrukuniversiteiten.pdf.

Foley, M. (2012). *Embracing the Ordinary. Lessons from the Champions of Everyday Life.* London, New York, Simon & Schuster.

Geertz, C. (1998). Deep hanging out. *The New York Review of Books, 45* (16), 69.

Geertz, C. (1973). *The Interpretation of Cultures.* New York, Basic Books.

Geppert, M., & Hollinshead G. (2017). Signs of dystopia and demoralisation in global academia: Reflections on the precarious and destructive effects of the colonization of the *Lebenswelt. Critical Perspectives on International Business, 13*(2), 136–150.

Ginsberg B. (2011). *The Fall of Faculty: The Rise of The All-administrative University and Why It Matters.* Oxford, Oxford University Press.

Harling Stalker, L.L., & Pridmore, J. (2009). Reflexive pedagogy and the sociological imagination. *Human Architecture, Journal of the Sociology of Self Knowledge, 7*(III), 27–36.

Haynes, D., & Wynyard, R. (eds.) (2006). *The McDonaldization of higher education.* Charlotte, North Carolina, Information Age Publishers.

Honoré, C. (2004). *In Praise of Slow. How a Worldwide Movement is Challenging the Cult of Speed.* London, Orion Books.

Jansen, J. (2009). *Knowledge in The Blood. Confronting Race and The Apartheid Past.* Stanford, Stanford University Press.

Kets de Vries, M. (2014). Doing nothing and nothing to do: The hidden value of empty time and boredom. (Faculty and Research Working Paper, INSEAD, 2014/37/EFE.). Retrieved from http://www.k12accountability.org/resources/For-Parents/Hidden_Value_of_Empty_Time_INSEAD.pdf.

Martell, L. (2014). The slow university: Inequality, power, and alternatives. *Forum: Qualitative Social Research*, *15*(3), art. 10.

Moshman, D. (2003). Intellectual freedom for intellectual development. *Liberal Education*, *89* (3), 30–37.

Mountz, A., Bonds, A., Mansfield, B., Loyd, J., Hyndman, J., Walton-Roberts, M., Basu, R., Whitson, R., Hawkins, R., Hamilton, T., & Curran, W. (2015). For slow scholarship: A feminist politics of resistance through collective action in the neoliberal university. *ACME: International Journal for Critical Geographies*, *14*(4), 1235–1259.

Navarro, Z. (2006). In search of a cultural interpretation of power: The contribution of Pierre Bourdieu. *IDS Bulletin*, *37*(6), 11–22.

O'Reilly, K. (2012). *Ethnographic Methods*. London, Routledge, Second Edition.

Pachirat, T. (2011). *Every Twelve Seconds. Industrialised Slaughter and The Politics of Sight.* New Haven, London, Yale University Press.

Parker, M., & Jary, D. (1995). The McUniversity: Organization, management and academic subjectivity. *Organization*, *2*(2), 319–338.

Pink, S. (2009). *Doing Sensory Ethnography.* Los Angeles, London, Sage Publications.

Reading, B. (1996). *The University in Ruins.* Cambridge, Harvard University Press.

Rossie, F. (2010). Massification, competition and organizational diversity in higher education: Evidence from Italy. *Studies in Higher Education*, *35*(3), 277–300.

Schweizer, H. (2008). *On Waiting.* London, Routledge.

Sutton, R., Vigneswaran, D., & Wels, H. (2011). Waiting in ritual space: Migrants queuing for Home Affairs in South Africa. *Anthropology Southern Africa*, *34*(1&2), 30–37.

Toohey, P. (2011). *Boredom. A Lively History.* New Haven, London, Yale University Press.

Turner, V. (1967). *The Forest of Symbols. Aspects of Ndembu Ritual.* Ithaca, London, Cornell University Press.

Victor, T. (1969). *The Ritual Process. Structure and Anti-structure.* Chicago, Aldine.

Vostal, F. (2016). *Accelerating Academia. The Changing Structure of Academic Time.* London, Palgrave MacMillan.

Watson, C.W. (ed.) (1999). *Being There: Fieldwork in Anthropology,* Chicago, University of Chicago Press.

Wels, H., Van der Waal, C., Spiegel, A., & Kamsteeg, F. (2011). Victor Turner and liminality: An introduction. *Anthropology Southern Africa, 34*(1&2), 1–4.

Yanow, D., & Schwartz-Shea, P. (eds.) (2015). *Interpretation and Method: Empirical Research and The Interpretive Turn.* London, Routledge, Second Edition.

Ybema, S., & Kamsteeg, F. (2009). Making the familiar strange: A case for disengaged organizational ethnography. In Ybema, S., Yanow, D., Wels, H., & Kamsteeg, F. (eds.) (2009). *Organizational Ethnography. Studying the Complexities of Everyday Life* (101–119). Los Angeles, London, Sage Publications.

Ybema, S., Yanow, D., Wels, H., & Kamsteeg, F. (eds.) (2009). *Organizational Ethnography. Studying the Complexities of Everyday Life.* Los Angeles, London, Sage Publications.

CHAPTER 6

Timescapes in Academic Life. Cubicles of Time Control

Ida Sabelis

Abstract

Under current conditions, it seems not enough to construct a plea for 'slow science'. Temporalities of academia under TINA require close scrutiny in order to bring out the time regimes of academic life. Economy, efficiency, and effectiveness have produced measures by which not only work processes are uniformized and controlled, but especially the design, the character, and the pace of work, including the embodied experience of working. Consequently, (academic) work determines a lot of other aspects of our existence and it tends to uniformize work load as a given. The image arises of not only 24/7 availability for academic work, but the inevitability of compliance to working in individual bubbles of time control, causing a narrower focus for 'the academic' and possibly less space for the rhythms of academic creation and creativity. Autobiographical 'vignettes' illustrate this development, highlighting the working of regimes that are not questioned on a daily basis.

Keywords

timescapes – *Bildung* – education – time regimes – workload – work-life balance

1   Introduction

In the opening scene of the film *About Smith* (2002), we see how Smith/Jack Nicholson waits. He sits, fully dressed in his winter coat, briefcase on his lap with his hands folded on top. The camera cuts to the clock over the door. We see the hour hands move, tick, tick, tick... the hour hand reaches five, the minute hand twelve, until exactly five pm. As if he feels that the time he has waited for has arrived, Smith just gets up and walks out the door, on to his retirement. A final leave? – or just what he always does: he leaves at exactly five o'clock, a neat split between work and other parts of his life. But he leaves, seemingly with clock time internalised, as if an inner metronome permits him to change scenes.

This scene has been with me since I first saw it; I could forget other details of that film, but this... Why did it stay with me in all clarity? It could be the punctuality associated with professional life – for a certain type of profession, that is. It could be the breath-taking tension caused by presenting work time and space in this manner. Or maybe it's also the immense experience of a tempo-spatial marker between working life, and – what, another life? or even retirement as a definitive phase, perhaps more than any other phase instilled with irreversibility? There is no going back after retirement – only old age, decline, and death await: a clock reaches five, and the cage of the office opens to freedom. Professional identity, so important in our type of society, is gone from literally one minute to the next. Smith does not seem to regret it – he is about to start a new life, liberated from work and from the straitjacket of working time. Most of all, I contend, this scene represents a timeframe of work that we do not experience anymore: work is, or was, an activity bound to an office and certain times of the day; it used to be a solid marker of life's activities (Elias, 1982/1985). Times and places for work and private life – rhythms of days, weeks, months, and years were embodied parts of our life's rhythmicity. Steady, and reliable, providing a pace of life.

Increasingly now, neither the office nor set times for work guide our working days, especially not in academia and other *free* professions (Lorenz, 2012). Economy, efficiency, and effectiveness have produced measures by which not only work is controlled, but especially the design and the character of work, including the embodied experience of working, and al lot of other aspects of our existence in its wake. Office times meander right through the times we spend at home, or on vacation, or wherever else in the world. Working times, in the 1990s problematised from the perspective of 'tele-work' (Paolucci, 1996) can hardly be set apart from 'other times'. Telework has developed into the experience of being 'always on'; it is not just an extra option to follow up on tasks, or work from home from time to time, it has established itself fully as the norm. Telework was succeeded by 'new ways of working', a specific type of open office use applied at random for a more efficient use of workspaces over time.[1] At the root of this development seems to be an increase in both standardisation and control of work, partly driven by technology, but mainly by the primacy of economics and an attitude based on consumerism (Parker & Jarvey, 1995; Ritzer, 1996; Roderick, 2016) as a consequence of what is called the neoliberal

---

[1] And yes, perhaps 'new ways of working' are an expression of recent changes in working time imperatives. It is hard to pinpoint what was first, and how working time/s and New Ways of Working (HNW) feed into each other.

turn (Van der Pijl, 2006; Davies et al., 2006; Lorenz, 2012). Of course, not all organisations produce or demand office times and spaces, but our society does require a lot of 'office work' in the form of service institutes and maintenance organisations providing supervision and control. Higher education and academia especially seem to produce and require offices under the guise of the growing importance of education (in the form of institutes of higher education) as a commodity, along with an increase in bureaucracy as a format to control the times of the people in it, as a function of the desired output.

Meanwhile, Martha Nussbaum, in her book *Not for Profit* (2010) argues along similar lines, adding that the humanities' purpose to promote reflection, critical thinking, creativity, and an interest in what cannot be predicted (or measured) must be pruned and curbed in a society that requires quantification as proof (of the benefits, the 'truth') and that ultimately serves the bureaucracy of the sciences and academic life.[2] And it is exactly this bureaucracy, with its time-consuming systems, that needs to be fed, and the promise of equal international comparison and competition[3] that ultimately takes up so much time that the raison-d'être of universities is called into question.[4] There is some kind of a niche in academia comprised of authors writing and complaining about these changes. And there is a vast body of work about neoliberal ways of higher education. But one of the main problems seems to be that nothing really changes the way things are going. Bauman and Donskis (2013) argue how this development is linked to ongoing managerialism. Academia seems to be contextualised and pervaded by a closed circuit: changes are announced with the argument that there is no money to act otherwise – and that changes provide real chances for revision, reflection, and improvement in education and research alike. A case of TINA, as Donskis and Bauman would put it; there is no alternative, thus compliance to the new, and this closed circuit is inescapable. Nobody dares to resist an opportunity to improve, of course. But the message of change also triggers ambiguity – ongoing change implies that 'things were never right', causing fear and insecurity, which in turn invites even faster change. No change, no progress as the saying has it; but even that expression has a different feel to it, as it has become a seemingly unquestioned, driving force. As Bauman and Donskis put it: 'Permanent change becomes a perfect form of social control' (2013, p. 139). What does that mean on a daily basis for academics, and what does that mean for the development of academic knowledge?

---

2   See also Kamsteeg in this volume.
3   See also Bianchini in this volume.
4   I use higher education, universities, and 'academia' alternatingly: HE, where mere education is meant, academia for the combination of education and research (knowledge production).

Vignette 1: Daily Routine

- Morning: try to make my desk free of tasks to be able to think. I start out by reading, responding, and filing emails.
- Some replies can be quick, just a note, but some take more time, or postponed action. In between, it seems better to make some phone calls. And, while working at home, the to-do-list also entails some domestic chores: dentist appointment for next week, neighbour with a query, some private emails to respond to.
- I phone a colleague about a research project and add some tasks to the main to-do-list.
- A colleague phones about a deadline – I deflect the process by involving another colleague.
- Then the main task begins: reviewing for the international journal I am involved with. The Manuscript Central system shows some 8 new articles to be desk reviewed, another 4 to 6 papers in the review process that need to be checked for delays, for paper to be accepted, and some correspondence with the central secretariat.
- After four hours I have ticked nine different tasks, and still feel as if I have not really done important work. Chores, small duties, but no real thinking, let alone reading.
- Have to switch off the automatic email notification. But also have to be available for the workers' council, in which the annual budget has its own rhythm. Hurry to read the documents for tomorrow's meeting – small notes, a glancing over them, and a little walk to think things over.
- Email again – I forgot to send an honorarium application after a PhD committee. Should not forget to send a card to congratulate.
- Project team calls for signed letter – forward the message to an assistant.
- Check Uni's central system for tasks – and find a course evaluation that needs response. Put on to-do-list for later this week.
- Evening: almost ten working hours spent.
- Exhausted – allow myself a little Netflix to unwind.
- Hot tea and early (?) to bed.
- Note: the main thing is not the character of the work, but the constant switching of scenes, of required energy, of starting again with never any relief after finalising – next thing already there. It is like a bicycle trip with too many traffic lights: constant acceleration, too many stops, no flow.

IS- summary from to-do-lists

If we feel so stressed, if so many colleagues report being 'always on', and if indeed we cannot escape giving in to the consumerist demand to think of knowledge and education as products totally subjected to market demands on a global scale, it seems pivotal to look at how this has become normalised and negotiated, and maybe even neglected, in our time use and perception. Of course, acceleration, the striving for moving ever faster, plays a role here. But that is not the only thing; other temporal traits are involved in terms of the neglect of long-term effects and immediate health risks (Clegg, 2010). Therefore, in this chapter, I propose to look at academia from a timescape viewpoint (cf. Adam, 1998; Sabelis, 2002), going beyond the mere analysis of acceleration and the call to slow down (Wels, this volume; Mountz et al., 2015). This requires looking at the education process with some reflections on 'Bildung', understood as classical Humboldtian education with specific assumptions about the temporalities of learning and knowledge production; and for the part of knowledge development (if not production), I will take a look at the experience in the work of colleagues who have researched the increasing time pressures and desperation of academics in the context of growing workloads and shifting temporalities. Together with some vignettes that serve as autobiographical reflection, this will then provide a view of how our total time experience is changing, our senses for temporalities curbed and controlled partly by the digitalisation of just about everything, and partly by the inescapability of control mechanisms setting the paces of our work and lives.

2 Bildung / Education in Terms of Time

One of the core tasks of universities is the education of students on to an academic level, either for further study as academics or for necessary life luggage for work and career. This notion of education is nicely illustrated via the German concept of *Bildung*, which is an activity engaged in via different, not always prognosticated temporal elements.[5] In this concept, relationships between learning, reflecting, acquiring certain ways of thinking, and especially coming up with new questions is of paramount importance. *Bildung* has no satisfactory direct translation into English; it derives from a 'romantic' ideal, a middle-class appeal for emancipation via education (see, for instance, Oelkers, 1999). *Bildung* covers education, but is generally speaking a far broader concept. A polite or civil person (*gebildet* in German) may have had a good education, or a great deal of education, but this is not always necessary – at least not in the

---

5 Some of what is written here derives from my former career in the realm of *Bildung* (organisational consultancy, general education). See also Abrahám in this volume.

sense of school or university education. Bildung/education in the classic sense seems to refer to both temporal as well as normative social qualities that are acquired to be (become) a valuable member of society. Obviously *Bildung* in this sense takes time and provides time; the latter in terms of enabling a broader horizon of insights for the proper assessment, analysis, and enacting of the knowledge and skills to be a citizen. But what is the relationship to time when reflecting on *Bildung*/education? Just a switch in perspective, from contemplation to reflection, to planning, constitutes far too brief a summary of how the historical development of *Bildung*/education can be seen. Let us look at a take on *Bildung*/education from different time perspectives: its relationship to past-present-and-future, its different rhythms and requirements of time elements or timescales, the role of tempo in terms of fast and slow, and its *Eigenzeiten*, the inherent social/physical temporal dimensions that belong to the different, mutually implicating elements of *Bildung*.

A specific, socially relevant issue regarding *Bildung*/education is that it has a relationship to past, present, and future, not just producing 'knowledge' on the spot for today or next week only. *Bildung*/education prepares for a future context as well; it makes envisioning and planning possible, or avoidable for that matter, for various futures through the accumulation and intrinsic connectivity of knowledge. A specific aspect to remember here is that both the content and the learning systems derive from past experience, 'what worked well', but are geared towards the future, 'what will come of this'. Thus, a crucial element in educational systems is that we use the past to provide for, or at least take account of possible futures, while we more or less consciously produce or prevent futures in our present (Adam & Groves, 2007). We may wonder if and how this works in its present form(s), as well as in the current guise of being promoted via neoliberal assumptions of 'usefulness' and efficiency.

VIGNETTE 2: TALK TO A FRIEND

When I started out as an academic, the educational programme attracted more students than we could staff. I learned to work fast, and sometimes graded theses in an hour, just to help out a colleague. I liked the tension, the stress, and the pride in succeeding in those tasks. But before we knew it that type of hurried working became the norm. It is tempting sometimes to sit back and read interesting work by students, but that just takes too much time – the new systems we work with assign hours to tasks; and thus, we face an accumulation of tasks based on what can be measured against the money the university makes available. With this, our time has become measured, controlled, and accounted for. We have fixed times for different tasks now. This actually means that a lot is not calculated in, and this heightens the pressure.

Another Rhineland concept, that of *Eigenzeiten*, or 'proper times' (Nowotny, 1992), can be helpful here. It refers to the inherent (system) times necessary to 'keep things going'. In other words, how, for instance, children and adults need different amounts of time, different rhythms, sequences, duration, and paces for various tasks, especially in education and learning activities. We all know how different chunks of knowledge require different paces; for instance, learning a language requires learning by heart, and a lot of repetition and pure use. While learning to do math requires, apart from choosing an area (algebra, goniometrics, calculations, differential equations), deep and 'criss-cross' thinking, following certain systems, and enjoying solving puzzles. Obtaining a certain level of critical thinking again demands different paces, learning cycles, periods of thought and reflection, and time for the ripening of insights. Basically, learning times/times for learning are the first time dimensions that teach us how there 'is a time for everything', for pace and rhythms of learning, for short- and long-term memory, for the role of accumulation of knowledge, and for the combination, deepening, expanding and sometimes also the loss of certain types of knowledge. This is also coupled with different times of day, week, or year (seasons) that are considered better or less proper for various activities of learning and study. It is a lot more difficult to be up and about reading and thinking early in the morning when it's winter rather than summer. And, to add a dimension, this is again different for owls and larks, or morning and evening people. All thinkable contextual and inner details together build conditions for learning in different combinations, on group (school/cohort) level, as well as for individuals.

Additionally, the concept of *timescales* links up with the variation of thinkable temporalities (Kümmerer, 1996; Lemke, 2001) inherent in both teaching and learning. Some timescales are pretty much fixed, such as heart rate; the maturing process of different animals, trees, and plants; the life cycles of various species; or the times required to obtain certain types of knowledge and skill. There is also some flexibility or resilience that allows one to cope with unexpected changes in a system; this illustrates that rhythmicity and cyclicality never refer to the same but always to the more-or-less similar, an important distinction to remember because the suggested space in more-or-less similar allows for resilience and sets rhythmicity apart from metronomic tact (Young, 1988; Adam, 1995). Time compression is only possible if rhythmicity is acknowledged, if there is room for variation, for a periodic 'free flow', and, at other times, for pressure (Sabelis, 2002). Because everyone has his or her own personal rhythms, educational systems will enable learning for some, while hindering it for others (e.g. morning and evening people, but also related to the changing of seasons, age-related differences, and personal combinations of adaptability and creativity). If we think about learning in this manner, we are all somehow aware of our personal rhythms that often turn out to be at odds with the social rhythms required of us by society. On the one hand, we choose to participate in societal activities that we like or need, while, on the other, social activities create a necessary evil – such as obligations or 'culturally defined times', among other things. Nothing wrong with deadlines and schedules until one's *slow* pace becomes a problem or when acceleration leads to stress (Rosa, 2003). In these cases, we end up suddenly having to take 'time out' in the form of a holiday or an illness, so we can check to see what is going on and what needs to be changed to prevent inefficiency or a burnout. Yet, increasingly, because of neglect of *Eigenzeiten* and personal temporal needs under clock-time working conditions, the result is burnout or neglecting one's sense of balance in the everyday pace of our lives; our sense of time becomes confused and a sense of pressure tends to dominate. How time perception is learned is easily observed with children, who sometimes combine time elements in unexpected ways. When she was four, my daughter once commented, 'Mum, you have to buy time', referring to the fact that I had to put money in the parking meter. Indeed, as small children learn about time, they often make us aware of the tensions involved in how we use time in our daily lives.

In sum, *Bildung*/education, as learning, developing, forming, preparing, sustaining, building, and combining essential elements of survival, knowledge, interest, curiosity, and then conjoining those elements in useful ways in (and for) specific situations, requires different, embodied ways of time perception and time spending, sometimes slow and sometimes fast. Education as a way to open us up to certain areas, while also focussing on others; it enables or hinders us in our goals based on particular physical, psychological, and systematic conditions present. In other words, *Bildung*/education provides knowledge in the widest sense, to be used according to one's need, and it allows us to see how *Eigenzeiten*, as the various times that comprise the total of our interrelated temporalities, are threatened, or how they build a reliant framework for action and preparation. Maybe we could even state that *Bildung*/education in its multiple qualities is closely related to resilience. These qualities emerge not only in how human beings learn – in the broadest sense of acquiring skills and knowledge – but also how people use a multitude of strategies and ways, which they combine in sometimes very complex short- and long-term ways to produce insights and skills that help make sense of our lives and provide logic for others.

Bildung/education deals with our own personal survival and maintenance, as well as that of the society we are part of. So, what happens if we compress and rationalise that vast vision of learning, what happens if we can only see a standardised mode of time for learning and reflection? It is one thing to accept that *Bildung*/education reflects the needs of the society it serves, but what if this brings along with it vast uniformization, and what if it more or less discourages queer (out of the box) or serendipitous thinking, or even dismisses that as superfluous under neoliberal conditions? More importantly, what if, as Zygmunt Bauman suggests (Bauman & Donskis, 2013, p. 134), utopia, the ideal society, has become privatised into a space where we all strive for our own individual success stories, rendering *Bildung* superfluous as long as the audits are all right? Acceleration of work processes and fluidity of relationships present a picture where we do not even need *Bildung*/education, since the rational frames and context promise almost ready-made career paths, like fast food for the mind.

3 Timescapes of Academia

As Tom Keenoy (2005), Heather Menzies and Janice Newson (2007), Rosalind Gill (2009), Chris Lorenz (2012), and Paula Baron (2014), to name just a few, observe: Western time use and perception are limited to clock time as a result of the developments of industrialisation – and, as we may add, are further trimmed under neoliberal conditions (also Mountz et al., 2015). This rationalised and managerialist time-use radiates the ultimate utopian promise of efficiency as a core value, after the flexible office – now also via digitalised systems enabling cooperation on a global level. We can depart from the premise that, in general, managerially controlled working time is a variation of clock-time rationality: simply linear and logical, often geared to relatively short-term outcomes, and dismissing time complexities as not rational, or at best less important. This leaves out the intricate play of multiple, yet differing rhythms, durations, and sequences, outcomes, and beginnings of different timescales, and products that have short- and long-term effects on the different parts of academic work. Additionally, rational clock-time-oriented managerialism tends not to incorporate possible future effects (Sabelis, 2002) due to the notion that what has not happened yet cannot be measured, and thus drops out of the managerial scope. This goes for academics living (in) the present, and almost running-in-place, while pretending that the future is unknown or something to be dealt with only in futures when and if they present themselves (e.g. Clegg, 2010) – only then as a possible issue to deal with (a present future view, cf. Adam & Groves, 2007). Accepting this as the mode of being for work and organisation, clock-time rationality presents itself as a sequence of sometimes overlapping but always forward-stretching tasks in linear forms, for example, piles of successive to-do-lists, a huge interest in planning, and a firm belief in growth as the main paradigm for survival. In my view, and in the view of a generation of time scholars combining the study of time with their own daily (embodied) experiences, this clock-related perception of time narrows down a wide range of other temporal possibilities, and perhaps necessities as well. Perceptions dealing with cultural difference, varying emotions, and more encompassing, bigger, or explicitly plural understanding of time(s), in which relationships between views, uses, and understandings of time prevail indeed require a more intense, sometimes confusing reflection on time in our daily lives, especially as these are not so straightforwardly captured in models, graphs, and measurements. However, a clock-time view helps increase the pressure put on people, because it leaves out the non-measurable everyday times that do not add to accountability but which we always feel. Clock-time rationality thus implicitly adds tasks and, at the same time, prevents one from looking beyond to-do-lists to other more encompassing, culturally diverse, interlinked, and mutually influencing modes of time and temporality, such as differences in energy, bodily markers like age, and the *Eigenzeiten* of people. As a result of fixation on clock time, we thus lose sight of time scales, different cultural norms regarding time, different paces and experiences of time, the role of duration, sequences, in the sum of timescapes: encompassing modes of time and their interrelationships (cf. Adam, 1998). Actually, the clock-time paradox – where 'big' time is equated with clock time, and other times, broader temporalities are dismissed as less important – influences how we reflect on current developments in higher education, and thus also on possible other outcomes, other modes of organising, and other opportunities for curbing the downsides of the time regimes as brought forward by the limited focus of what is also called the metronomic character (Young, 1988) of present-day life and work.

Over the years, a plethora of studies have appeared about how time and time(s) are utilised by academics in contemporary university contexts and how time pressures lead to loss of quality via increased workloads and risky managerialism, the latter especially causing stress due to fragmentation of work and the rise of audit cultures and accountability cultures (Keenoy, 2005, Menzies & Newson, 2007; Gill, 2009; Clegg, 2010; Ylijoki, 2013; Baron, 2014; Gill & Donaghue, 2015; De Vita & Case, 2016). It is not my intention to provide a full overview of the debate here, but it seems necessary to present some of the main arguments in order to have an idea of the debates and highlight some of their most important elements so as to grasp the complexity and the reach involved in looking at academic work from a timescape perspective.

VIGNETTE 3: WORKING DAY

Wake up shortly before seven – startled and with something stinging in my head. What again? – Oh, yes, the pile of manuscripts to be processed. Processing manuscripts, some 120 per year, goes with the position of being EC for one of the journals. Does not pay, is not calculated anymore, but the workload is increasing. Brain active in seconds. Get up; want that pile done before turning to writing that article.

Breakfast, bread and cheese, coffee and a smoothie, while reading the newspaper of today. Computer is starting up. Late messages from colleagues, and some early ones from that one colleague who manages to only process his mail in the morning. Before long, it is 09:00 – head is working, on top of things. Already handled two requests from students, engaged in an ongoing debate over teaching reform and organisational (department) politics, and looked at flights for next month.

Message from dean comes in. Make an appointment for next week. Don't forget to email thesis students. Make a list for today. The list will probably swallow up the rest of the week. Mails, phone calls, reading, reviewing and having a look at a PhD manuscript. Get those little things out of the way – yet, when done, a large part of the day is over.

(IS – Spring 2016 – personal diary)

The overall picture is not a happy one. Most authors who have done research into the ins and outs of changing time use and perception in higher education and academic life agree on the need for analysis of the effects of neoliberalisation, with as its main effect a change in the character of academic work from process to project driven (Ylijoki, 2013; 2016), the first step in losing out on embodied, diverse, and not-always-accountable time use. But some also point to implicit health risks via 'hidden injuries' in the current systems (Gill, 2009; Gill & Donaghue, 2015), and the effects of increased stress on content and context of our work (Baron, 2014). Additionally, Sue Clegg (2010) demonstrates how the time use currently imposed on academics reveals short-term characteristics aimed at stimulating ever faster cycles of academic production, both in teaching (students) and in research pursuits (journal articles). This assumes that there is a market for knowledge that determines the inner processes of academia – and this market obviously demands more or less direct return on its investment. Academic knowledge production as a commodity, a tradable goal in itself and generating profit, entails short-term orientation by its very nature. And a short-term, almost metronomic production of articles, project grants, and student output accelerates the flywheel of academic life. But not just that, it also extends fragmentation in academia itself. With a given tact on article output, longer-term work is discouraged. And the 'lottery' traits of project grant application (without which no academic these days gets a promotion) additionally adds to cutting corners and possibly desperate moves to... cut out time for the *really interesting work*. What about sustainable, long(er) term knowledge that requires other timescales for observing societal phenomena? What about time for reflection to include both past and future issues? What about bigger relationships and interlinkages in thinking if we produce in increasingly standardised formats? It seems important to look at what we lose by faster production – and what we can gain by at least a flexibilization of strict and general output demands.

VIGNETTE 4: HOLIDAY

Valorisation of results for the last batch of exams is due this week.

Due to a tight annual schedule (this is a summer holiday week), there is no other option than combining a holiday in Croatia with a little work.

Search a site with good Internet, close to the reception of the campsite.

Adolescents there: playing games and keeping in touch with their peers elsewhere in the world.

I sit down on my towel, open the laptop, and start working. It is a hot day; I hear the sound of children playing and the drum of waves in the distance.

Focus required; the university's system needs a lot of reloading pages before all the steps are done.

And yes, it takes a lot more than the envisioned hour. Lunchtime passes before I shut down.

Hopefully there will be no errors.

Within the hour, students' queries start coming in on the phone, I decide to have no Internet for the next two days.

(IS – personal diary, summer 2017)

Ylijoki (2013) identifies another temporal trait; one of the consequences of marketization and *McDonaldisation* is that academics first work hard to get the admin. out of the way before turning to the 'core business', meaning the joy of reading, reflecting, and writing, not just of research but also of students' work, and taking time to deepen discussions. 'Getting the admin. out of the way' tends to take more and more time, and of course this causes stress and frustration leading perhaps to even less time for the desired academic tasks. As administrative duties increase, including disruptions via digitalisation, academics end up working ever longer hours, because they get to 'the real work' later; and this leads to the conclusion that universities tend to increasingly exploit staff engagement. Administrative personnel (support staff, secretariats, policy-makers) often get annoyed when 'academics take their time'. But just one look at the amount of time one spends on emails or journals makes it fairly apparent that 24/7 has been the norm for a long time now, and that 'smart working' adds to the pressure and is nothing new (cf. Keenoy, 2005). Support staff, however, are also under pressure via project obligations involving output and via the audit culture's ongoing new demands. The rise of different temporal demands (regimes) is one of the reasons why it has taken so long for the two groups to join together to protest against mounting institutional pressures.

In 2004 we carried out a small explorative research in my own faculty of social sciences.[6] It turned out that the first cracks due to time pressure and mismatch between academics and support staff were visible at the time. The temporal patterns of working days between the two groups of colleagues were totally different. Due to the new digital systems, we could trace what these patterns were and how different time regimes served in miscommunication between staff and academics. Academics would mainly spend time at the university (buildings) for teaching, meetings, and the odd chat with colleagues. Staff would, as ever, work their nine-to-five, or eight-to-six working hours; they would be irritated by academics 'taking their time' and coming in, for instance, by eleven o'clock. What they did not observe were the emails late at night and the deadline-driven articles sent in the early morning hours. Staff suffered from the then-rising workload due to the combination of digitalisation of work coupled with the new form of accountability and control (Keenoy, 2005; Keenoy & Seijo, 2009; Clegg, 2010). Academics then still enjoyed the rising options coming from the chance to work from home and the new opportunities for

---

6 The report *Werkdruk* FSW/Workload FSC, 2004, Cootje Loggers & Ida Sabelis, was never externally published but is available upon request from the Faculty of Social Sciences, VU Amsterdam. A next check on the situation was planned a couple of years later, but not granted by the faculty management.

worldwide cooperation with colleagues (see also Menzies & Newson, 2008). However, the different paces and rhythms of work were not really seen as different in terms of time(s) – the presentation of our small-scale research results before the faculty population produced at least exchange of habits and indeed triggered mutual understanding for diverse work practices and times. However, the eye-opening effect of this small-scale research soon faded, and what remained was the frustration of not being able to synchronise work processes, which in turn led to more 'systems' being introduced (digital diaries, for instance) in order to keep track of what people were doing and where. Additionally, planning cycles became more visible and important – these would also cover larger timescales, as planning demands more precision and resilience to be taken into *account* (literally).

Paula Baron (2014) argues how academics' time use – in keeping with the *Bildung* concept – should be task-oriented, which is actually a craft, and crafts require various time dimensions. This is quite contrary to the fragmented, industrial image of production, be it that historically there seems to be a nice parallel in the development from time orientation to clock-time compliance under industrial pressure (Elias, 1982; Virilio, 1986; Zerubavel, 2012). Our head-and-hand-work to produce academic quality requires a lot of time in order to bring to the fore the proper skills, to develop programmes, to teach, to study, and to *produce* outstanding research. Our products, or output, take different amounts of time, and different levels of intensity and product quality, to create a valuable, transferable entity. This requirement cannot be met, for instance, by the present three-year PhD programmes for ever younger students; it is counterproductive for the annual demands involving journal production and it undermines the rhetoric of institutional brochures that tout their lofty mission statements of 'excellence'. Sue Clegg (2010) presents another angle on this by stressing the present-future character of contemporary university education. This implies that the projected image of university output is geared towards short-term results, towards 'timescapes of employability' – and this produces another case of TINA in which employability is core. This means that employability, providing instant use for the labour market, has become more important than a future present notion of academia, for example, with a long-term orientation and a fuller or wider idea of accompanying young people in a search, an adventure of science and intellectual development, in order to become resilient, creative, and flexible citizens prepared for diverse future options. The nature and purposes of the modern university have been substantially reworked, encompassing not just a reductionist discourse of employability but fundamental shifts towards what Slaughter and Rhoades (2004) describe as 'academic capitalism', and Marginson and Considine (2000) as the 'enterprise university' – no need stressing the metaphor of MacUniversity (Parker & Jarvey, 1995; Ritzer, 1996).

Yet, these observations address daily work in higher education, and only hint at the underlying power processes at work. For the latter, we can look at the work by Ulrike Felt (2009). Departing from four narratives of time, she analyses the complexity of academic timescapes and demonstrates how hegemonic time regimes prevent re/action of the actors involved. According to Felt temporal regimes governing contemporary academia build an invisible infrastructure guiding the ways in which we know and the kinds of lives we can have in academic environments (Felt, 2009, p. 130) And Felt elaborates: '...this allows us to think of higher education as a set of nested relations between different temporalities in which change happens at different rates' (Felt, 2009, p. 132). Finally, this reveals how landscapes of higher education are deeply intertwined with timescapes and how researchers have to be understood in terms of their local embeddedness in an environment of ongoing processes of change in different temporal, material, and spatial dimensions.

VIGNETTE 5: IMPROVISATION ON THE DIGITAL CLASSROOM

Digitalisation projects are always announced with the promise to make our lives easier: work faster, gain more time for other things, liaise all over the world, and enjoy the comfort. Grading, controlling assignments, keeping track of results, what have you – we don't need piles of paper but can do it all online. Students can immediately see the feedback on their work. Peers can control the grading process. Flip-the-classroom provides students with exactly what they need to know – and management can control teaching processes to manage the next peer control of education programmes. But in whose time do we learn to work with the software? Where does the saved time go? And how do students benefit from online teaching where individualisation demands personal contact?

Last year, I returned to the black-board and chalk system – by providing students with half of a class' information on a note-sheet an hour before class, so that they need to make their own notes during a lecture, while I complete notes on the (black or white) board. Students reported that this requires another type of involvement and mental activity, by which they had to think themselves, instead of just consuming. They reported that this enhanced their capacity to remember what was said in class.

IS – personal diary, 2017

4 Cubicles of Time Control

So, what about the current state of time, acceleration, workload, and a future image of where we are heading, towards or from the academic office? The disappearance of set working times and spaces, as so present in the observation in *About Smith*, have also appeared in academic life. Instead of escaping from the controlled office, including the total and even inner control of times, we have moved towards an open and flexible yet also highly controlled virtual office. It is my contention that this is a highly contradictory development of academic work over the last decades. Our work has become rationalised under novel forms of not-always-visible control via new ways of rationalising both offices and what has replaced offices, the digitalisation of work. May we state that academic work had also become fluid following Bauman's (2000) understanding? Are we '…just a piece of fiction-writing away from a non-fictitious dilemma exposed by Aldous Huxley and George Orwell, and (…) reinterpreted by (…) Michel Foucault…' as Bauman and Donskis argue in their last book, *Liquid Evil* (2016, p. 146)?

Digitalisation has brought huge benefits along with it, like cooperation on a global level, fast exchange with colleagues wherever they are, and the option to work whenever we feel inspired. But that option at the same time became imperative, as the radiating panorama of global academic life and education apparently blended out the risks. The reflexive consequences of these developments, often appearing later than the benefits, have not been highlighted as often as the downsides. This may well be due to fragmentation of effects; as Menzies and Newson (2007) pointed out, the possibility of being online soon turned into a necessity to browse the web and to be always on. What made us not see that development coming? One answer is that change never happens as a straightforward process but is bridled with diverse temporalities; it happens in different timescales of effect and reverberation. And it happens with different effects for different people, thus partly preventing collective action, as the need for action occurs in different times and situations. Acceleration can bring short-term benefits that are harvested before the downsides become apparent, and the downsides work out differently for people doing different tasks. And of course, often, as with burnout and other structural effects that take a long time to appear, it is very difficult to rationally track down the causes of the damage.[7] It is in this context that Ulrike Felt's (2009, p. 59) call for a chrono-political analysis becomes important. Forging an analysis in which

---

7   This parallels the pollution debates in the natural (sustainability) sciences, as in Kümmerer's (1996) work on toxic matter in the environment, which built the foundation for developing

times and organisational politics are considered simultaneously, as temporal regimes, brings to the fore not only the power dimensions at work but also and especially the fragmentation of interests preventing a coherent diagnosis. While we take time for granted (Adam, 1998), we do not see the workings of intricate time control (Felt, 2016, p. 132ff) especially not in its multiplicity and the different time scales linked up in systems of (managerial) power.

Maybe some of us have more influence on our own working conditions than others, especially in terms of the time = money mantra. But most of us can only comply with what is framed as progress and efficiency, leading to more output and more administrative and digitalised tasks. Can we detect a specific kind of TINA here? The There-Is-No-Alternative stamp on our time, as originally promoted by Margaret Thatcher, indicates that '...that there is no reality outside the free market, individualisation, deregulation, and dissemination...' (Donskis, 2016, p. 134). How ironic that the utopia of the free market should lead to loss of choice – and how limiting that planning and control should pervade all areas of development, for students and academics alike.

My personal inclination is still to pursue the question of why there is currently such a lack of interest or motivation on the part of university colleagues at all levels in terms of reflecting on the time spent on learning, education, and future conditions, on the one hand, and how knowledge should be developed, on the other. In other words: why does nobody seem to bother about what knowledge is developed and 'produced' under current clock-time-inspired regimes as long as the output criteria are met? Why do we not question the usefulness of knowledge and academic attitudes apart from meeting the audit criteria? And how come we do not interfere or protest when we see losses and risks in the current system? Under neoliberal rule, or TINA, the reasons for this are part of the same regime that promotes the linear, compartmentalised mode of temporality on daily academic work. Clock-time managerialism is, in a sense, simple, measurable, and plannable, and with that quality it provides a kind of certainty and reliability that feeds well into managerialist cultures, no matter the organisational or individual effects. If The System becomes more important because of its auditability, all else becomes insignificant. Acceleration and commercialisation of the academic industry have caused increased anxiety and have rendered academics cautious, toothless, and small, while consuming their time to the point where they believe their work to be the only *Zeitgeber* in their lives. During a visit to Kaunas University in October 2015, colleagues would approach me after my lecture on academic time to tell me how

---

the concept of timescales [toxic matter in the environment may take up to thousands of years to produce its negative effects].

truthfully and recognisably I had pictured their situation, and it was only then that I fully comprehended, really felt, how individualisation works: it took a fairly simple message to realise that the pressures of time we feel should not be an individual responsibility. Gill and Donaghue (2015) present the growing evidence of unease and desperation to be seen in blogs and forums. It becomes acutely visible that time pressure serves two masters: on the one hand, coupled with individualisation, not meeting the demands of the pressure it is characterised (and internalised) as an individual shortcoming, for instance via output demands and the prevalence of research over teaching. On the other, it leads to the trend of people 'running in place', with no time to reflect on what is actually going on, let alone to take collective action against the increased pressures. And this is exactly the message that lies at the foundation of Bauman and Donskis' (2013, pp. 96–97) argument: be careful not to lose your sense of morality because living a life of fear and forced compliance as a result of a lack of (broad) knowledge and less and less time to develop that knowledge results in increased ignorance, impotence, and humiliation. It is in this situation that we lose our ability to comprehend a broadened time horizon and maintain our capacity to use our time effectively, not in an economic sense but as a measure of human proficiency. The control systems have become our own personal robots. We become, however linked to global communities, caught up in our own individual time cubicles that float around like juggling balls of a managerial time-provider, a global belief in the rationality of academic life.

Post script: writing this chapter was a fair example of the TINA character of academic work. Essay-like reflections for an edited volume are not what our audit-culture values. And therefore, it takes sometimes a long, long time before a publication can be finalised – especially if it does not 'count' in the system.

VIGNETTE 6: ON FADING ENERGY

...It is not the amount of time spent, but the number of times you have to turn your head around for diverse tasks. Reading an article is different from reviewing one. Grading a research proposal requires a different level of attention from replying to a list of emails. And, if on one morning the to-do list requires that many different tasks, the energy flows away in the process of adapting to the different kinds of energy those tasks need and consume. Head spinning after a few hours. Cannot grade, think, and write all at the same time.

IS – diary February 2018

References

Adam, B. (1995). *Timewatch. The Social Analysis of Time*. Cambridge, Polity Press.
Adam, B. (1998). *Timescapes of Modernity: The Environment and Invisible Hazards*. London, Routledge.
Adam, B., & Groves, C. (2007). *Future Matters: Action, Knowledge, Ethics*. Leiden, Brill.
Baron, P. (2014). Working the clock: The academic body on neoliberal time. *Somatechnics*, 4(2), 253–271.
Bauman, Z. (2000). *Liquid Modernity*. Cambridge: Polity Press.
Bauman, Z., & Donskis, L. (2013). *Moral Blindness: The Loss of Sensitivity in Liquid Modernity*. Cambridge, Polity Press. (especially chapter 4).
Bauman, Z., & Donskis, L. (2016). *Liquid Evil: Living with TINA*. Cambridge, Polity Press.
Clegg, S. (2010) Time future – the dominant discourse of higher education. *Time & Society*, 19(3), 345–364.
Davies, B., Gottsche, M., & Bansel, P. (2006). The rise and fall of the neo-liberal university. *European Journal of Education*, 41(2), 305–319.
De Vita, G., & Case, P. (2016). The smell of the place: Managerialist culture in contemporary UK business schools. *Culture and Organization*, 22(4), 348–364.
Donskis, L. (2016). Three modern sensibilities: Machiavelli, Shakespeare, and more. *Deeds and Days*, 66, 121–135.
Elias, N. (1982/1985). *An Essay on Time*. Amsterdam, Meulenhoff.
Felt, U. (2009). Taking European knowledge society seriously. In *Science et devenir de l'homme*. 59, Fascicule thématique Science in Society: Dialogues and Scientific Responsibility. European Conference, Paris, France, 2008-11-24. MURS. Retrieved from http://ec.europa.eu/research/science-society/document_library/pdf_06/european-knowledge-society_en.pdf.
Felt, U. (2016). Of timescapes and knowledgescapes. *New Languages and Landscapes of Higher Education*, 129–148.
Gill, R. (2009). Breaking the silence: The hidden injuries of neo-liberal academia. Secrecy and silence in the research process. *Feminist Reflections*, 228–244.
Gill, R., & Donaghue, N. (2015). Resilience, apps and reluctant individualism: Technologies of self in the neoliberal academy. *Women's Studies International Forum*. http://dx.doi.org/10.1016/j.wsif.2015.06.016.
Keenoy, T. (2005). Facing inwards and outwards at once: The liminal temporalities of academic performativity. *Time & Society*, 14(2–3), 303–321.
Keenoy, T., & Seijo, G. (2009). Re-imagining e-mail: Academics in the castle. *Organization*, 17(2), 177–198.
Kümmerer, K. (1996). The ecological impact of time. *Time & Society*, 5(2), 209–235.
Lemke, J.L. (2001). Articulating communities: Sociocultural perspectives on science education. *Journal of Research in Science Teaching*, 38(3), 296–316.

Lorenz, C. (2012). If you're so smart, why are you under surveillance? Universities, neoliberalism, and new public management. *Critical Inquiry, 38*(3), 599–629. https://doi-org.vu-nl.idm.oclc.org/10.1086/664553.

Marginson, S., & Considine, M. (2000). *The Enterprise University: Power, Governance and Reinvention in Australia.* Cambridge, Cambridge University Press.

Menzies, H., & Newson, J. (2007). No time to think: Academics' life in the globally wired university. *Time & Society 16*(1), 83–98.

Menzies, H., & Newson, J. (2008). Time, stress and intellectual engagement in academic work: Exploring gender difference. *Gender, Work & Organization, 15*(5), 504–522.

Mountz, A. Bonds, A. Mansfield, B., Loyd, J., Hyndman, J., Walton-Roberts, M., Basu, R., et al. (2015). For slow scholarship: A feminist politics of resistance through collective action in the neoliberal university. *ACME: An International Journal for Critical Geographies, 14*(4), 1235–1259.

Nowotny, H. (1992). Time and social theory towards a social theory of time. *Time & Society, 1*(3), 421–454.

Nussbaum, M. (2010). *Not for Profit: Why Democracy Needs the Humanities.* Princeton, NJ, Princeton University Press.

Oelkers, J. (1999). The origin of the concept of 'Allgemeinbildung' in 18th-Century Germany. *Studies in Philosophy and Education, 18*(1–2), 25–41.

Paolucci, G. (1996). The changing dynamics of working time. *Time & Society 5*(2), 145–167.

Parker, M., & Jary, D. (1995). The McUniversity: Organization, management and academic subjectivity. *Organization, 2*(2), 319–338.

Ritzer, G. (1996). McUniversity in the postmodern consumer society. *Quality in Higher Education, 2*(3), 185–199.

Roderick, I. (2016). The politics of office design. *Journal of Language and Politics, 15*(3), 274–287.

Rosa, H. (2003). Social acceleration: Ethical and political consequences of a desynchronized high-speed society. *Constellations, 10*(1), 3–33.

Sabelis, I. (2002). Hidden causes for unknown losses: time compression in management. In Whipp, R., Adam, B., & Sabelis, I. (eds.) *Making time: Time and Management in Modern Organizations* (89–103). Oxford, Oxford University Press.

Slaughter, S. & Rhoades, G. (2004). *Academic Capitalism and the New Economy. Markets, State and Higher Education.* Baltimore, The Johns Hopkins University Press.

Van der Pijl, K. (2006). A Lockean Europe? *New Left Review, 37,* 9–37.

Virilio, P. (1986). *Speed and Politics. An Essay on Dromology,* New York, Semiotext(e).

Ylijoki, O.-H. (2016). Organising logic: Project time versus process time in the accelerated academy. *Impact of Social Sciences Blog.*

Ylijoki, O.-H. (2013). Boundary-work between work and life in the high-speed university. *Studies in Higher Education, 38* (2), 242–255.

Young, M. (1988). *The Metronomic Society*. Cambridge MA, Harvard University Press.
Zerubavel, E. (2012). *Time Maps: Collective Memory and the Social Shape of the Past*. Chicago, University of Chicago Press.

Further Reading

http://blogs.lse.ac.uk/impactofsocialsciences/the-accelerated-academy-series/ (March 2018).
Gibbs, P. Ylijoki, O.-H., Guzmán-Valenzuela, C., & Barnett, R. (eds.) (2014). *Universities in the Flux of Time: An Exploration of Time and Temporality in University Life*. London, Routledge.
Ylijoki, O.-H. (2016). Projectification and conflicting temporalities in academic knowledge production. *Teorie vědy/Theory of Science, 38*(1), 7–26.
Ylijoki, O.-H. (2014). Conquered by project time? *Universities in the Flux of Time: An Exploration of Time and Temporality in University Life*. London, Routledge, 94–107.

CHAPTER 7

A Nomad of Academia. A Thematic Autobiography of Privilege

Joost van Loon

Abstract

Written from an autobiographical perspective, this chapter describes experiences of being an 'international academic' during the radical transformation of university life into a system that is usually referred to as 'neoliberalism'. Taking up some of the ideas of Baumann and Donskis (2013) regarding 'liquid evil' and the liquidation of the humanities, the emergence of 'audit culture' as serving an autopoietic technocracy is being analysed as part of a stroboscopic experiment that has led to the gradual destruction of the university. First hand experiences from the Dutch, British and German universities are compared to argue that although one might be inclined to treat the entire process as completely determined and thus inevitable, fragments and smithereens of resilience might also be considered – and in spite of the otherwise justified pessimism – as moments of disclosure of a possible saving power.

Keywords

privilege – austerity – efficiency – institutional reform – the Netherlands – United Kingdom – Germany

1   A Preamble

In my life as a member of the privileged internationalist class of higher education, there are only a few traces of my class background left. As Didier Eribon (2016) has shown so well in *Returning to Reims* and has been analysed in such a harrowing detailed fashion by Simon Charlesworth in this book, students with working-class backgrounds have been systematically set up to fail in that system of modern higher education, at least since the 1970s. In order to succeed, I had to erase most of my class background, and my success in doing so has been the consequence of at least three factors, which I was lucky enough to have been affected by: (1) a privileged trajectory of the differentiated (pre-comprehensive) Dutch secondary education system; (2) a long-standing partnership with a woman from a well-to-do family; and (3) an international university experience. In this contribution, I am exclusively focusing on the third, as this is of direct relevance to the theme of this edited book. It is exactly the ideals that ultimately led to the Bologna-process in Europe (see for example also the contributions of Abraham, Bianchini, and Donskis in this book), that have made a strong impact on my academic career. The fact that these ideals have all but vanished in administrative procedures of what I will refer to as 'audit culture' are also key issues in the aforementioned contributions.

My university education in sociology stretches across three different countries: I did (the equivalent of) my Bachelor's degree in the Netherlands, completed my Master's of Arts in Canada, and obtained my PhD in England. My university career as a lecturer and researcher has been shaped by four different countries: in chronological order, Wales (18 months), the Netherlands (12 months), England (14 years), and Germany (8 years).

Of course, no autobiographical experience can be used for a systematic comparative analysis of universities, let alone university systems in different countries, because too many variables cannot be controlled. Moreover, by their very nature, autobiographies are anecdotal, impressionistic, and deeply subjective. Their primary value lies in providing a symptomatic illustration of what would otherwise remain mere generalised abstractions, enabling readers to identify in a more concrete manner with the matters of concern being raised. It thus fits well within the established, and currently reviving tradition of 'autoethnography' (cf. Holman Jones, 2005).

2   The Institutional Reproduction of Privilege

Because of the nature of this book, I want to illustrate the impact of – for want of a better word – the neoliberalisation of higher education. However, it must be stressed from the outset, that what is normally referred to by this label is neither new nor liberal (let alone liberalising) by any stretch of the imagination. It is exactly one of these zombie concepts (also see the contribution by Donskis in this book) that mediate what he referred to as 'liquid evil': it intervenes, seduces, manipulates, and then withdraws again into the shadows, like an intangible, shallow Prometheus. What this label 'neoliberal' perhaps more accurately stands for is the recapturing and securing of a reproduction of a social order most commonly described as 'capitalist' (Boltanski & Chiapello, 2017), but manifesting itself in a more limited fashion as the naturalisation of white, male, bourgeois privilege.

In *Moral Blindness*, Zygmunt Bauman and Leonidas Donskis (2013) reflect on the transformations of university life under the condition of what Bauman (2000) once referred to as 'liquid modernity', which is a sociologised version of what is often referred to as neoliberalism. '[T]he present day strategy of commercialisation coupled with a refusal to recognise any value that is not commercial and any potential except sales potential [has not] necessarily augured a more secure life for the endemic university values...' (ibid., 142). However, what they have failed to recognise is what is at the core of Simon Charlesworth's contribution to this book: The entire liquidation of the traditional academy was only possible because of the manufacturing of a reserve army of doctoral students, many of whom turned to a mere 'standing reserve' of sessional lecturers, part-time tutors, and teaching assistants, or simply cast off as 'failures' to the growing pool of overqualified, overeducated, unemployed postgraduates. The liquidation of the academy required such a standing reserve exactly because it enabled those, privileged enough to work within it, to continue the institutionalised pretence of value accumulation.

Whereas the academics with secure positions inside universities might lament the 'good old days' of the academy operating under the conditions of 'solid modernity', their suffering is nothing compared to those who have been at the receiving end of the circulation of devalued credentials. However, it is exactly the generation of this standing reserve that has enabled the unfolding of this liquid evil of inconsequential instantaneity. The main brunt of the costs of liquid modernity has been externalised and as a result those inside the academy have been able to actively participate in these processes, as '...accomplices in that accomplishment' (Bauman & Donskis, 2013, p. 140).

In what follows, I am autobiographically engaging with my own accomplishments as an accomplice of the liquidation of the academy. When I entered the Dutch university system as a student in 1985, access to higher education was still somewhat of a political issue. Students from families with limited economic means were allowed to have a stipend; there were no tuition fees and there were no severe repercussions for not finishing your degree within a certain period. This all changed in the subsequent years. With the introduction of student loans, tuition fees, and punitive measures for exceeding the maximum duration of study, university life in the Netherlands succumbed to the logic of rationalisation. All of a sudden, I had to organise my life and studies to maximise efficiency rather than the pursuit of knowledge or research-related interests, face considerable future debt, and worry about how to transform my university degree into an asset on the labour market. As I had chosen to read sociology (having switched from psychology), this of course was by no means self-evident as it raised the question: what is sociology good for?

Already during my second year of studying sociology, it became apparent that one possible way to deal with the inevitable threat of future labour market insecurity was to compete in the university's internal market of student-assistantships. Until then, competitiveness was restricted to grades for exams and discussions during seminars and – being a highly competitive person (a legacy from being an outcast in a more elitist grammar school) – I might have been better prepared than most of my cohort. I became a research-assistant in my third undergraduate year, and this enabled me to interact and socialise with academic staff on slightly different terms.

When the first opportunity to study a year abroad in Canada emerged, I was the first to apply (because of my position, I knew of it sooner than the other students did) and got it. This enabled me to enter a Master's programme before even finishing my undergraduate degree. University life in Canada was more competitive than in the Netherlands, although at that time, I had no idea this might have been institutionalised as part of concerted effort by the elite to ensure they always ended up on top.

Grades function as a means of differentiating between students, transforming cultural capital into educational capital (Bourdieu & Passeron, 1990), and classifying and selecting students according to what are believed to be 'their cognitive abilities' (Bowles & Gintis, 1976). Simon Charlesworth (2000; also see his contribution to this book), however, adds to this an extremely important insight: the institutional processes of higher education function to value and devalue, not simply by means of imposing a grading system but also by means of personalising this (de)valuation, so as to present success and failure as the natural consequence of pre-established personal qualities. However, because universities do not offer opportunities to actualise the potentialities they create as part of their everyday practices, they are setting up to fail exactly those students that do not have access to such means of actualisation outside of the university.

My own autobiography is a perfect example of this. By becoming a research student in the second year of my undergraduate degree, I was already privileged, because working as part of a research team already allowed me to actualise what it meant to be a sociologist, without even having finished my first degree. From that moment onwards, being a sociology student had a certain objectivity, because I could be objectively constituted within the institutional setting of a university. This gap between possibility and actuality, which marks the condition of being a student just as much as being unemployed, was thus being reduced by the mere fact of activity, from which significance is being derived. This significance finds its realisation in evaluations of both others as well as myself. One does not need to become a research or teaching assistant as a student to be able to succeed, but if one is unable to be objectified outside of the university, which is the privilege of those in possession of sufficient (economic, social, cultural) capital, it is one of the few ways that are left.

There is, however, another way and that is 'going international'. Being a foreign student erases most of the hallmarks of a class-based *habitus*, as one becomes recoded as 'foreign'; hence traits that would be considered 'vulgar' to indigenous elites can all of a sudden become interesting in their own right, as they are attributed to some exotic, foreign national culture, whilst simultaneously being able to claim 'intercultural competences' (also see Bianchini, in this book). Being an overseas student in Canada wiped away the stigmas of being a student from a working-class background. I could subsequently reinvent myself and intensify my elite trajectory. Gaining the confidence to speak in public, deploy intimate knowledge of a foreign culture, being bilingual, etc., all helped to propel my early career as a promising young scholar. The fact that I was white and male constituted equally important aspects of my normalisation. Whereas Charlesworth (in this book) is absolutely right that exactly these two features work to your disadvantage if you are unable to avoid the stigma of being a working-class low-life, it is amazing how easily these codes switch once you are adopted as one of the middle class. Different from all other 'traits' of what feminists have referred to as 'intersectionality', class is not simply a factor among many, one that adds up to the others; class is a polarity switch for the privileged. White working-class males are the pariahs of university life, whereas white middle-class masculinity is the norm-setting ideal.

Being set in my favour, the modes of selection of higher education enabled me to compete on unequal terms, first during my Master's in Canada, secondly when obtaining my first-degree summa cum laude in the Netherlands, and thirdly by being awarded a scholarship to do my PhD at Lancaster University in the UK. After arriving in Lancaster, I was immediately offered the opportunity to work as a seminar tutor, thus closing the final gap between possibility and actuality, as I could then build up the teaching-experience that had thus far eluded me.

3   Austerity and Efficiency

From the start of my life in higher education (in the 1980s) onwards, I have been confronted with an almost uninterrupted series of reforms, instigated by both national governments as well as university administrations. These reforms all went in one and the same direction: a reduction of input and an increase in expected output. There have always been cutbacks in resources and reductions of time, at the same time, students were expected to become more instrumentally oriented, to focus on acquiring skills (rather than knowledge) that are relevant to the labour market (rather than intellectual pursuits), and to complete their studies faster and according to fixed programmes. Relevance had been redefined as that which served the needs of business and industry, and critical thought was generally considered to be at best a luxury and at worst a hindrance.

In the UK it is commonly accepted that this transformation coincided with the biggest cultural-political revolution in the British Isles since Oliver Cromwell: Thatcherism. Thatcherism is basically a clever mixture of: (a) crude capitalist political economy, which comes down to a kleptocratic transfer of resources from the poor to the rich via institutional means (such as 'deregulation' and 'privatisation'); (b) a sugar coating of inequalities and injustices under the label of 'liberalism' and 'free markets' (even if these markets were already completely oligarchic); and (c) a nationalistic form of authoritarian populism. Thatcherism preached a neoliberalism – as an expression of There Is No Alternative (see Donskis, in this book) – that it did not practice. It did not create free markets but destroyed them; it did not establish equal opportunities but amplified distinctions based on class, ethnicity, and gender, and it made sure those at the receiving end of the stick blamed foreigners (most notably the EU but also immigrants) for their 'misfortunes'. In this sense, it is a prime example of what Donskis (in this book) has referred to as 'liquid evil'.

However, contrary to my dear British colleagues, I am not convinced this model – though extreme it certainly was – was in essence unique to the UK. At exactly the same time as Thatcher declared war on the unions and civil society, the Netherlands was also experimenting with similar forces, albeit in a spirit of consensual hallucination (the so-called *poldermodel*: see Kuypers, 2015). During the 1980s, the most progressive Dutch public broadcaster, the VPRO, declared that the nation was at risk of *verloedering*, that is, succumbing to a culture of sleaze. Pointing to the work of the culture industries – television, film, radio, music, newspapers, and magazines – it was apparent that Adorno and Horkheimer's (1979) thesis from 1944 was still remarkably accurate, perhaps even more so than during the time of its publication. Inundated with sleaze of the lowest common denominator, Dutch popular culture turned anti-intellectual, celebrating its own ignorance as bliss, insisting on 'speaking your mind', whilst refusing to listen to anyone else.

In the Netherlands, the 1980s sowed the seeds for the populist demagoguery of Dutch right-wing populists such as Pim Fortuyn and Geert Wilders.[1] It was the same cultural breeding ground for a new type of student, for whom a university degree was merely an affirmation of their entitlement to superiority. They flocked to the burgeoning degrees in economics, business administration, and public administration. They were both the beneficiaries and executives of the 'neoliberal turn'. Austerity served them well, because their accumulation of wealth was never going to be affected by the quality of public services or education. Universities in the UK had been caught-up in this process as well. They were actively encouraged to marketize their research and teaching: deliver products and services to customers and users. One of the first domains where this took place was the acquisition of international PhD students, of which I was a beneficiary. It is no surprise that this was the favourite strategy of universities from the outset, as (overseas) PhD students do not require a lot of investment of resources (as a PhD is to a large extent based on self-directed learning), but they can be charged very high fees. Moreover, because of the fact that these students would mostly go back to their native countries, the risks of a reputation loss for the supervisor could be minimised to those involved in the behind-closed-doors affair of the *viva voce*.

The second strand of the 'neoliberalisation' of higher education in the United Kingdom that started in the early 1990s was the introduction of auditing for research and teaching. Audit culture is often 'sold' as a necessary corollary of deregulation and deployed as a means of controlling that the levels of quality of research and teaching are of a standard considered appropriate. For research audits, however, this was blatantly ignored, as it became the means for justifying decisions related to resource-allocation. The exercise was from the outset an assessment rather than an audit and subsequently turned into kind of credit rating linked to a selective distribution of rewards. Competition between universities was thus now fought in the arena of the research assessment exercise, that is, a peer-based affirmation of credibility and sign value. The criteria for assessing quality are of course all very subjective and – as with all aspects of cycles of credit – based on the relative strength mustered by the networks of 'evaluation': that means they are political.

---

1 Pim Fortuyn was instrumental in transforming the financing of student loans, having set up a system during his time as a senior civil servant in the Ministry of Education, which forced all students to transfer parts of their student loans into rail cards, managed by a privately-owned limited company, of which he became the managing director. Ten years later, he became the voice of racist, Islamophobic, Dutch nationalism, having left the Dutch Labour Party, which had served him so well during his time as a civil servant and director of the quango 'OV Studentenkaart BV'.

4 Audit Culture and the Rise of Social Constructionism

That Thatcherism fosters a politicization of science was, however, hardly visible to social scientists at that time, primarily because these were engaged in arguing that the products of scientific work were social constructions. In a perverse way, the argument that scientists were not engaged in 'making reality speak the truth' but in hermeneutic negotiations over the establishment meaning – which was the hallmark of social constructionism – perfectly fed the Thatcherite reforms of higher education. The actual fall out of this, however, would not be visible until the rise of climate change denial, and above all Trumpism and its deployment of alternative facts nearly three decades later.

Universities in the Netherlands and the UK both experienced the rise of audit culture during the 1990s. Audit culture is closely associated with blame culture (Van Loon, 2002) and the culture of fear (Furedi, 2002; also see Donskis in this book) and is a perfect example of a reflexively modern response to the 'risk society' (Beck, 1992), which marks a reinvention of politics (Beck, 1997) that no longer adheres to any humanist understanding of the political but has become deeply technocratic (Bauman & Donskis, 2013). The idea was that the state needs to be able to trace how 'its' money has been spent in terms of research and teaching, as a means of controlling risks and governing actions. Financial audits had already been established long before the rise of Thatcherism or the Polder Model, as capitalism and kleptocracy are often very close bedfellows. However, rather than using the suspicion of theft as the reason behind the audit, policy makers had adopted another phantom of 1980s sleaze culture: quality-management, which a bit later was to be rephrased as the 'management of excellence'.

Politicians and policy makers in governments and universities established a discourse of auditing that could be linked easily to promoting and even producing 'quality' (or 'excellence'). Enhancing quality was not just the objective of auditing; it became its equivalent. In order to compare different universities, quantities had to be produced. That is, the discourse of quality required technologies of quantification to enable comparisons and establish the normal of best practice. The same quantities were also associated with the redistribution of financial resources. 'Quality Speak' thus became entangled with the circulation of credit. Although this has been part and parcel of the modern university system since its reconfiguration as an institution of the nation state at the turn of the twentieth century (Gouldner, 1970), cycles of credits were the exclusive domain of scientists; with the turn to audit culture, however, they became the property of university administrators.

Quality enhancement as the result of auditing, which itself is based on technologies of quantification that translate differentially enhanced qualities into cycles of credit, has of course nothing to do with good research or good teaching, but with the ability to optimise quantification. The current deployment of impact factors is a perfect example of this. An impact factor is a compound of the frequency of citation and the weight of the publishing venues where these citations appear. Impact is measured as the consequence of impact measurement. The impact factor has nothing to do with the quality of the research to which it has been attached, but with the social process of imitation that grants it its reputation.

Whereas the quantification of research quality still has a pretence of objectivity, no such thing has been remotely achieved by audits of university teaching. These are formalised impressionistic judgements based on highly subjective student evaluations, screenings of curriculum materials, and samples of observations of class-room-based teaching. Doing well in teaching and learning audits usually means that you need to tick the right boxes and speak the right lingo (see the contributions of both Sabelis and Wels in this book).

Auditing practices have led to the formalisation and standardisation of 'quality speak', a bit of jargon championed by university administrators, also known as 'managerialism' (Bauman & Donskis, 2013). In due course, all universities have become experienced in deploying quality speak for the sole purpose of being successfully audited. It is, however, dangerously wrong to suggest that 'this is mere speak', as if it were without consequences. During my first years as a university lecturer, first in England, followed by Wales and the Netherlands, we were trained to perform for audits. We were actively encouraged to adopt 'quality speak' in our course material and handbooks; we were also instructed to plan our publications exclusively with an eye to the Research Enhancement Audit years before its due date. My work as an academic has been influenced by audit culture from the very beginning.

Audit culture has thereby become an example par excellence of what Beck, Giddens, and Lash (1994) collectively referred to as 'reflexive modernisation'.[2] Generating data constituting their own objectivity is equally well described as autopoiesis (Luhmann, 1984). Auditing research as well as teaching and learning has moulded the objective forms of academic life and fine-tuned the

---

2 I should say that the three social theorists were actually referring to different processes. Whereas Beck deployed it to describe the inevitable backlash-effects of intended consequences (e.g. risks) on institutional practices, Giddens was referring to cognitive (reflective) operations in the realm of subjective consciousness, and Lash was primarily concerned with aesthetic judgments of a decentred, post-humanist mode of subjectification.

academic disciplines to imitate the modes of subjectification designed to enable 'management'. This self-referential closure also meant that the 'neoliberal turn' seemed to be natural, self-evident, self-explanatory, and without any alternative.

As I moved from Wales to the Netherlands and a year later again back across the North Sea to England, one thing that struck me was that despite considerable differences in the organisation and administration of university life in Cardiff, Amsterdam, and Nottingham, all three universities were facing similar pressures to economise and rationalise university education, streamline research to the needs of business and government, and embrace audit culture as the means to achieve these. Also, remarkably similar was the lack of organised resistance. In my case, being so highly attuned to the competitive nature of university life also meant I was deeply sceptical about any allusion to the collectivisation of interests. Having been well-trained in the techniques of individuated performativity, I knew how to respond to the requests for data for the purposes of quality control, was able to adopt the quality speak in terms of self-representation, and always made sure that quantities rather than arguments based on justice or fairness formed the basis of claims for recognition and rewards.

However, perhaps an additional reason why universities were so slow to sense the danger and so pathetic in organising alternatives, was that their own decision-making bodies were made up of academics, who often had no clue of what they were doing, whereas the administration was in the hands of professionals, who knew exactly what they wanted and where to get it. For example, at the Vrije Universiteit Amsterdam, where I worked during the academic year 1996/1997, over 50% of employees were working for the administration. That means: more people were involved in 'supporting' (and above all regulating and controlling) the primary processes than actually delivering anything. Of course, it might also be the case that they knew very well what they were doing.

It should therefore come as no surprise that the neoliberal turn in higher education has not resulted in a reduction of bureaucratic overhead expenditure, but has in fact increased it. The people who most emphatically advocated the reforms that were in line with the wider political-economic restructuring of (at that time still globalist) late-capitalism were also those who were able to self-referentially operationalise it, as a result of which they themselves became the measurement of 'their' success.

During the same period in which the neoliberal turn was able to transform institutions of higher education into self-referential, self-valorising quality-machines, whose 'impact' was exclusively measured by its ability to meet the needs of business and government, there was also a significant paradigm shift within the magical, secluded world of 'science theory' (Philosophy of Science, *Wissenschaftstheorie*, etc.). What had been problematically labelled during the late 1980s as 'the postmodern turn' was in effect a shift in orientation on the question of validity. Whereas 'methods' formed the cornerstone of most scientific disciplines until the arrival of postmodernism, they became the target of intense scepticism and incredulity afterwards.

The social sciences and humanities were at the forefront of this shift. By being able to show that scientific truths are – in the final analysis – nothing but truth-claims, they were able to use the opposition between reality and representation, which had been the cornerstone of notions of Truth (for both its rationalist and empiricist variants), and deploy it as an antidote against itself. If truths cannot be separated from truth-claims, then every truth always bears the mark of a particular interest or a combination of interests as the motivation behind the claim. Then scientific truth becomes a matter of politics (Latour, 2007; Van Loon, 2002; also see Kamsteeg in this book).

For those who – perhaps inspired by Karl Mannheim as a founding father of the Sociology of Scientific Knowledge – had already taken this position as part of a critical stance, this initially might have had a positive resonance, but its critical sting quickly vanished with a more nihilistic turn. If all truth-claims are political, and thus an expression of the will to power, then this also applies to truth-politics itself. There is no critical 'time out' from where to judge the cynical deployment of claims ironically. When one can no longer claim naïve sanctuary (because God is dead and we killed him), the ironic distancing itself becomes the expression of a deep cynicism.

Avoiding the abyss of realising the fatal strategy of cynical nihilism, those convinced that truths are inseparable from truth-claims preferred to embrace a milder version: social constructionism. This preached that whatever truths might be 'out there', we do not need to concern ourselves with them but only with what is said about them. By being agnostic about the question of truth, social constructionism cultivated a more pragmatic orientation. The dangerous nihilistic sting of situating truth-claims as political could be circumvented by addressing social constructions as cultural forms: they are more often than not the consequence of negotiations, subjective expectations, and hermeneutic traditions.

Depoliticising the paradigm shift transformed social constructionism into an ideal counterpart of the neoliberal turn. After all, as universities were valued primarily for their impact on business and government, deliberating the political or metaphysical nature of truth-claims became simply obsolete in the face of the more pragmatic question: is it working? Social constructionism did not pose a threat to the reforms of higher education exactly because it had already adopted a post-nihilistic stance. Likewise, theories of reflexive modernisation and autopoiesis may perfectly describe how auditing practices establish their own objectivity; they are unable to instigate critical thought that might generate alternatives. This is a well-known phenomenon as part of wider processes of bureaucratisation (cf. Luhmann, 1998).

5 Stroboscopic Practices of Institutional Reform

In breath-taking analyses of processes of environmental de(con)struction, James Morrow (2017) described one example of how the town of Sheffield itself had become the bedding ground of the Thatcherist revolution during the mid-1980s. Environment establishes everyday life and not the other way round. By destroying the infrastructure of the coal-mining industry, the Thatcher government choked the life out of the working-class communities in and around Sheffield. By the time the miner's resistance had been decimated, it was fairly easy to establish a new, post-industrial landscape deploying the destitute, precarious remnants of the working class, who were no longer able to collectivise and resist. Expanding higher education to accommodate for this now obsolete 'labour force' was both clever and effective. Promising skills that were never taught, which were held like the proverbial carrot that makes the donkey pull the cart, credentialism and meritocracy were mere public-relations window dressing and enabled those inside the academy to produce accounts of value accumulation without having to significantly increase their workloads.

This analysis would have been equally suitable to institutions of higher education in the United Kingdom. After a series of reforms and cutbacks, a new era of managerialism had been established during the 1990s, in which those involved in university education were completely individuated and the vast majority of students put in a position of permanent precariousness. That many university degrees had no value, because nothing was being taught and the only usable transferable skill was the ability to deploy exclusive means of self-actualisation that were not offered by universities themselves, only worked to its advantage as there was no exteriority which could serve as a reality check (in the sense of Ulrich Beck's version of reflexive modernity).

Morrow referred to the destruction of the working-class environment as stroboscopic. With this he means, that there are many individual instances, facts so to speak, that seem to be disconnected and are therefore not linked as part of one and the same process (of class warfare). For example, different pieces of legislation related to trade unions, education, the funding of community arts, public transportation, housing, and financing local authorities may not seem to add up. However, once lined up in a sequence, they suddenly display a complete unfolding. Many individual changes may appear to be very local, gradual, and very slow, but then all of a sudden everything is different. Stroboscopic reforms unfold as if they were meticulously planned, 'under cover' so to speak, even if this might often not have been the case.

The gradual destruction of university life in England and Wales took a sudden, radical turn with the introduction of tuition fees in 1998 (by the then Labour government). This, however, was eclipsed in England by the Higher Education Act 2004 (again by a Labour government). Under the Act, universities in England could begin to charge variable fees of up to £3,000 a year, as the system had been deregulated further. This was much more radical than it had been in the Netherlands during the 1980s, because they were not accompanied by a generic financial support (topped up by loans). In England and Wales, students were not offered generic stipends but still had to pay tuition fees that were steep from the outset. At the same time, central funding for universities was cut and linked to performance indicators derived from research audits, learning-and-teaching audits and above all student numbers.

Universities were now competing with other universities (for the right to call themselves 'centres of excellence'), departments within universities were competing with each other, and even the competition between individual academics became attached to much more serious consequences such as 'performance-related pay'. Additionally, obtaining 'international students' became imperative for universities and departments to sustain themselves. These students had to be treated as customers who expected services in exchange for the high tuition fees. They could therefore not be failed easily, and, as a result, departments started to perform all kinds of additional services in order to satisfy customer need and minimise the risks of litigation.

These processes went hand in hand with a systematic reduction or expenditure on staff or students. Whereas during the first decade of the twenty-first century, the salaries and bonuses of university executives increased dramatically, and many universities were engaged in high-risk financial investments and high-profile building projects, actual per capita investment in learning and teaching decreased. At the same time, however, the salaries of lecturers have dramatically stagnated and their pension funds have been raided. Additionally, research funding was increasingly concentrated mostly in the hands of elite institutions that were already wealthy, creating a university system with a very small but well-funded elite at the top and an increasingly marginalised and underfunded 'tail' of mediocre institutions jostling for positions that hardly matter.

At least in Europe, England and Wales were at the vanguard of this slash-and-burn tactic of neoliberal institutional reform. This was not some haphazard, opportunistic political process, but strategically planned with full knowledge of the consequences because it was based on decades of experience of downgrading public services as a means to enable (cheap) privatisation (cf. Morrow, 2017). The fact that in 2018 many universities in England declared that they were unable to sustain the pension schemes for their lecturing staff is merely one consequence of the transformation of higher education.

Although I have not had any personal experience of working in a university in the Netherlands since the mid-1990s, I am quite certain the developments there have not been as radical as in England and Wales (but unfolding in a similar direction). This is largely because the radicalisation of the elite establishment in the Netherlands has been less draconian in socioeconomic terms, and been more preoccupied with xenophobic identity politics vis-à-vis migrants and refugees. Even if the preaching of radical neoliberalism has ceaselessly deployed the minarets of the national newspapers and broadcasters to enable a normalisation of the underlying economic violence – for example with the threat of capital outflow terrorising any government that suggests holding the business and finance sectors more accountable – the Dutch form of right-wing populism has never held a majority government in the Netherlands. To put it differently, the timeframe of the stroboscopic practices of institutional reform could be drastically reduced in the UK because there were and are fewer checks and balances in place there.

It should come as no surprise that the consequences for those involved in academic work have been enormous. Ever since returning to work as an academic in England in 1996, I have had to face a year-on-year increasing workload and, although my salary has not been curbed as much due to successive promotions, those starting at a lecturer level in 2010 were in a far worse position than I was 10 years earlier in terms of pay, job security, and work load. For example, in 1996, the average university lecturer at my university (Nottingham Trent) would be teaching eight contact hours per week; by the time I left the UK in 2010, this had been increased to 15. Increased student numbers, necessary for the university to meet its business targets, meant that the class and number of Bachelor's theses had also doubled, whereas the number of staff available for teaching and marking has remained the same for 15 years. As a result, contact hours per student were reduced as were time for supervision and feedback. While students had to pay more and more tuition fees, they obtained less and less 'value for money'.

During my final years at Nottingham Trent University (NTU), I had the privilege of becoming involved in middle management. Here, the language of neoliberal reform had been fully incorporated. During the first wave of major institutional reform, NTU had abandoned its organisational structure and merged several faculties into 'schools'. This enabled the university executive to devolve responsibility for success, and above all failure, to lower levels, whilst at the same time creating internal markets to enhance 'competitiveness'. Schools may seem to have greater financial authority, but the Quarterly Business Review ensured that schools had to adhere to performance indicators that were centrally imposed and evaluated. As with many other universities, the main emphasis in these QBRs was on generating more income, either through greater numbers of domestic and above all overseas students or through the acquisition of 'third stream income'. Because NTU was not a high-performing research university, a significant part of the latter was geared towards the generation of 'transferable knowledge' that could be of direct service to commercial enterprises. Schools that were unable to generate more income were forced to cut expenditures.

Within less than 10 years, Nottingham Trent University had ceased to be a university but had become a business. For example, whereas in 2001 the Research Assessment Exercise was still the most significant measurement of the standing of the university, this was much less of a priority in 2008. Instead, one of its new key performance indicators was 'employability', for which it boasted an extremely high success rate in terms of graduates finding employment. By contrast, the university's standing in terms of research is comparatively modest: in 2014, it occupied the 84th place (out of 128 and six places lower than in 2008).[3]

6   Exit Neoliberalism?

Moving to Germany in 2010 to take up a Chair in General Sociology and Sociological Theory at the Catholic University of Eichstätt-Ingolstadt was an extremely important decision for the whole of our family. With the return of the Conservative Party to power in 2010 on the back of the collapse of the financial markets in 2007/2008, the urgency to leave the island could not have been greater. As a result, I did not have to think long before accepting the offer of a permanent professorship.

The system in Germany is very different compared to both the Netherlands and the UK. In Germany, as a rule the only academic staff holding permanent positions in universities are professors and 'Akademische Räte'. The latter are, however, more of an exception. At first sight, this looks even worse than in the UK and the Netherlands because most teaching staff in universities are on

---

3 https://www.timeshighereducation.com/news/ref-2014-results-table-of-excellence/2017590.article.

fixed-term (and often part-time) contracts and these can stretch over 12 years. However, the purpose of this is not as much cost-reduction but obtaining qualifications. Most lecturers at German universities are in the process of obtaining PhDs or *Habilitations* (a post-doctoral degree). Unlike in the UK, a doctorate is not exclusively relevant for higher education but is a qualification that is in greater demand in the labour market, both in the private as well as in the public sector. Hence, despite the fact that most lecturers and researchers in German universities are not in permanent positions, their precariousness is moderated by a greater amount of opportunities outside of the higher education sector.

German universities still bear some of the traces of their pre-modern predecessors and still adhere to a guild-like structure revolving around patron-client relationships between a professor and her/his assistants and the wider student-body. The 'chair' (*Lehrstuhl*) is the key organisational actor and therefore the central unit of administration. Unlike in the UK, therefore, a professor is not some honorary title that allows for an increase in salary and a bigger office (alongside a reduction in teaching load and administrative responsibilities). Instead, a professor is responsible for all the teaching, research, and administration of the chair, and professors are expected to also play a leading role in fulfilling administrative and organisational duties beyond the realm of the chair, for example, in faculties and other administrative bodies and committees. In other word, professors in German universities have much more autonomy but also bear greater levels of responsibility than their British and Dutch counterparts.

This older structure has proven to be a major factor of resilience against the neoliberal onslaught. Of course, German universities have not been immune to this and, especially in relation to research and teaching audits, attempts have been made to introduce rankings. The German Research Funding Council (DFG) has had a major impact on the concentration of research in certain universities (via so called 'Excellence Initiatives', Special Research Areas (SFBs), and Graduate Colleges) and thus the formation of 'elites', but these have by and large not pandered to the immediate needs of business and government. That is to say, the German system seems to have kept a closer affinity to the notion of 'academic freedom' as a prerequisite for the pursuit of knowledge. Impact-factors and bibliometrics, for example, are not deployed as some kind of Holy Grail to decipher the relevance or significance of research. Audit culture and its corollary of quantification are actually quite frequently frowned upon as instruments of 'banalisation' and 'managerialism'.

The resilience of German universities against neoliberalism, however, is much less ideological than I may have suggested. Indeed, in the face of neoliberal reform, ideology is of little significance. Much more important for explaining the German resilience to the neoliberal onslaught (or the inertia of its impact) is law. As a result of the experiences with the Third Reich, the post-war German state has been legally configured in such a way that most institutional processes are based on written statutes that cannot be changed willy-nilly but have to go through lengthy procedures involving a wider-range of official bodies, some of which consist of elected members (like the Senate). Resistance to reform thus forms the very core of institutional operations.

Most neoliberal reforms have taken place with little legal anchoring; they thrive exactly there where law is most easily instrumentalised to fit the needs of elites. The German experience with the Third Reich was exactly that: law was being instrumentalised and had no built-in resilience. However, in the age of Trump, Putin, Erdogan, Orban, and Brexit – which contrary to common belief is not a contradiction to neoliberalism – the German system shows its durability and strength, not because it somehow magically pre-empts authoritarian populism but because it resists its normalisation in legal terms. Unfortunately, the lessons learnt from the Third Reich seem to affect only certain nation states.

However, Bianchini (in this book) suggests that it is a mere matter of time before the Germans will also embrace the same fate as their British and Dutch counterparts. Indeed, universities such as the Technische Universität Munich are explicitly modelling themselves on the Ivy League in the USA. The legal inertia that was a consequence of a built-in institutional resistance to radicalisation is unlikely to withstand the sheer economic power of global capitalism indefinitely, especially as this form of power has been able to circumvent the alleged sovereignty of nation-states so effectively in the last 40 years. The relative ease with which German politicians, for example, supported far-reaching trade agreements such as Comprehensive Economic and Trade Agreement (CETA) and the first drafts of the Transatlantic Trade and Investment Partnership (TTIP) suggests that there are already many forces at work that seek to put the law firmly under the control of the interests of multinationals.

It is from this perspective that the Netherlands is such an interesting case. Having embarked on quite radical institutional reforms that enabled the neoliberal onslaught very early, Dutch higher education has not (yet) been reformed as radically as its Anglo-Saxon counterparts (although insiders have said this is changing fast, which is to be expected following the successive shifts to the right of politics in the Netherlands). This relative inertia is certainly also due to the legal anchoring of the institutionalisation of universities in the Netherlands and, if the resilience may be less ideological than in Germany, this still has some impact on slowing down the instrumentalization of research, learning, and teaching. Anti-intellectualism and authoritarian populism have a much stronger footing in the Dutch public sphere than in Germany, but it has not (yet) been as effective in binding higher education exclusively to the needs of the powerful.

For me personally, working in German higher education has offered me a lifeline for now, but not likely for much longer. However, 'where danger is, the saving power grows also' (Hölderlin, quoted in Heidegger, 1977, p. 42). If one is able to continue to pursue knowledge for the sake of knowledge, develop critical faculties without suffering financial repercussions, and cultivate thinking as the most vital 'transferrable skill', one might perhaps collectively generate sufficient staying power to go against the grain or at least to slow it down. If neoliberalism is merely a subsequent phase in the tragedy of capitalism's attempts to overcome its contradictions, then it too will be washed away, 'like a face drawn in the sand at the edge of the sea' (Foucault, 1970: p. 387).

References

Adorno, T., & Horkheimer, M. (1979). *Dialectic of Enlightenment*. London, Verso.
Bauman, Z. (2000). *Liquid Modernity*. Cambridge, Polity.
Bauman, Z., & Donskis, L. (2013). *Moral Blindness: The Loss of Sensitivity in Liquid Modernity*. Cambridge, Polity.
Beck, U. (1992). *Risk Society. Towards a New Modernity*. London, Sage.
Beck, U. (1997). *The Reinvention of Politics. Rethinking Modernity in the Global Social Order*. Cambridge, Polity.
Beck, U., Giddens, A., & Lash, S. (1994). *Reflexive Modernization. Politics, Tradition and Aesthetics in the Modern Social Order*. Cambridge, Polity.
Boltanski, L., & Chiapello, E. (2017). *The New Spirit of Capitalism*. London, Verso.
Bourdieu, P., & Passeron, J. (1990). *Reproduction in Education, Society and Culture*. Thousand Oaks, CA, Sage.
Bowles, S., & Gintis, H. (1976). *Schooling in Capitalist America Revisited*. New York, Basic Books.
Charlesworth, S. (2000). *A Phenomenology of Working Class Experience*. Cambridge, Cambridge University Press.
Eribon, D. (2016). *Rückkehr nach Reims*. Berlin, Suhrkamp.
Foucault, M. (1970). *The Order of Things. An Archaeology of the Human Sciences*. London: Tavistock / Routledge.
Furedi, F. (2002). *Culture of Fear*. London, Continuum.
Gouldner, A.W. (1970). *The Coming Crisis of Western Sociology*. New York, Basic Books.
Heidegger, M. (1977). *The Question Concerning Technology and Other Essays*. New York, Harper & Row.

Holman Jones, S. (2005). Autoethnography: Making the personal political. In Denzin, N.K., & Lincoln, Y.S. (eds.) *Handbook of Qualitative Research* (763–791). Thousand Oaks, CA, Sage. Second Edition.

Kuypers, S. (2015). *Het Begin van het Moderne Nederlandse Poldermodel. De Hoge Raad van Arbeid van 1920 als eerste manifestatie van het Nederlandse tripartiete sociaaleconomische overlegmodel.* Nijmegen, Radboud Universiteit. Retrieved from https://www.academia.edu/11843938/Het_begin_van_het_moderne_Nederlandse_poldermodel (accessed, 20 April 2018).

Latour, B. (2007). *Elend der Kritik. Vom Krieg um Fakten zu Dingen von Belang.* Zürich, Diaphenes.

Luhmann, N. (1984). *Soziale Systeme. Grundriß einer allgemeinen Theorie.* Frankfurt am Main, Suhrkamp.

Luhmann, N. (1998). *Observations on Modernity.* Stanford CA, Stanford University Press.

Morrow, J. (2017). *Where the Everyday Begins: A Study of Environment and Everyday Life.* Bielefeld, transcript.

Van Loon, J. (2002). *Risk and Technological Culture. Towards a Sociology of Virulence.* London, Routledge.

CHAPTER 8

The Truth is Out There: 'Educated fo' Bollocks. Uni's Just Institutional Daylight Robbery'. Universities in Crisis? What's New?

Simon J. Charlesworth

Abstract

This chapter considers a variety of materials that make clear the absurdity of educational processes in divided societies in which institutional processes relating to the public value of economically powerful groups take precedence within a state apparatus that must constitute the appearance of an equality that is everywhere disavowed via the effects of different distributions of capital. What is clear is that those whose social conditions mean they require the most educational action get the least, and that the education of the poor tends to be poor education.

Keywords

status difference – class relations – education of the poor – un-employment – auto-biography

I am loath to engage in biographical detail concerning a system that is as impersonal and de-realising as the English system of higher education. When the appearance of a 'system' is materialised via abstracted administrative processes involving little co-presence, then it's very difficult to even validate the reasons for an individual's treatment, not even one's own. As one academic expressed it, 'I don't know that you're the best example to base a general argument on'. Singularity of trajectory masks the effects of trajectory as the individual, separated from the conditions that make visible the reasons for their being, can no longer validate their experience as an effect of the de-realising process they endured.

1   Occupying the Disadvantaged

I entered university via Rotherham College of Arts and Technology (RCAT), which, historically, educated local people for the available employment but by the 1980s, with local industry gone, its function was eroded and it became a place where the most disadvantaged were occupied. The nature of the experience emerges in the following:

> University connects to nothing. It connects us only with instability. It's just an unofficial dole office. It amazed me after School how many People I later saw in the Rotherham dole Office and then again later at RCAT and then later again in the dole office.

Connection requires involvement. Involvement requires the management of transitions so that individuals can project successfully via forms that physiognomically regenerate dispositions that inhere in belonging and if there is no organisation of transitions, then there is no connection, no realisation, no experience of being-situated, of being-there, nothing for the individual to achieve integration or coherence via, and they experience the same de-structuring of their existence arising from their being 'nothing there' no 'there' for them to experience being via, beyond the absence they experience via being displaced. The physiognomic regeneration of the sense of positions via ways of being realised that constitute different relations to being arising from experiences of a different interpersonal medium, a different 'there'; a different 'world'; are fundamental aspects of institutional processes that situate individuals very differently, transposing different statuses into differences of competence whose grounds are effaced by the anonymity used to obscure the nature of what is occurring. A generic administrative process can be used to materialise the appearance of public functions that mask differences of treatment; differences of trajectory; different forms of transition arising from recognitions, which constitute different ways of being-there so that some experience a realisation that embeds dispositions, while others undergo an absence of any interpersonally realising process; and their CVs manifesting their insignificance via breaks in ascent. Subtle human distinctions, and different modalities relating to the nature of being-there, are realised via mediums of interpersonal contact rooted in the perception of difference. For example:

> I was a scholarship boy … That means that I was constantly pushed out of comfort zones, but perfectly equipped to adapt and cope. Primary school,

Independent school, uni, Cambridge, law. All part of a consistent trajectory. Each confirming the bias. I'd venture to suggest that the reason you didn't benefit from it is because you were 'in Cambridge' rather than 'at Cambridge' for the time that you were there.

Differences of status can be casually rearticulated via different ways of being situated arising from perceptions of difference that surreptitiously contextualise individuals in relation to a different experience of being-there, of presence.

The education of the poorest tends to be affected by the same limiting parameters that, in turn, constitute the meaning of being-from such areas, the education they receive as stigmatising as the conditions they try to escape via it: 'Rotherham leaves no one ... You can't escape by leaving. It marks you. You are always "from Rotherham"'. Being 'from Rotherham' arises from processes of differentiation that render individuals legible so that they are subject to circumscriptions, which constitute them objectively. The circumscription arising from these processes obviously leads those who experience barriers, whose sense they bear, to encounter perceptions of this sense, mediated via others, as one professor said: 'When I talk to you, I never get the sense that you know anything outside Rotherham'. The paradox is that the educational process forces you back onto the domestic sphere because it doesn't connect you with anything publicly because of the way such people refract the appearance of their function via institutional relationships that are private. You are forced back onto whatever your familial resources are because the process connects with nothing, especially resources: you have to turn yourself into a resource in order to experience any viability and once you lose the ability to function as a resource-bearing-administrative-entity, contact ceases. When you have to develop a project to secure financing to purchase a PhD via an administrative process these people associate their names with, then judgements of parochialism are not made because they require you to do whatever you can in order to produce a thesis they can judge. This academic didn't say this when being paid to read my thesis on Rotherham for Cambridge University Press. In a world constituted via the effaced monopoly of elites, any deviation becomes significant. I have an autism spectrum disorder, which impairs me interactionally, one indication being poor eye-contact, and at one interview, as I looked away, the professor clicked her fingers in front of my face, snapping: 'If you look away when you answer questions, you'll never get a job'. At another I was asked, 'Can you deal with the social aspects of being a fellow?' One can appreciate the difficulties that the discrepant face in an institutional economy dominated by the forms of the valued.

2 Administration Refracts the Appearance of a Process

For the students I knew, possible futures, like the nature of the educational processes available, were never discussed because there was, 'now't the'er'. The type of education available required us to project via a vacuum. There was no organisation of transitions and no involvement in anything beyond abstracted administrative processes that involved little by way of co-presence: form-filling across distances and then the production of documents that materialised the appearance of a process that objectified others. Everything is so temporally distant that you end up forgetting what your reason was for ever starting because any opportunity to do anything is displaced so far into a future you must perform a series of miracles to ever realise that you experience your attempts to project via the meaninglessness of a decontextualization that constitutes the insignificance of what you are doing:

> University made me less hopeful than before I went. It disenchanted me and took a lot of my enthusiasm away. It was meaningless. Made me look bad before I even got going in life. I never knew actually what future I was studying for, I only knew it seemed a better option than the dole. I did it not to go back to that shit hole office in Rotherham. I had ideas but they died on the way. I was doing more before I studied than when I left, just lost the connections to do anything and ended up stuck.

We see the structuring constancy of absence, experienced as meaninglessness via the physiognomically materialised effects of non-mediation and un-realisation. These problems with 'looking bad' are effects of objectivizations rooted in the nature of the process itself. Poorer students have little control over their self-objectification because they have little power to situate themselves so that they can develop appropriately via relational processes that objectify them. It is the exact opposite of what education should provide and of what elite education does. The same, public, valuationary processes are constitutive of your objectivity within education and the processes of claiming and studying are analogous, involving abstracted, de-realising, administrative mediations.

Institutions were appropriated by a generation who used an administrative shell, whose labour was largely carried out by secretaries, to materialise the appearance of processes that involved almost nothing beyond self-education. Little wonder many say, 'Ah dun't know what yer pay fees fo'. Anyone who has been through it can appreciate the logic manifest in the words of one PhD student:

> There is loads of teaching available, if you are a PhD student at Cardiff, all you have to do is sign-up. It's easy work you don't really have to teach anything, you just have to make sure the students have filled in the forms properly to submit their essays and that's about it.

Given that the appearance of a process is materialised via administrative acts, it's not surprising that academics would council, 'just make sure you hand something in': provided students submit, the appearance of a process is materialised. Whilst I was, as one professor said: 'lucky to be here', because it was 'very difficult for English students to get money'; a comment made to evade an obligation manifest by the fact that he continued, 'it isn't like you're very unusual; it's not like you're a black woman', which overlooked that, as a postgraduate student, I accessed nothing beyond a self-generated process that objectified those who associated their names with the administration of the products of my labour.

The problem your education forces you to resolve is the overcoming of the provision and mediation of nothing via a labour itself struggling with the effects of the absence of anything making self-constitution reek of the absence constitutive of its form. At one interview one professor noticed, 'there's nothing on your CV'. We can appreciate the importance of extra-curricular culture or what one application form called an 'impressive co-curricular activities record', that is: middle class culture because working class culture is classed as doing-nothing even when a student is forced to attempt to constitute it as 'research' because they access no sphere of practice via a university process that requires them to constitute the illusion of their own education in order to realise the illusion of the 'research practice' of those who experience the authenticity of their own commitments via association with the administration of student labour (see the chapter by Donskis in this volume). When your educational process reduces to minimal contact and to strategies of evasion and displacement that obscure a withholding born of the inability of academics to involve you because of the way institutional space is used to constitute exclusive forms, that operate via tacit reference to the generic processes that materialise the appearance of a 'public' system, then, is there, really, a system there? If involvements constitutive of experiences of being competent are not forthcoming, then, is the underlying condition constitutive of unemployment, devaluation, being addressed or does education merely become another form of its public inflection? Without income, you are not viable because nobody will engage with you unless you have the capacity to attach money to yourself. Once you lack significance, how do you mediate access? Approaching a research group, I was told, 'We don't have anyone available to do this'. If you belong to an insignificant group, how are you supposed to attract research funding, and by what means?

The devalued have bad luck because they can't connect. Processes degrade as academics exploit individuals via ever more abstracted interpersonal processes and individuals find it more difficult to connect themselves and come to bear the sense of absences that are effects of an insignificance that the process reproduces as the sense of processes are extorted via relationships that involve little situating of individuals and no opportunity for them to accede to a self-composure arising from being-realised in relation to interpersonal forms that disclose possibilities so that they accede to an experience of capacity arising from experiencing being subject to such actualising moments and, thereby, able to sustain a hold on forms because they experience their physiognomic regeneration.

As the process available to one becomes insignificant, the degradation is manifest via inabilities born of insignificance and, lacking contextualisation or realisation, one struggles to represent oneself conversationally because one doesn't access the grounds of representational forms of intentionality. If one doesn't access, interpersonally, disclosures, which constitute aspects whose sense one bears via experiences of being significant, of counting to others, then one's expressivity will manifest the sense of a will-less-ness born of an inability that is an effect of degradation. What can one say about one's person when one's objectivity leads one to be unable to access any public sphere, which itself is an effect of an objectivity made determinate via experiences arising from ways of being rooted in the interpersonal forms of such significances? The very same judgements are made about them, throughout, concerning a social experience devoid of objectification in which they are perceived (usually via communicative relations that are abstracted and electronically mediated) via an absence that is itself an effect of being-perceived to lack aspects required to solicit contact. If you are not socially viable then the ways of being arising from being-perceived to lack legitimate forms physiognomically regenerates the grounds of a sense incorporated via experiences of being subject to such dynamics. Attempting to mediate opportunities, I had to wait eight years for a response from a professor who said, 'I sense that you lack the experience of everything ... that conducting research in an applied social science field ... involves'. What are being perceived are effects of a reality as the sense of relational processes is born via expressivities arising from being situated via precisely such mediations. If individuals are perceived to bear the sense of an absence of capacity, as an effect of absences of opportunity, then how are they to accede to the interpersonal conditions constitutive of being competent? Notice how objectivities function as absolutes precluding opportunity and thereby eternalising the condition reproduced via the recognition of an incapacity born of a condition arising from impoverishment: 'you lack the experience of everything' and notice how this alludes to a global sense indicating the absence of a fundamental relation constitutive of the sense: involvement in a world: 'you lack the experience of everything', the professor senses the absence of a totality of relationships that subtend functionality. This is testament to the way individuals face circumscriptions arising from experiences of being-perceived via expressive physiognomies rooted in institutional forms that constitute legibilities that only further reconstitute precisely what education is supposed to address: absences of opportunity. Given the sense arising from expressive physiognomies rooted in the absence of connection, the absence of realisation, the absence of the interpersonal grounds constitutive of intentional states that presume such conditions that render individuals capable of appropriating forms via modalities rooted in realisations arising from disclosures which constitute capacities for projection that physiognomically regenerate the sense of such temporally and spatially sustained personal properties, can we really consider people subject to such conditions educated?

The absence of the interpersonal conditions constitutive of intentional states that arise from involvement in a circumscribed sphere of legitimate encounter is perceived via the professor when he observes, 'I sense that you lack the experience of everything ... that conducting research in an applied social science field ... involves', given that such a criteria debars me from accessing any context that might allow me to appropriate the forms constitutive of the sense of such an objectivity, how can a decontextualized education address the deficits arising from structural dislocations arising from institutional command of the instruments of objectification? Products of educationalism, who self-finance a process of self-education bereft of anything but the solitary task of producing the forms which materialise the appearance of institutional processes devoid of anything beyond the administrative actions that materialise the appearance of functions bereft of any interpersonal reality, are not being prepared for anything. If the education leaves individuals perceived by the same sense of absence characteristic of unemployment then in what sense have the poor been educated? The process merely legitimates discrimination by hiding a condition that is personalised by the charade of provision which, robs individuals of any authority in the face of what they are perceived to be as effects of a mutilating process that provides access to nothing. Individuals are exposed to responses which constitute the inert pressure of the order of things, operating via the inscription of differences whose forms are imbibed via disclosures which trigger responses that manifest the 'subterranean complicity that a body slipping away from the directives of consciousness and will' maintains 'with the violence of the censures inherent in the social structures' (Bourdieu 1999: p. 170) so that it appears individuals exclude themselves. You are exposed to an order awareness of which leads to exclusion, reclassification merely legitimates differences via appearing to provide opportunities that are as spurious as the administrative process constitutive of their illusion is vacuous. The greatest discrimination individuals' face arises via the conditions constitutive of different actualities so that individuals face experiencing being realised in relation to forms that constitute different possibilities. The power of destiny arises from the social magic whereby some are consecrated and others condemned to futures proposed by a collective perception that ensures that the very fabric of being constitutes realities that are difficult to countermand because negation precludes opportunity: once you are perceived to lack required forms, you cannot situate yourself so as to accede to the conditions of possibility that those forms make accessible, you can't be subject to the disclosive conditions of modalities and remain enmired in an incapacity that is a really attributed effect of forms whose physiognomic materialisation constitute you objectively. Perceptions of the sense of the absence of required characteristics should always alert us to a deprivation of the conditions required to satisfy intentional states because personal characteristics have temporal, spatial and interpersonal conditions, if individuals are perceived to be useless, then it is a failure of the institutions that underpin the economy. Cognitive barriers are social barriers: the practice of difference: the recognition and disclosure of the sense of different forms has cognitive effects because it constitutes sense appropriated via being subject to processes that not merely circumscribe but actualise.

The real issue of competence concerns the forms of involvement constitutive of the acquisition of forms via actualisation and this becomes ever more remote as educational functions replace what becomes ever more mediated: employment. Without involvement there isn't a 'there' experienced and a fundamental medium of disclosure is absent, which explains why the devalued articulate an absence they experience being constitutive of them, as there being 'nothing there', nothing they experience via being-there: no 'there' for people to experience being via. The fundamental fabric, interpersonally constituted, of meanings experienced via being subject to disclosures, which realise us, is affected by devaluation. It is possible to use abstracted administrative processes to materialise a commitment experienced via association, whilst neglecting individuals and one-to-one processes obscures the way distinctions are materialised. As one PhD student describes:

> From my experience, there are far too many PhD students coming through, with at least 10 people per job ... The contact time on the PhD

is so poor. I have become quite numb to how bad it is ... In social science departments like these 'work' is like a mirage.

As another PhD student described:

> It was interesting ... for me to discover how unhappy most postgrads feel concerning the quality of supervision ... Last night, we all sat around ... discussing our various experiences of academia. It appears to me that the whole system is flawed ... and that we are all ... victims. One guy resigned from his PhD in his final year and has gone it alone ... He had major conflicts with his supervisor (female ... social psychologist) and has no publications to help him get a job. So, he's hunting round for a position as research associate and is completely shattered by the whole situation... You need money to pay for the degrees, you need money to pay the conference fees ... money to travel, to live away and eat when you struggle to pay your rent.

The censures individuals face in a system in which access is mediated via prestigious, exclusive forms, not competencies whose manifestative conditions remain unavailable, causing pain implied in simultaneously developing needs that cannot be satisfied, emerges clearly in the words of another PhD student:

> ... Academia is quite a terrible joke. It is a closed shop system for the ones who play by the rules... It is so terrible that I cannot laugh anymore at it. It just sicks me. So, I avoid the theme at all. I am so hurt with Academia that I refuse to hear and talk about it ... I refuse to talk on academic subjects because it is useless and only does me harm.

The devalued just face the same conditions via institutional reclassification. As one person put it, 'All Ah did was pay to bi in a buildin' fo' three years, thi' taught mi absolutely nothin' an' Ah learned absolutely nothin'.' If people aren't involved in anything realising or consequential, are deficits born of dislocations themselves economically rooted in the interpersonal-institutional processes that subtend resource-access being addressed?

3   If You Are Rich Enough, You're Clever Enough: the Marks of Intelligence Are Bought

Getting onto a PhD I had to develop a project, unaided, in isolation and then secure one of twenty-four Economic and Social Research Council (ESRC) awards.

When I finished, I didn't get a single interview in two years. When individuals can't even get interviews, how can they be expected to adapt? If your process reduces to self-teaching and submission of work, how can you compete with those involved? Despite achieving three minor-miracles: securing an ESRC award, publishing my PhD, and getting a Cambridge fellowship, a professor of sociology at a nearby university wrote via email:

> From your point of view, I suspect that one of the biggest difficulties that you face at the moment is a combination of your age, and the fact that you haven't been in 'proper' employment for a long time ...

What is disturbing is that a professor of sociology is one of the few people who might take my work seriously. When a professor of sociology can say, 'having a first-class degree doesn't mean very much these days', then you realise those instituting the charade know the reality: when the best-case scenario is worthless, people are wasting their time. It is clear that the context students exist in relation to affects the significance of their production: that their class position constitutes their objectivity as an effect of institutionalised differences that constitute legibilities that practically refer to the sense arising from the way such forms are instantiated. The reason this matters is that it is both an effect of public value and a manifestation of the conditions constitutive of competence: being socially valued and recognised constitutes the disclosive conditions for the forms required to function. This is why 'experience' counts in selection criteria because it functions as a guarantee of conditions which satisfy intentional states yet this is precisely what is unavailable and, whilst education is supposed to function as a parallel institutional apparatus, it clearly can't.

For those who can't access the legitimating and humanising processes of employment-specific training that are the preserve of those on elite trajectories, outside 'the specifically scholastic market, a diploma is worth what its holder is worth, economically and socially; the rate of return on educational capital is a function of the economic and social capital that can be devoted to exploiting it' (Bourdieu, 1984, p. 134). As another product of RCAT narrates:

> I realise my degree was basically just humouring people to process them and get them out the other side. Three years not on the dole stats. It was just the same as being unemployed, nothing much to do, no reason to be anywhere, nowhere to go, no money. When I finished, I was in a worse hole than if I'd not done it. Better off getting a trade ... I should have joined the army ... Least I'd not be stuck and I'd have some worthwhile skills. I can't do ow't with the shit I did at university, total waste of time.

It's a fraud. It is the dole, it's a fraud and it's becoming more and more the norm too ... People are studying until they are like thirty and then ending up doing un-paid work as 'experience' ... all it is is the dole with a false hope at the end as bait and now I'm cleaning bogs part time ... I'm just sick of going to work knowing it won't even pay the rent. No Motivation. It's like that Soviet saying 'they pretend to pay us, we pretend to work or should we say 'they pretend to educate us, we pretend we've got a future'. Most of it is like someone sticking an obstacle in front of you and asking you to pay for the ladder to get over it.

Manifesting the effects of such conditions, and calling from a phone box in Rotherham while on benefits, the external examiner of my PhD berated me, 'it's ok for you to deny the value of education, it isn't like you've been rotting on the dole', maybe because he was too eager to realise his own commitment to education via constituting me as a 'great example of the success of second-chance education' via a process that involved no personal contact so that the reference he wrote for me was so inadequate as to be ineffectual because such people are paid for judging people outside of contact or access to any sphere of practice other than one that narcissistically realises them and their sense of a system via the administered judgement of the labour of others who access none of the institutional relationships that objectivise them. Letters of reference are inadequate because there is little that academics can claim about individuals they have little contact with: they have the same problems that the subjects of the 'education' have, lacking access to anything, individuals are unsure as to characteristics whose interpersonal conditions are not satisfied for them leaving them confused and insecure. Letters of reference have always been a problem for me because I was never introduced to any sphere via education so, consequentially, nobody knows me, let alone knows what capacities I might be capable of manifesting were any process available to me that might elicit human qualities. The truth was well articulated by one academic: 'I actually couldn't write you a reference because there isn't anything, I could honestly say I believed you were fit to do'. Is there really much of a difference between rotting on the dole and living the same form of life in a city under the guise of being educated?

Generally, what those from non-standard trajectories get is non-specific education bereft of contextualisation, which directly reproduces the meanings they experience being via an aimless, pointless, existence that education simply reproduces. Any detailed elucidation of labour market criteria that they will confront via education is ignored, as the words of one academic make clear:

Well don't say Sociology is shit – they don't need to hear it. They're starting a social science degree of some kind – sociology, education, etc. – and that will just demoralise them. And they won't have any way to connect to ideas about social science research funding. Most of them don't even know what class is – they don't recognise it. Of course, it is a dead end for the majority. I know it's not open and equal – you only have to look at the majority of people in lectures to know that.

What is interesting here is the spontaneous connection of the link between social science and a general education degree: 'a social science degree of some kind – sociology, education, etc.', the 'etc.' manifests how interchangeable the areas are since they are financed via the general malaise that feeds those without determinate educational choices onto general degrees which entrench the dislocation manifest by the acknowledgement that 'they won't have any way to connect to ideas about social science research funding'. What are they being educated for?

I'd like to consider the extent to which educational space reduces to economic imperatives. The words of one academic seem relevant:

> ... It's run now by business people, something terribly corrupt has happened, there's no respect for scholarship, it all about getting money, that's the main criteria now, if you can bring money into the departments then they'll have you ... We had a dreadful meeting the other day with our head of department, he called us in and said we didn't have enough post-graduates, that we didn't have enough on the MA that we needed to get more doctoral students, he said we need to get a lot more overseas students, that's what it's all about now, they want to get these overseas students, they pay these huge fees, you see, nobody cares if they're any good ... it's all a business now, it's like in America ...

How all this affects university selection processes is clear in the following:

> I am intrigued by your somewhat strange academic career to date... Just to repeat what it says in the advertisement concerning the sort of person we are looking for, it would be someone who has published ... in the area of culture, has obvious promise and potential as well as relevant teaching experience. It would seem, from what you have said, that your research might fall under the heading of culture, but that remains unclear. I should stress, however, that preference would be given to an active researcher (preferably with grants) above someone who is simply a scholar/writer.

Notice how the term 'active researcher' reduces to those who can successfully procure grants and we can see the reduction and devaluation manifest in the 'above someone who is simply a scholar/writer', the valuationary dynamics constituted spatially manifest distinctions operationalised via networks that make available such objectivities. Valuationary processes constitute spatial divisions that circumscribe individuals determining the meanings they experience being via forms, which disclose such objectivities, actualised via such processes. Studying from a bedroom clearly doesn't count, negating my work. If you belong to a non-literate group, how do you avoid appearing to be 'simply a scholar/writer' and if these categories manifest the real schema constitutive of value in the academic field, how would someone in such conditions ever operationalise contacts? Looking at an application process for the University of Coimbra, I found the following, 'CES gives priority to those applicants who already have connections to research networks'. This is to be expected since private networks in the public sphere are the source of validation and valuation that function as guarantees of a competence rooted in recognition of forms that assure individuals, and institutions, of the individual value that functions as a guarantee of competence because it is a constitutive condition. There are issues concerning access to the interpersonal grounds of competencies: elite students usually access direct mediation, realisation, and contextualisation, and lower-class students experience educational processes consisting of dislocation, abstracted mediation, and de-realisation that constitute differences in expressive physiognomy. For the poor there is a problem with objectification because of a decontextualization that the education reproduces. What is valued is labour arising from employment and labour producing its own income via grants. And yet the devalued cannot situate themselves institutionally so that the form of their labour is affected by their dislocation: how can they direct their consciousness appropriately without a shared horizon of disclosure arising from involvement? Without access to the same nonintentional or preintentional conditions that enable intentional states, how can they constitute appropriate forms? This is the devalued face, the re-articulation of the sense of a barrier that arises from the continuous perception of a difference that re-constitutes a barrier whose perception is evident in the sense of my academic career as 'strange'. That the discernment of difference, that legibilities are inextricably constituted via the way space is used to materialise the sense of such forms via deviation from a modal trajectory is manifest by: 'I am intrigued by your somewhat strange academic career to date'. In a system whose processes are instituted with so little engagement with the poor and in which income can be transmuted into early-arrival, we see how easily class differences can be legitimated by a mass system whose anonymity obscures the processes constitutive of differences in objectivity relating to different ways of being-there, different forms of treatment, and different lineages constituted via different contextualising mediations privately materialised. Bourdieu makes the important point, 'Individual corruption only masks the *structural corruption* (should we talk about corruption in this case?)' (Bourdieu, 1998, p. 17), the corruption is legitimated as part of the constitution of the public realm. All one has to do in order to select the privileged, is to select the best: those with the cultural tokens manufactured in this domain in order to objectify the dominant who pay to access the private spaces of the institutional sphere in order to access exclusive forms that operate via tacit reference to the mass of students undergoing generic processes whose significance arise from the use of such space to constitute such distinctions.

Because valuationary processes are institutionally private: relating to the exclusive forms that manifest the interpersonal effects of recognitions which physiognomically regenerate the sense of differences incorporated via experiencing being privy to such recognitions, the devalued are cut-off from the spheres whereby the elites produce the objectifications required to access employment. The institutional machinery of objectification is financed via a mass process that materialises the sense of its legitimacy, but, if you look at the interpersonal processes occurring, it is not legitimate because it involves the de-legitimation and invalidation of those who lack economic capital. What these spatial divides do is lock the devalued outside of channels of legitimation and leave them unable to solicit contact, leaving them without any sphere of actualisation, and, thereby, no experience of efficacy or viability. This is why 'experience' is such a key differentiator: without access to a context of realisation, how can individuals accede to a sense of possibility? 'Public' institutions can be commandeered by groups who surreptitiously subvert the institutions' imperatives to satisfy their own needs. Moreover, there is a contradiction between the way value is constituted via the institution of exclusive forms via access to private networks that require recognition and mediation, and the generic, anonymous process that lower-class students undergo, devoid of direct mediation because they function as a foil for the elaboration of character, narcissistically, like props, part of 'the proven games and tricks of the theatricalization of pedagogic action' (Bourdieu, 1996, p. 96) used situationally, by academics to enact commitments that their practice disavows. The results are a monopolisation of resources because of the spatial divisions constitutive of the sense of the positions underpinning the objectivities individuals experience being materialised.

There were academics I was infrequently in contact with throughout my postgraduate study, yet never was I invited to speak. Upon completion of my PhD, never was I invited to speak, and never did I ever present any material at any point during my 'education'. The readers who read my thesis for Cambridge University Press never enquired into my situation; no one acted to involve me: I was trapped on benefits in a condition perpetuated via such processes. The reason it is like this is because individuals are used as objectifying nodes via relational processes in which people manifest concern to one-another without students even being privy to the processes. All decisions on my book were made without contact with me, and I never had contact with anyone involved except over the phone. Most of my postgraduate education reduced to conversations over the phone because there was no context of co-presence. When I published the book, one of the academics who dealt with me as an undergraduate, invited me to speak, although this was never finalised. Contacting one professor, upon completion of my PhD, I was ignored, when the book came out, I contacted him again and he responded. This raises the question: do academics take the certificates seriously or do only exclusive forms count because of the ubiquity of credentials that finance the apparatus of objectification they appropriate under the guise of a universal good they subvert via their own private use of institutional space? When the few points of contact arising from a process that is anonymously constituted can't involve you in anything, how do you accede to the objectifying 'experiences' arising from modalities rooted in recognitions that are clearly unavailable because of the generic nature of what is available: the behaviour of those who institute the processes clearly manifests that they don't take seriously either the process or its products. The issue is not merely how do you become objectified when you can't access any interpersonal sphere beyond form-filling and submitting written-work, but how can you develop?

In reality, what happens is that one condition is merely perpetuated because the educational process continues it because of the way the reclassified unemployed function as resources, aids for the elaboration of character and sources of disclosure, which constitute forms appropriated via being subject to such relational mediations for those who experience being capable of instantiating the sense of forms because they are subject to such possibilities because they are contextualised, relationally, via the extortion of the sense of a process out of associating their names with the non-contextualised labour of others. The fact that individuals can undergo these processes without access to experiences of being situated in relation to the conditions of possibility of representational forms of intentionality that presume recognitions which in turn constitute opportunities to emerge from the insignificance of a process, whose generic nature is manifest by the absence of access to any such possibilities – this fact manifests the way individuals are subject to the grounds of judgements which are materialised effects of significances which become crystallised by conditions of existence arising from aspects that arise via the interpersonal constitution of such processes which subtend the forms of intentional life individuals experience via being subject to experiences of being circumscribed via such conditions. Individuals are subject to ways of being-perceived that physiognomically regenerate differences of objectivity born of a contestation that competition merely exacerbates, so that, for the poorest, education is not a break-from unemployment but a continuation of its essential forms via other mediations. Human beings need to be contextualised and interpersonally realised for them to accede to the grounds of actualities that constitute them capably via an experience of the meaning-of-being-there, realised and contextualised, via disclosures which physiognomically materialise the grounds of possibilities that they experience being actually able to appropriate because they experience the availability of the forms constitutive of such objectivities. How can people compete when they cannot experience the interpersonal grounds of actualities as possibilities of their being-for-others?

Without actualisation, individuals find themselves experiencing the chaos of abortive projection as they face the frustration of un-realisation, unable to extend their corporeal schema, and accede to a fuller experience of being more self-composed because they experience their flesh being imbibed with the sense of interactional forms that intersubjectively donate capacities whose sense they grasp via being subject to such modalities as possible aspects of their being-for-others. Without access to a sphere of practice, the processes of valuation individuals are subject to are identical with unemployment, they endure the same experience of ostracism characteristics of the anonymity of those unable to signify themselves appropriately and engage with informal abstracted communicative mediations in which they are ignored because they are insignificant because they lack access to the spheres of existence that constitute objectivities arising from recognition. Without immersion in a sphere of disclosure that constitutes not merely a horizon but the very conditions of intuiting appropriate responses, how can individuals synchronise the form of their labour?

The problem is that different ways of being-perceived constitute different ways of being-there so that individuals are not involved in the same space, different relations of involvement which constitute subtle differences in objectivity that are responsively manifest: 'That's one thing I notice. I can't socialise in those groups ... it's like they tag you as a scrubber before they even speak to you. The way people interact is completely different and you can't fake it either; it's like you are giving off a smell or something as a sign'. Without experiences of being involved via the same disclosive forms, individuals do not face the same nonintentional or pre-intentional conditions that enable intentional states and, consequentially, hold different beliefs about the nature of reality. The devalued are exploited not merely economically but symbolically, that is existentially, they are, essentially, victimised via educational processes that derive an experience of being competent for those who do little beyond associate their names with the administration of their labour, and their dispropriation is perpetuated by processes that extort the sense of forms whilst exploiting them economically. A world in which the poor must skill themselves places an undue burden upon them because they cannot contextualise themselves in order to provide themselves with the opportunity to accede to mastery of forms whose grounds remain unavailable. The devalued lack the means to elicit recognition and solicit contact. Without engagement, they lack access to the interpersonal fabric constitutive of competence; education is supposed to function as an analogue of contextualising mediations, but the problem is it tends to reproduce the same spatial processes that constitute the problem.

Education as a class process is obvious: it is a way of keeping people out of the labour market, increasing competition for positions, and making money out of the competition for the symbolic forms required to access employment. It is a process that only makes more valuable forms relating to elite trajectories, and competition suits dominant groups because the worthlessness of credentials has had the effect of pushing the criteria of value back onto the social criteria that credentials used to guarantee, *'unification benefits the dominant*, whose difference is turned into capital by the mere fact of their being brought into relation' (Bourdieu, 2003, p. 83). The process whereby educational institutions function as mediators between groups and the labour market, is becoming manifest, as one Cambridge academic confided:

> All they want is that we filter them out; they'd be happy if we never taught anything; all they want is as many prestigious Cambridge students as they can get; and they just want us to act as a sorting mechanism and to filter out the thousands of applications that we get and filter them down and give them a rubber stamp saying these are good enough people to come out of Cambridge. So, they're not interested in what we teach them ... (S: Yes, but how do you know that, how do they show it?) They show it by the fact that they're happy for the degree to get shorter and shorter: at first it was three years, then it went down to two years, then it went down to twelve months, now it's nine months; it clearly shows that they don't value the learning because they're happy for us to reduce content.

As a postgraduate student describes:

> One of my Chinese friends, she is doing a course which was supposed to be 2 years but now 10 months, and she has to produce 40k in 10 months. Those stupid Master's level students write primary level English, and they get Master's degrees easily because they pay the money for the course. I can only say that the society is totally unfair. I see that poorer kids study hard and get unemployed. These rich kids didn't go to class and get decent jobs ... I just heard from my friend today that Greenwich universities are full of rich kids paying 20k per year for a stupid MBA certificate; the ranking of that university is even worse than mine. They get 15% commission fee for taking one student, PhD supervisors. And, yes, if you can bring even one Master's student (self-funded), you get 15% from his/her tuition. That is how it works in my university. That's why there are many university application agencies that are helping students to apply for free.

As the process of turning income differences into symbolic differences is rationalised, its logic becomes manifest. What this does is secure the transfer of forms of capital via tethering achievement to income: the rate of exchange on symbolic forms arises via private institutional processes, accessed via income: validation is a class process. Sadly, the devaluation that ensues only further empowers those rich in economic capital who have the means to access the institutional machinery of objectification that secure a return. The reality is captured by the words of one academic:

> They give you a place if you agree to pay the 8000 or whatever the ridiculous sum is per year, but from that point onwards, they just don't care what happens to you. In fact, I have witnessed how they accept overseas students who barely speak any English, to do a PhD, just because they are paying the full overseas fee. They obviously are not overly concerned about the academic standard these students are going to achieve.

As one overseas student describes the reality:

> Personally, I prefer to do my degree overseas than stay in China. There are two reasons behind this: learn English and get rid of the junk teachers in China. Cameron thinks international students can boost British... According to the Education department of China, over 100,000 Chinese students are currently studying in the UK. But I assure you, 80% of them are there only for the degree, they bunk the class, buy luxury sports cars, sometimes try to bribe teachers ... There is no chance that we will make friends with native students. They put all Asian students in the same

cohort. 90% in my class are Indian, rest of them are from Pakistan, Cambodia, and Thailand, etc. I can tell from teachers' eyes that we are second-class students in the uni ... Thus, it is very hard to get a grade above B for us ... Even my work was perfect, they will still give me a B- with the comment 'you need to practice your English' ... Universities in UK want more Chinese students. My tutor told me that the 'management team want me to have some international PhD students in order to raise more money. But I will feel bad if I accept low quality proposals, so I refused'. On the flight back to Beijing, I talked to a few passengers who are doing their PhD in the UK. Their stories shocked me: they did not have any proposals or interviews, they went through the 'back door' (pay money and get the offer letter) ... Anyway, the way that universities treat us and the way we survive are both sick and meaningless. Once you surrender to the money, you compromised with the quality. The students know it is a deal, they pay the money and they can get a degree. So English degrees, are they any good? I see students who just party, party, party, look down on others, they just do as well as anyone, so family and connections are important. Just imagine if the population structure in university is exactly the reflect of the society, 10% rich and 30% mid class and 60% working class, they the rich won't bully and ignore the majority. And ideas and creativity will bloom. Now it's like only the rich go to university, and they don't fucking care about study. They ... act like overlords.

The function described here used to be served by lower-class students who were treated this way. For many lower-class young people, university was a process of being denied recognition without anything being provided that might constitute qualities anyway. At the end of my first year I was summoned to see one academic who suggested I needed remedial lessons in English, even though, as another academic, after my PhD, in a letter of reference, noting deficiencies in my mastery of grammar, wrote, 'UK universities don't run freshmen English Language courses', his own description exhibiting how colonised the institution was by the terms of the dominant American clientele and also manifesting the absence of any means to address the deficits via which they perceived lower class students. After asking about a low grade from another I was told 'I'd like to tell you it's worth more but it isn't. I've seen students like you before they usually go on and get a two-two'. People who teach little in disciplines offering few opportunities to acquire skills, could easily justify poor grades, in terms of 'the sources you used'; although generally no reasons were given and none sought in an anonymous, impersonal, process that, throughout, instead of concerning the affirmation of qualities elicited via involvement, arose from a negation rooted in barriers the education was supposed to address but merely reproduced. This is why most of the young men I studied with in Rotherham went on to get two-twos at a time when there was nothing they could use degrees for. On entry to postgraduate study, having no supervisor, I went to see a potential supervisor and had to talk about my intellectual preferences, expressing a negative opinion, the academic said 'is it too abstract for you?' which manifest, not merely, a prejudicial perception based on a judgement of an expressivity arising outside of any access to any kind of display of competence, but also negligence because the comment showed what was also manifest by me having no supervisor, a lack of effort on the part of the department I was entering: any glance at my CV would have indicated that I studied philosophy before university.

4   Economic Imperatives Affect the Form of the Process

It can hardly be surprising that this international trade in credentials effects a difference between the universal and the particular, or, between the international and the local, and a key schema constitutive of value becomes an individual's relation to these: the poor are mired in locality by the very valuationary processes that degrade them. As Bourdieu puts it, 'the "new economy" ... is global and those who dominate it are ... international, polyglot and polycultural (by opposition to the locals, the 'national' or 'parochial')' (Bourdieu, 2003, p. 33). We should not therefore be surprised that in the institutions that the rich use to constitute the international realm, via which their experience of actualisation is constituted, issues to do with locality, indeed, the 'national' itself, become degraded, as a trans-national class constitutes itself internationally in relation to representations of the world so that they produce the interpersonal conditions of validity for by constituting referential practices that allow them to accede to experiences of being competent via the use of categories embedded in a horizon disclosed via their use of cultural spheres to materialise such possibilities. We should, not, therefore, be surprised that there is a relation between the syllabus, the personnel, and the clientele:

> Anything to do with locality is sullied, polluted; the institution won't go near it. There are two posts in the pipeline here and the emphasis is on international things, stuff to do with international media. (S: And what benefit will that have for your students?) Nothing, but it's just about the international focus of the department.

The department must have an international focus because they want to focus on topics that are of interest to the modal group. There is thus an inherent bias in recruitment. One of the hidden mediations being satisfied here is the need for those with economic capital to be validated, their dispositions affirmed, via institutional agents who disclose forms that regenerate their expressive physiognomy because they are congruent. That these assessments of the suitability of staff are considered is manifest by words from a selection meeting in a Cambridge College in which the following recommendation was made:

> His congruence with the life of this college ... his keen interest in international students, he has studied in many different countries, he would suit the life of the college ...

The 'life of the college' has to be physiognomically regenerated as part of the experience of being part of a circumscribed realm of legitimate encounter that universities ensure so that those being consecrated experience belonging and involvement: status, personhood – forms the devalued rarely experience. It is clear that the personnel are the policy from the words of one Cambridge academic:

> We're under a lot of pressure on the MBA to get the students, people who are, suitable ... so most students are American ... they are the largest ... group, so people have to be carefully selected to do supervisions ... and it is the same with the materials ... we have to find stuff that is ... suitable for them.

Moreover, given that, whatever discussion is able to take place, takes place within a discursive space dictated by the syllabus, how can this *not* affect the educational experience of lower-class students? The absurdity is well captured by the words of one person:

> I'm exhausted. I'm so behind now my times running out to finish the assignment. I've had virtually no sleep, and I have to work tomorrow again, and I just think I want to cry. I can't get my head around infrastructures of transnational civil society, etc., all a load of old toss – I can see every part of the argument, it's basically common sense, and there's never a real conclusion to draw! Just more questions!... When people ask 'where did you go to university?' I will answer – my bedroom! That doesn't sound good does it? I have been to three tutorials in five years – a complete

waste of time – the last one was last year and it was like watching paint dry!

There is no relation between the towns, villages, and the universities. This affects the experience of studying because working-class students cannot be engaged in relation to the phenomenal realities that their lives issue from. They are assessed in relation to schemas of classification that issue from a different relation to a reality that is alien because they aren't privy to its constitutive grounds.

5 Distorted Communication and Bankrupt Education

British universities, as communicative spaces capable of responding to the resonance that societal problems have found in the private sphere, have been in crisis for decades. We see why, at the heart of the communicative relations constitutive of the pedagogic processes at the core of the institutions, there is systematic deceit, which means that recruitment has to carefully screen out people of integrity in order to protect the institutional interests constitutive of the space. Given that those with the money to travel internationally have access to a global experience of the world, we should not be surprised that they want to study things that have an international aspect. Luckily for them, having the income that British universities desire, a syllabus is being compiled by people who have acceded to position via the same trajectory, as one academic's CV shows:

> Organizing the setup, course-design, curriculum, and validation of a Postgraduate Course ... the MA in International Cultural Studies to become the MA in Globalisation, Identity, and Technology.

Institutions are producing courses that are constituted around schema that relate to the forms of disclosure arising from a social position that the appropriation of forms arises via, so that the mobilisation arising from the economic power that the institutions recognise by offering such administered products ensures that a hidden mediation of competence is the actualisation involved in experiences of being-validated via the operationalisation of a culture able to naturalise itself via sedimenting itself in the classificatory practices of those who institute the charade. There is a symbiotic relation between clientele and producers of the forms because the recognition of the needs of those with capital leads institutions to select agents able to produce appropriate forms because they have a constitutive relation to the grounds of the competence: shared lifestyle. The key technologies, which identities arise via, are those systems of institutional relations that veil class relational processes. What is interesting is how the clientele affect the terms, via which the course is drawn up; it seems that, when significant groups are being catered for, then their need for consecration must be recognised via careful attention to the schema used to constitute a sense of optics arising from an international position that actually precludes any local function because these positions are being repressed by the economics of the institutions, manifest by the fact that, on the course, there isn't a single British student. As one overseas student confided:

> My friend is very disappointed here because the lecturers are from overseas and speak with foreign accents ... She wanted to be taught by people with good English ... I don't know any English students; all are from overseas.

As the system organises around favoured clienteles, tutors must be selected to mirror the clientele, and the whole exercise collapses into the false culture of a multicultural charade. As one overseas student described the reality, 'The Indian lecturers suck; they speak worse English than me; when I talk fast, they don't understand me. We even have Pakistani guest lecturers; they don't even know what they are talking about. All the case studies they gave us are like *Apple* and *Coca Cola*, everyone knows them'. 'Waste of time', or as another student observed, 'the foreign lecturers are the worst', yet the institutions need to accommodate individuals whose expressive physiognomy mirrors the significant clientele, and they must teach materials constituted via schemata that are common to the position of outsiders that the dominant are, relative to the cultures they are condemned to spectate, thus constituting the grounds of sense of the optics that render sensible a pedagogic exercise rooted in estrangement that is common to a de-contextualised process that makes a virtue of the necessity of an understanding arising from nowhere except the artificial conditions of the excess competition that makes closures constitute the reality of the multitude.

Our universities can develop courses that allow wealthy overseas students to study their own cultures, with tutors who are far removed from any of the personal realities of those cultures, and can produce courses that produce symbolic capital; whereas when it comes to our own indigenous students from poorer families, in equally distant regions of social space, the universities simply force upon them an irrelevant syllabus. An institutional system that serves the needs that those with wealth have to transmute their income into instituted distinction for carrying out routinised ideological processes in administrative sites that exchange private wealth for public distinction is clearly exactly what they want. And a university system that renders the culture of the wealthy constitutive of knowledgeability is perfect. You don't need to be well read; you just need to transmute your own culture into an ideological product administered through a routinized assessment. What is more important in the space is the culture of affluence that is shared: a knowledge of airports and multiplying fluid identities so that your identity is realised in precisely the ways analysed by cultural theorists, so that you don't even need to think because your cognitions issue from an experience of being realised appropriately because you share the position inscribed by those constituting intellectual culture: exchanging private wealth for public culture and constituting an institutional culture that objectifies one-another in the process. In reality, what these mobile students are offered is the opportunity to constitute their experience via frameworks that, in being operationalised, are then validated: cognition is an effect of realisation in relation to a culture whose incarnation is part of its developmental conditions. We find traces of this organisation in conferences like this: 'Transnational Anthropologies: Convergences and Divergences in Globalised Disciplinary Networks' where:

> The papers in this panel analyse how professional as well as personal engagements of anthropologists with a variety of mobilities (e.g., migration, trans-local fieldwork, and global academic exchange via conferences, visiting programs, and online networks) strategically positions them within the social sciences to ethnographically describe, critically assess, and theorise the current 'mobility turn'.

Because the international rich now 'migrate' internationally and network so as to produce the forms they require to objectify themselves in relation to students condemned to locality, they can now organise conferences on their transnational intellectual practices, objectifying a 'turn' toward the issue of mobility, and then make this a delineating organisational possibility excluding the resourceless and constituting their experience as something they can be expert upon. In other words, competence is an effect of status differences that relate to ways of being that constitute possibilities that are effects of appropriations of space used to produce such modalities. What we see is the way in which those with resources segregate and interpersonally constitute the terms of their existence, objectifying their existence via a command of the public realm they constitute as a resource begetting distinction; they also constitute the legitimate terms of perception of their own objectifications: they are *never* constituting capital as part of an accumulation strategy: no, they are producing advances in our understanding of processes they are 'strategically' positioned to describe because this is their chosen mode of existence turned into an income-generating lifestyle, a vocation.

Academics are more familiar with most of the major cities in the western world than they are with poor areas in the cities in which they work. This might be why they are happier interacting with international students than with those who live in the villages that surround the cities in which they work. The poor are offered an impoverished experience of their own possibility because they cannot be realised in relation to a culture constituted in distinction to them. Academic staff perceive international students as manifesting a broader range of culture and greater intelligence. Knowing nothing of the intra-worldly aspects of lives in localities, they are unable to engage with poorer students whose silence is merely enlightened self-interest and who are perceived to manifest a discomfort born of an inability to acculturate to a superior culture, as one postgraduate student described:

> The problem is that a lot of these intellectuals, this petite-bourgeoisie that reigns over the academia, is full of pretentious bullshit and actually very ignorant ... Once I was presenting a work ... on migrant construction workers and ... trying to describe ... those workers' mode of living in terms of a sociology close to Bourdieu's terms linking them to a phenomenology of migrant daily experience. And this American lady, this academic 'expert', just said: 'Well, that's nice, but you should just leave the theory and tell us all about those gory aspects of the everyday life and work of the construction workers; that's what people want'. And I said that she told that because she didn't have the means to access what we were trying to say, since she didn't know shit about the working class, and she hadn't read shit about the concepts and the authors... I was obviously 'rude', but I couldn't contain myself ... The problem with the young poor ... is exactly that of 'the attitude' ... They can't appear ... without exactly being that self-fulfilling prophecy, without showing themselves as exactly as the others think they are ... The bodies, the clothing, the words, the talking out loud, the way they look to the ... the middle classes, they're all things that denounce them and underline their background and their 'inappropriate' way of being.

If you create an economy based on hidden unemployment, in which educational institutions repress social positions while reproducing their interpersonal grounds, then what you do is create a lot of burdened, hopeless people amidst a game that is rigged in favour of those who have the income to transfer economically into other forms of capital and thereby materialise the appearance of a system in which class differences are irrelevant because institutions are used to obscure complex mediations that produce the objective grounds for the miscognition of class because of the autonomy of institutional processes secured by the financing of a mass system that offers increased security for the privileged, at the expense of an increased burden of debt and despair for the poor who find their routes into worthwhile *public* forms of existence, ever more difficult to attain. Instead of clarity, foresight, and well-being, we have confusion, antipathy, and malaise.

References

Bourdieu, P. (1984). *Distinction*. London, Routledge.
Bourdieu, P. (1996). *The State Nobility*. Cambridge, Polity.
Bourdieu, P. (1998). *Acts of Resistance*. Cambridge, Polity.
Bourdieu, P. (1999). *Pascalian Meditations*. Cambridge, Polity.
Bourdieu, P. (2003). *Firing Back*. London, The New Press.

Epilogue

Ida Sabelis

This book was in the making for four years: we consistently called it *Academia in Crisis*. It became a book in process, a longer process than ever envisioned. With a *dystopic* element coming from Leonidas's debates with Zygmunt Bauman (2013; 2016), albeit with some optimism deriving from his personal quotes; and what we like to call *postalgic realism* pointing in the direction of the hope we expect to provide with this volume.

In September 2013, Zygmunt Bauman and Leonidas Donskis came to VU University in Amsterdam, to address the university's leaders: the university board, management staff, and deans. Who would have imagined how a great, though brief friendship could have evolved from that meeting? The occasion was to present their book *Moral Blindness*, especially Chapter 4 'Consuming University', which deals with system thinking and the increase in bureaucratic measures. Or in other words, the university as a 'consumerist' and market driven institution, or as 'cookie factory',[1] which is how VU staff and students called the process: a factory or institution that sells students as products and treats staff as machines, very much like Parker and Jarvey (1995), as well as Ritzer (1996) predicted, not so very long ago. Bauman and Donskis argue that '…a consumerist attitude may lubricate the wheels of the economy, [but] it sprinkles sand into the bearings of morality' (2013, p. 150). Of course, this is meant as a warning to universities that are supposed to produce 'useful' knowledge as well as the graduates who will promote and utilise it – and put it 'up for sale' as soon as new trends break. But it is also an explanation of why university staff and management remain compliant in the current fast, gripping and consumerist culture: consumerism by its very nature serves as a drug, preventing us academics from taking action via its ability to seduce us into compliance.

More specifically, cooperation between editors and authors participating in this project has emerged from ongoing discussions and exchanges since 2013, over that Bauman and Donskis' chapter in *Moral Blindness* in combination with our own experiences, thinking, and views on current 'life in academia' in various European countries. We are delighted to present our effort to put critiques, protests, and tensions in current academic life in the spotlight

---

1   The university as a 'cookie factory' was the ironic slogan of students and staff at VU University, Amsterdam, during their protests against new cutbacks (and 'reorganisations') starting around 2013.

via this volume. Experiences from the European countries we come from and work in are combined: Lithuania, Britain, Germany, the Netherlands, Italy, and Slovakia. Inspiring debates have taken place in each of our countries on what to think about the current state of academia and where to go from there, in some cases linked to recent university protest movements.

As we have seen, dystopia and utopia mingle in contemporary reflections on academic life, under pressure of economic developments and an increasing emphasis on the 'production' of knowledge, specific forms of 'internationalisation', and on an increase in the numbers of students, simultaneous with cutbacks, 'corporatisation', and 'commercialisation'. The tone of the contributions ranges from dystopic vistas all the way to utopian or 'postalgic' (cf. Ybema, 2004) visions of European-inspired cross-boundary options for students and scholars. However, between the university as 'accommodating tradition', on the one hand, and 'anticipating the modern world', on the other (cf. Donskis in his chapter), we encounter pleas for changes in structure, character, pace and direction of what started out as the 'Bologna Project' in the late 1990s. This might entail radical steps and initiatives to demonstrate what we have in common: an interest in engaged scholarship embodied by a Humboldtian community of learners, working in an intellectual space rather than a place where knowledge is commodified, controlled, and compressed into a rat race of 'citable' journal articles.[2]

Are we indeed facing the 'end of the university', as Donskis warned in his lecture to the rather stunned VU managerial staff in 2013? We cannot really know while in the midst of this turbulent development, in which we try to be critical, but also find ourselves complicit, since we must admit that in the recent past, we have helped build our universities in their present forms. Indeed, from a future-present perspective, in which on a daily basis we open up and close down future possibilities (Adam & Groves, 2007), we may fear for loss of content and independence, if McUniversity continues, if we do not find ways to counter disruptive measures from politicians, and, more pressing still, from the administrative and bureaucratic bodies of universities who rule by numbers, graphs, and standardised measurements rather than via academic creativity and inspiration. We have decided and discussed that it is worthwhile to look at current development in academia, at 'academia in crisis' from different perspectives: internationalisation and the European project (Stefano Bianchini and Samuel Abraham), a deeper exploration of the TINA context of

---

2 A quite recent experience in this regard was a well-meant wish by a close colleague to the publication of an article: ... 'congrats to this nice publication, may you receive loads of citations'...

academic life (Leonidas and Frans Kamsteeg), a temporal view on academic work (Harry Wels and Ida Sabelis), and autobiographical accounts from the UK and from NL-UK-Germany (Joost van Loon and Simon Charlesworth). Where do we go when the economic paradigm tells us that TINA rules?

The book thus reflects and builds on the 'Consuming University' chapter in Bauman and Donskis' *Moral Blindness* (2013). In absolute terms, it has taken us quite a long time – and indeed, the writing of and discussions about our chapters have not always enjoyed top priority in the daily tasks and fragmented duties of our work. But is that 'Werdegang', this development, not exactly at the heart of what has been taken from us through compliance with the TINA effect of economy first, in academia as elsewhere? What about the 'production of scholars' and journal articles in ever larger numbers, with preferably less ever money but with ever more control systems? No matter, the volume has now been completed, and we present it to the world, not just the world of academics, hopefully, but to all curious and broad-minded thinkers. And, yes, the process was sadly interrupted and delayed when Leonidas Donskis, our dear, dear friend, tragically passed away in September 2016, on his way, as always, to promote deep thinking, and to linking people together as he did with most of us. Coupled with that, Bauman passed on a couple of months later and left us without a foreword to this volume. In May 2017, we were invited to present about 'academia in crisis' during a commemoration seminar for Leonidas Donskis on the occasion of the opening of a grand new library now bearing his name in the city of Kaunas. At that point, we decided that 'an outsider' (from a European perspective) should perhaps be the perfect choice to compose the introduction to our book. Tamara Shefer, South African scholar of Lithuanian descent, turned out to be that person – a friend and cultural partner of Leonidas in so many ways.

I am afraid that, without the inspiring presence of Leonidas, we, as authors of this book, have been chasing our own tails, so to speak. We have tried, and are trying still, to do something that is neither desired nor valued by our universities... but we intended to proceed and finalise this venture anyway, despite and in-between the various measures coming from all directions, which seem to prevent us from research, academic thinking, along with intellectual well-being – if that really ever did exist. So, onwards to many readings, 'to many citations', as the new motto seems to be in academia. And perhaps then onwards to... a way out of the crisis and to finding a common cure for these dystopic vistas.

Ida Sabelis – May 2018 – two years after travelling South Africa with Leonidas and Jolanta.

References

Adam, B., & Groves, C. (2007). *Future Matters: Action, Knowledge, Ethics*. Leiden, Brill.

Bauman, Z., & Donskis, L. (2013). *Moral Blindness: The Loss of Sensitivity in Liquid Modernity*. Cambridge, Polity Press. (especially chapter 4)

Bauman, Z., & Donskis, L. (2016). *Liquid Evil: Living with TINA*. Cambridge, Polity Press.

Parker, M., & Jary, D. (1995). The McUniversity: Organization, management and academic subjectivity. *Organization*, 2 (2), 319–338.

Ritzer, G. (1996). McUniversity in the postmodern consumer society. *Quality in Higher Education*, 2 (3), 185–199.

Ybema, S. (2004). Managerial postalgia: Projecting a golden future. *Journal of Managerial Psychology*, 19 (8): 825–841.

Index

Autobiography / ical / ly   3, 129, 133, 150–153, 197
Acceleration   16, 112, 132, 133, 136, 137, 144, 145
Africa / n   4, 36, 60, 65, 73, 119, 119n
Artes Liberales   89, 95, 96, 96n, 98n, *see also* under Liberal Arts
Arts   3, 12, 34, 63, 68, 72, 101, 114
Audit(s) / ability / ing / ors   4, 39, 47, 48, 137, 138, 141, 145, 146, 150, 151, 156–159, 161, 162, 165

Bachelor / s (BA)   82, 84–90, 92, 93, 96n, 97, 103, 105, 107, 108, 116, 118, 123, 151, 163
Berlin Wall   64, 69
Bildung   36, 84, 89, 93, 95, 129, 133, 134, 136, 137, 142
Bologna (New)
    Declaration   82, 84, 85, 85n, 86, 86n, 92, 96n, 97, 103, 108
    process   54, 61, 64, 69, 77, 85, 85n, 87, 151
Boredom   20, 48, 113, 114, 123, 124
Bureaucracy / cratic / tisation   1, 3–5, 16, 26, 31, 36, 40, 54, 56, 74, 100, 131, 159, 161, 195, 196
Business   1, 4, 14, 25, 28, 30, 43, 45, 46, 64, 65, 72, 74, 89, 118, 141, 155, 159, 160, 163–165, 180

Capitalist   1–3, 152, 155
Care
    ethics of   4, 7
    self   7
Christianity   64
Citizen(s) / ship   2, 6, 7, 16, 39, 44, 47, 54, 55, 56, 57, 58, 63, 69, 88, 93, 97–99, 134, 142
Class   1, 4, 6, 9, 14, 30, 150, 155, 161, 173, 178, 180, 194
    lower   29, 181, 182, 187
    relations   169
    process   185, 186
Clock-time   5, 130, 136, 137, 138, 142, 145
Cold War   8, 53, 70
Commodity   89, 131, 140
Complicit / y   9, 10, 43, 47, 175, 196

Communist   82, 85, 96
Competition   3, 60, 112, 131, 156, 162, 184, 185, 191
Consumerism   130, 195
Consumption   18, 24, 30, 46
'Cookie factory'   3, 195, 195n
Creativity   13, 66, 112, 113, 114, 123, 124, 129, 131, 136, 187, 196
Critical / critique(s) / criticism   1, 3, 6, 7, 9, 10, 12, 18, 30, 32, 33, 37, 38, 46, 48–50, 54, 62, 65, 66, 78, 90n, 91–94, 97, 112, 115n, 118, 125, 131, 135, 155, 160, 161, 167, 192, 196
Culture(s) (of)   4, 5, 11, 13, 15–17, 22, 23, 26–28, 34, 37, 39, 53, 61, 67, 68, 69, 71, 74, 83, 113, 116, 123, 145, 154, 155, 173, 180, 190, 191–193, 195
    accountability   4, 47, 138
    audit   47, 138, 141, 146, 150, 151, 156, 157–159, 165
    blame   157
    bureaucratic   5
    confessional   26
    determinism   20–22
    extra-curricular   173
    faculty   49
    fear   157
    middle class   173
    salon   12
    sleaze   155, 157
    surveillance   5
    university   11
    violence   4, 6
    wars   32
    working class   173
Curiosity   6, 58, 97, 136
Curriculum   60, 75, 88, 89, 94, 100, 101, 112, 158, 190

Decolonise / ing / ation   1, 7, 37, 49
Devil   17, 27, 47
Donskis, Leonidas   1–3, 8, 11, 11n, 21, 32, 37, 39, 46, 111, 112, 113, 115, 125, 131, 137, 144–146, 150–152, 155, 157, 158, 173, 195–197
Dystopia / s   11, 14, 24, 27, 196

Education (higher) / al   1, 4–8, 11–13, 16, 37, 38, 38n, 44, 45, 49, 50, 53–55, 58, 58n, 60–65, 67–75, 77–79, 82–96, 96n, 97–108, 115, 118, 119, 122, 125, 129, 131, 131n, 133–139, 142–145, 151–154, 156, 157, 159, 160–163, 165–167, 169, 171–173, 175, 176, 178, 179–181, 183–185, 188–190, 193
Efficiency   3, 4, 33, 36, 37, 39, 121, 129, 130, 134, 137, 145, 150, 152, 154
Eigenzeiten   134–136, 138
Elite / ist / s   22, 30, 70, 71, 76, 78, 79, 91, 153, 154, 162, 163, 165, 166, 171, 172, 178, 181, 182, 185
Emotion / al / ally / s   7, 9, 21, 38, 42–44, 70, 73, 78, 92, 108, 113, 138
Engagement   2, 4, 17, 19, 53, 73, 79, 141, 181, 185, 192
Erasmus Programme   53, 55, 60–62, 76, 77
Ethic / al / s   4, 7, 27, 31–33, 42, 89, 90, 94n, 95, 97, 98, 101, 108, 124
Ethnography   111, 112, 113n, 114–117, 119, 123–125
Eurocentric   4, 7
European   1, 3, 8, 9, 11–13, 27, 29, 33, 35, 37, 53–57, 60, 61, 62, 64, 67–71, 74, 76, 83, 85–89, 92, 95, 96n, 97, 107, 115, 195–197
European Union / EU   8, 56, 82, 83, 85
Evil   1, 11, 14–20, 25, 27, 98, 136, 144, 150, 152, 155
Experience / d / s   1, 6, 8, 9, 24, 27, 33, 36, 37, 45, 46, 48, 58, 60, 62, 65, 68, 92, 102–104, 106, 106n, 111, 113–115, 118–121, 123, 124, 129, 130, 133, 134, 138, 150, 151, 154, 157, 158, 163, 166, 169, 170–185, 188–190, 192, 193, 195, 196, 196n

Fast food   5, 112, 119, 137
Fear / s   5, 14, 16, 17, 19, 27, 28, 33, 66, 73, 76, 77, 91, 131, 146, 157, 196
Freedom (academic)   3, 17, 18, 19, 22, 24–26, 29, 31, 32, 38, 39, 47, 48, 69, 111, 130, 165

Global / isation   29, 30, 37, 53, 55, 59–62, 64–66, 68, 69, 70, 72–74, 78, 79, 88, 94n, 111, 119, 133, 137, 144, 146, 166, 175, 188, 190, 192
God   13, 15, 18, 28, 160
Graduate / s   6, 7, 40, 58, 84, 88, 102, 105, 107, 164, 195

Hegemony / ic / ies   1–5, 9, 64, 143
Hope (false)   10, 15, 47, 70, 99, 111, 179, 195
Humanities   1–3, 7, 13, 30, 33, 34, 37, 44, 48, 49, 60, 63–65, 67, 68, 74, 74n, 85, 88, 89, 98, 131, 150, 160

Identity   6, 11, 12, 19, 26, 55, 56, 71, 72, 115n, 121, 130, 163, 192
Independence   24, 32, 65, 90, 196
Inequality / ies   6, 30, 112, 155
Integration   54, 55, 60–62, 68, 72, 76, 78, 79, 85, 170
Intellectual / ism / ly   2, 5, 21, 22, 31, 39, 43–45, 48, 49, 67, 86, 87, 89, 90, 92, 94, 94n, 97, 99, 100, 107, 108, 112–116, 115n, 120–125, 142, 155, 188, 192, 193, 196, 197
   Anti-   155, 166
Intercultural / ism   59, 74, 78, 79, 154
Interdependence   65, 66
Internalisation   94

Knowledge   3, 4, 7, 11, 12, 36–38, 44–49, 53, 54, 57–60, 62–66, 68–73, 78, 79, 85–95, 98, 99, 105, 131, 133–136, 139, 140, 145, 146, 152, 154, 155, 160, 163–165, 167, 195, 196

Language   12n, 13, 28, 30, 31, 33, 41, 45, 53, 60, 63, 68–71, 73, 74n, 75, 93, 99, 135, 163
Liberal Arts / liberal arts   7, 8, 13, 49, 82–84, 87, 87n, 89, 93–108, 96n, 98n, 100n, 101n, 104n, 106n, *see also* under Artes Liberales
Liberal democracy   26
Liquidity   17, 19, 20, 53
Literature   13, 24, 27, 28, 33, 36, 39, 40, 42, 74n, 92, 119, 120n

Male   2, 4, 49, 122, 152, 154
Managerialism   2, 30, 131, 137, 138, 145, 158, 161, 165
Marketisation   3, 37, 64
Massification   6, 64, 83, 101, 118
Master / s (MA)   41, 82, 84, 85–88, 90, 95n, 105, 108, 116, 151, 153, 154, 186
McDonaldisation   118, 119, 140
Mobile / ity   53, 56–59, 58n, 62–65, 67–74, 76–79, 192

INDEX

Modernity 1, 12–14, 17–21, 24, 29, 43, 90, 152, 161
Money 42, 46, 57, 123, 131, 134, 136, 145, 157, 163, 173, 177, 178, 180, 185–187, 190, 197
Moral / ising / ity / isation 7, 18, 20–22, 27, 31, 33, 44, 82, 146, 195
'Moral blindness' 1, 27, 30, 152, 195, 197

Neoliberal / isation / ism 1, 2, 6, 8, 11, 16, 23, 31, 32, 36, 37, 47, 49, 65, 74, 131, 134, 137, 139, 145, 150–152, 155, 156, 162–167
  turn 4, 6, 130, 156, 159, 160
Network / ing / s 24, 30, 53, 54, 64, 66–69, 71, 72, 76, 77, 79, 96, 96n, 156, 181, 192

Passion / ate /ately / s 9, 16, 34, 38, 40, 44, 48, 98, 101n
Patience 120, 122, 123, 123n
PhD 61, 70, 79, 83, 85, 86, 88, 104, 105, 132, 139, 142, 151, 154, 156, 165, 171–173, 176–179, 183, 186, 187
Politics 7, 21, 26–28, 30–34, 39, 44, 72, 91, 124, 139, 145, 157, 160, 163, 166
Poor / er / est 6, 155, 169, 171, 172, 175, 181, 184–188, 191, 193, 194
Power / s 2, 4, 6, 11, 17–19, 27, 30, 32–34, 41, 42, 44, 77, 108, 112, 119n, 143, 145, 160, 164, 166, 167, 172, 176, 190
Precariat 29, 30
Privacy 19, 23–25, 27
Privilege / d 2, 6, 7, 37, 105, 119n, 150–154, 163, 182, 194

Quality 5, 6, 8, 36, 38, 40, 41–48, 54, 61, 77, 79, 82–84, 88, 94, 101–103, 102n, 104n, 107, 138, 142, 145, 156–159, 177, 187

Race / d 2, 3
Reading 5, 9, 42, 46, 112, 118, 119–125, 132, 139, 141, 146
Renaissance 12–14, 33, 34
Research 4–6, 38n, 42, 45, 49, 53–57, 59, 63–67, 72, 76, 79, 83, 85–89, 92, 93, 95, 103–106, 112, 113, 115, 115n, 124, 131, 131n, 132, 139, 141, 142, 146, 152, 156–159, 162, 164–166, 173–175, 180, 181, 197

Resistance / s 3, 5, 7–10, 53, 72, 79, 102, 105, 106, 119, 124, 159, 161, 166
Rhythmicity 130, 135

Shallow / ness 28, 30–33, 90, 151
  scholarship 2
Slow (ing) 5, 7, 10, 43, 75, 77, 111–113, 113n, 115, 118–122, 120n, 124, 125, 129, 133, 134, 136, 159, 162, 166, 167
Social justice 3, 7, 9, 17
Society 2, 8, 13, 14, 17, 19–22, 25–28, 30, 32, 38, 47–49, 63–66, 70, 72, 73, 78, 79, 83, 88, 93, 94, 97, 99, 114, 125n, 130, 131, 134, 136, 137, 157, 186, 187
  civil 13, 91, 155, 189
Solid evil 16, 17
Subjective 8, 9, 115, 118, 151, 156, 158, 158n, 160
Symbol / ic / ically 13, 17–19, 31, 32, 36, 37, 39, 42, 43, 112, 185, 186, 191

Teacher / ing 4–6, 8, 33, 38–42, 45, 46, 49, 50, 54, 59, 63–66, 69–71, 75, 77, 79, 84, 87, 88, 92–95, 100–106, 102n, 104n, 106n, 111, 116, 135, 139, 141, 143, 146, 154, 156–158, 162, 163, 165, 166, 173, 180, 186, 187
Temporality / ies 5, 129, 133, 135, 136, 138, 143, 144, 145
Thatcherism 155, 157
Timescape/s 7, 129, 133, 137–139, 142, 143
TINA / There Is No Alternative 11, 14, 19, 23, 129, 131, 142, 145, 146, 196, 197
Transnational 7–9, 53–55, 57, 59, 62–64, 66–72, 76–79, 189, 192

Unemployment 57, 173, 175, 184, 193
University College / s (UC) 92, 92n, 96, 99, 100, 102, 103, 104n, 105
Utopia / n / s 14, 17, 24, 32, 56, 137, 145, 196

Waiting 50, 114, 119, 122–124
Western 37, 39, 60, 85, 90, 91, 107, 113, 137, 193

'Zombie concepts' 3, 30, 32, 151